The Identity of
ANGLICAN WORSHIP

EDITED BY
Kenneth Stevenson and Bryan Spinks

MOREHOUSE PUBLISHING
HARRISBURG, PENNSYLVANIA

Published in the United States of America by
Morehouse Publishing

Editorial office
871 Ethan Allen Highway, Suite 204, Ridgefield, CT 06877

Corporate office
PO Box 1321, Harrisburg, PA 17105

Published in Great Britain by Mowbray, a Cassell imprint

First published 1991

Library of Congress Cataloging-in-Publication Data
The identity of Anglican worship / edited by Kenneth Stevenson and
    Bryan Spinks.
        p.   cm.
    Includes bibliographical references.
    ISBN 0–8192–1578–3
    1. Church of England—Liturgy.   2. Anglican Communion—Liturgy.
I. Stevenson. Kenneth (Kenneth W.)   II. Spinks. Bryan D.
BX5141.167   1991
264'.03—dc20   91–21640
                                                                    CIP

Typeset by Colset Private Limited, Singapore
Printed and bound in Great Britain by
Mackays of Chatham PLC

Character is an atmosphere rather than a sum of qualities. The great marks of character are teachable-ness and a capacity for growth.

Mandell Creighton
(*Life and Letters*, II, p. 196)

Contributors

Henry Chadwick is Master of Peterhouse, Cambridge

Kenneth W. Stevenson is Rector of Holy Trinity and St Mary's, Guildford

Bryan D. Spinks is Chaplain, Churchill College, Cambridge

Rowan D. Williams is Lady Margaret Professor of Divinity, Oxford

David R. Holeton is Professor of Liturgics, Trinity College, Toronto

Thomas J. Talley is Professor Emeritus, General Theological Seminary, New York

Martin Kitchen is Canon Residentiary of Southwark Cathedral

Christopher J. Cocksworth is Assistant Curate of Christ Church, Epsom

Paul F. Bradshaw is Professor of Liturgics, Notre Dame University, Indiana

Paul J. Roberts is Lecturer in Christian Worship, Trinity College, Bristol

Gianfranco Tellini is Rector of St Mary's, Dunblane

David S. Stancliffe is Provost of Portsmouth Cathedral

Donald C. Gray is Rector of St Margaret's, Westminster Abbey

George Mathew is priest of the Bethlehem Mar Thoma Church, Kollad, Kerala

Dinis Sengulane is Bishop of Lebombo, Mozambique

John F. Baldovin is Professor of Liturgics, Jesuit School of Theology, Berkeley

Gordon S. Wakefield is former Principal of Queen's College, Birmingham

Contents

Foreword

Geoffrey Cuming (1917–88) was both priest and scholar. His work happily lives on, not only in the books and learned liturgical papers which lit up with such lustre the second half of his life, but also in the other scholars whom he inspired and who have inherited his golden mantle. I first knew him as a musician, and recall him in 1934 introducing me, three years his schoolboy junior, to Stravinsky's *Rite of Spring*, an enthusiasm that made a splendid contrast to his otherwise quiet and bookish ways. During the Second World War he suffered a severe and permanent injury to his back in a parachute drop before the battle of Arnhem, and perhaps this lasting pain both made him so self-contained as to be hard to know and imparted his altogether remarkable powers of sympathy with other sufferers. As a priest and pastor he had the qualities of a suffering servant. Another quality which made him a great pastor, while simultaneously inhibiting him from becoming a leader, was his ability to see the other side of the case: he could enter deeply into the point of view of the person with whom he did not naturally agree. He was thereby enabled to influence those in training for the ministry at St John's College, Durham, American seminarists who took him to their hearts as teacher and friend, and people consulting him in his parish in Leicester diocese. They could unload their cares on him and find a spirit of rare understanding.

His exceptional gifts included an unerring eye for precise detail, and this came through in the scholarly work in English liturgy. For the history of the Book of Common Prayer in the seventeenth century no work is more cardinal than his edition of *The Durham Book*, with John Cosin's (largely unsuccessful) proposals for a moderate and balanced revision. This meticulous and nobly printed work was crowned by Oxford University with the degree of DD. It laid the foundations for a wider and more general *History of Anglican Liturgy*, first published in 1969 but then revised in 1982 with an account of the modern liturgies of 1980 to which he made so notable a contribution. The last decade of his life took him back to the editing of ancient liturgical texts, culminating in the splendid edition of the Liturgy of St Mark which appeared, sadly after his death on 24 March 1988, in the prestigious series of the Pontifical Oriental Institute, *Orientalia Christiana Analecta* 234 (1990).

'He was a very perfect gentle knight.' The present collection both honours his memory, and continues his quest for the forms of liturgy that express the Anglican spirit of worship.

Henry Chadwick

Editors' Preface

> ... now that many parts of the Anglican Communion have largely abandoned worship in the Prayer Book tradition, for all the high quality of some of the new rites ..., how [is] this cohesion going to be maintained in the future? Will it be possible to say what the character and ethos of Anglican worship is, in brief and simple terms, on a worldwide basis at the end of this century?[1]

This basic question has been on the lips of many observers of the phenomenon of Anglicanism in recent years. In that sharp form, it comes, appropriately, at the end of an essay on 'The Prayer Book outside England', by a scholar of classical Anglican liturgy, in a book to honour the 500th anniversary of the birth of Thomas Cranmer. The question that lies behind our book, therefore, is not new.

The ensuing collection of contributions to a book entitled *The Identity of Anglican Worship* is built around two opportunities. The first is that new liturgical books have been produced in many parts of the Anglican Communion, in company with other Christian Churches, and when second thoughts are in the air, now is the time to take stock of this upsurge in writing new services and prayers, and to probe behind them.

The second is that early in 1988, Geoffrey Cuming died, and all the present contributors (and many others) would like to honour his memory with a book that would express what his major concerns were, namely a genuine love for the Anglican tradition, and a commitment to ecumenism, and to the creation of liturgical shapes and prose that would serve a world that has changed greatly from the reign of King Edward VI of England.

The essays are, therefore, offered not to answer the question 'What is Anglican worship?' in some slick and hyperanalytical manner. We do not think that either possible or desirable; and in any case, the range of contributors precludes it. We believe, rather, that questions of this sort are better wrestled with than answered, and that there is an Anglican character and ethos that emerged in England in the sixteenth and seventeenth centuries, and that had as much to do with the creation of new liturgical *texts* as it had to do with the *contexts* in which these various rites were celebrated and interpreted, and reinterpreted.

In our own day, we believe, the same process is going on, with the essential threefold difference that the Anglican Communion is now a worldwide reality; that we know much more about worship in the early centuries than Cranmer and his colleagues could ever boast; and that liturgical work is now shared among Christian Churches that are no longer at daggers drawn with each other. But there are drawbacks to this glorious perspective: it is much more difficult to be part of a Church that wants to remain in Communion with others who live and work and pray within a milieu that seems light-years away from one's own. To know how Christians celebrated the Eucharist in the third century just a little bit better than the Reformers knew it does not necessarily enhance creativity – it can (and does) stifle it. Moreover, ecumenical liturgical work can run the risk of all contemporary international bureaucracy, and settle for flat, bland parlance, that may be acceptable to all but lack the push and the drive of Cranmer at his most poignant.

These essays, therefore, are offered to carry on Anglicanism's conversation with itself, with its sister Churches, and above all with its *roots*. It is our firm conviction that identity is not something that is self-consciously sought after. It is, rather, a quality of life that emerges with maturity. It is, indeed, an essential feature of the life of a Communion that has, over a period of time, listened to what the Spirit is saying to the Churches. In what is inevitably a vain attempt to put this into the severely practical form of a published book, the editors would like to thank Archbishop Robert Runcie for his encouragement, the contributors for working so hard at their offerings, and the publishers for seeing in our question something worth sifting and striving for.

When Geoffrey Cuming wrote his *History of Anglican Liturgy*, he followed a quaint tradition in prefacing each chapter with an apt quotation. The eleventh chapter, 'New paths', begins with some words of T. S. Eliot that somehow say it all:

> There is only the fight to recover what had been lost
> And found and lost again and again: and now, under conditions
> That seem unpropitious. But perhaps neither gain nor loss.
> For us, there is only the trying. The rest is not our business.

> T. S. Eliot, *East Coker*, V[2]

Kenneth Stevenson
Bryan Spinks   All Saints' Day, 1990

1 Richard F. Buxton, 'The Prayer Book outside England' in Margot Johnson (ed.), *Thomas Cranmer: Essays in Commemoration of the 500th Anniversary of his Birth* (Durham: Turnstone Ventures, 1990), p. 250.
2 G. J. Cuming, *A History of Anglican Liturgy* (London: Macmillan, 1982), p. 191.

1

Imagining the Kingdom: some questions for Anglican worship today

Rowan D. Williams

Exhortation at Communion

When did the Exhortations[1] in the 1662 Order of the Holy Communion cease to be regularly heard in public? I don't know the answer (though I should like to); I mention the Exhortations simply because they suggest some thoughts on the character of Anglicanism and the Anglican liturgy which may have some contemporary pertinence. In the text of the 1662 Book, the Exhortations precede the invitation to confession, though the rubrics confusingly instruct that the first or second Exhortation should immediately follow the sermon, while the third should be read while the congregation is 'conveniently placed' for the sacrament — that is, when they have moved into the chancel. The confusion reflects the different policies of 1549 and 1552; in the former, the Exhortations precede the offertory, and in the latter they follow the Prayer for the Church. Originally designed (as the 1549 rubric states) to reinforce the importance of communicating on occasions where the sermon had not made this clear, they have, in 1552, become much more evidently what they essentially remain in 1662, part of the penitential rite. My main concern is with the first Exhortation and its history, and more specifically with what it has to say about the diverse ways and means 'to worthy participation in the sacrament'.

Like the rubric which introduces the Communion Order in all three Prayer Books, this text assumes that a major obstacle to worthy reception is publicly visible sin against a neighbour, and that publicly visible restitution and reconciliation are a prerequisite for participation in the sacrament; where this is lacking, the minister has authority to refuse communion. 1549 is more specific, insisting that 'lands and goods taken away or witholden' are to be restored — a formula whose absence in 1552 and 1662 tells us a good deal about what could and could not be said against the background of the later years of King Edward VI's reign, when social rapacity had reached an unprecedented pitch. However, the point remains, even when veiled in generalities; admission to the company of faithful people who receive the mystery of Christ's body

1

and blood has something to do with *tangible* forms of love and charity. Or, to put the point another way, the relations between persons that are of pertinence to their share in Christ's Body are not abstract, nor are they restricted to the liturgical event. What can be seen in human relations outside the event of worship is allowed to 'invade' the language of liturgy.

We are fairly well used to vague petitions about social justice, and so may not see quite why this is surprising. The Communion Orders of 1549, 1552 and 1662 were, of course, political documents in a very strong sense, enforced by Act of Parliament for use in every place of worship in the realm; their authority was coextensive with that of the English Crown.[2] They were not authorized by a Church visibly distinct from the realm, with a different set of laws and distinct class of official interpreters of those laws. Hence, what is enacted in the laws enforcing the use of the Prayer Books is law for both Church and State; for the Church as well as the commonwealth of Christian people living under the rule of the English Crown, and for the State as the political community at worship. The collects for the monarch in the Communion Order bring this home very sharply; but so does the Prayer for the Church Militant, which assumes that the people who are to be 'godly and quietly governed' by the Christian Prince are *God's* people. This prayer for the 'Church' is, once again, telling us that human relations beyond the event of worship, the relations of political order, are matters of the Church's identity and the Church's welfare; prayer for the Church *is* prayer for rulers, pastors, magistrates and (common) people, not for clergy and laity.

It is not that the mediaeval Church declined to pray for secular rulers; we know that some great monastic houses like Christ Church, Canterbury, devoted lengthy prayers each day to the welfare of the royal house. What is new is the idea of praying for secular rulers as — in effect — office-holders in the Church, and to conceive the Church itself *as* political society. In this place, in this realm, the Church is both the company of all faithful people *and* that company as organized by the laws of the realm. The discipline of the Church is part of the health of political society, which exists under God's authority, borne by the monarch, and so must be, as a polity, obedient to God. As J.N. Figgis showed many years ago,[3] the effect of the Reformation, in England as elsewhere, was to remove from the body politic as an alien intrusion the 'clerk', as representative of another polity than the king's.

The Church ceases to be the ensemble of clerks and laity under the supreme magistracy of the Pope: those relations of power and accountability which, for the mediaeval canonist, might be governable by divine law but did not enter into the consideration of what the Church as such was, were now relations within the Body of Christ. Consequently, the abuse and distortion of these relations was a publicly scandalous wound to the Body. Once again, of course, this is not to say that the mediaeval Church lacked any sense of sin in the public or political order; far from it. But the novelty is in spelling this out as part of the common and tangible definition of active participation in the Body of Christ as a communicant, and in reinforcing this definition and its attendant disciplines by the monarch's laws.

Communion and responsibility

How should we read all this? Its malign aspects are all too clear. The 1549 and 1552 Books were indeed tools of Tudor ideology, elements of a major political revolution: the notion of a sovereignty independent enough to outbid the Pope's, the idea — very unmediaeval — of a source of law and right and honour from which the legitimacy of lower-level institutions derived, these things are not hard to find among the pages of the Prayer Books. The Catechism hurries past the unglossed complexities of doctrine to concentrate on what, practically, is owing to God and the social order. None of the Prayer Books could conceivably be a charter for social revolution, and the only appeal from the monarch is to God, to whom alone the monarch is answerable; such an appeal could only ever take the form of passive resistance, a patient commending of one's cause to the final purposes of God.

But before we write off the polity of the Prayer Book(s) too hastily, I want to ask whether there are less malign influences at work, and whether there are elements we should be reckoning with. My proposal is that we read the Prayer Books as setting out within the context of worship a vision of the Christian commonwealth, a kind of model of the relations which would have to prevail in a society in order for the members of that society to say their prayers honestly. By removing the boundary between Church and social order, it establishes within the rhetoric of the liturgy a recognition of Christ's sovereignty in this particular place, the place where the liturgy is occurring — which is not just anywhere. It occurs in a place where certain specific patterns of power prevail and where particular abuses in those systems of power are possible (like the unlawful taking away or withholding of goods and lands); and part of the function of the liturgy is for the political community to take cognizance of the authority to which it finally, as a community of Christians, must answer. My question is whether this kind of taking responsibility for Christ in this place and time can survive the dissolution of the monolithic and autocratic order which its Prayer Book form presupposes.

The politics of the Books of 1549, 1552 and 1662 could be seen as a way of 'imagining the Kingdom' — providing the materials for an

Anglican believer not only to locate him- or herself in society but to do so with a sense of responsibility to God for its maintenance in justice. Is this part of the job of liturgy? Isn't it in danger of degenerating into the awful human-centred moralizing of some twentieth-century hymns? I think the answer lies precisely in the way the Prayer Books spell out the 'grammar' of responsibility. First and foremost, we take such responsibility in the conviction of the greatness of the claim which God's holiness makes upon us: we cannot begin to understand this without understanding what it means to be accountable to God 'unto whom all hearts be open' and whose majesty is insulted by our lawlessness.[4] Thus our responsibility for 'imagining the Kingdom' in our society and acting upon our imagining, is sustained only by the evocation of that majesty. 'Judge therefore yourselves, brethren, that ye be not judged of the Lord', says the third Exhortation: to come to the sacrament unaware that our unjust and unreconciled and scandalous lives are at odds with the law of God means that we have not grasped the nature of God, and are in mortal peril. We are pretending to be more serious than we are, and that is, at least, a recipe for corruption, for the decomposition of our language and the selves we share in language. To know what seriousness requires, we must be brought up against the greatness of God in the language we use together as Christians.

But at the same time, that discourse about the greatness of God is not the evocation of an empty transcendence — and could not function as the cornerstone of our corporate moral seriousness as a community if it were only that. God's greatness enacts itself as grace — specifically as the invitation to the Lord's Supper; the greatness of God is set aside *more* decisively by deliberate holding back from Communion than by other sins. 'I bid you in the Name of God, I call you in Christ's behalf, I exhort you as ye love your own salvation, that ye will be partakers of this Holy Communion' says the priest in the second Exhortation of 1662 (and the first of 1552). The majesty of God is there for us, known to us, in the free act of grace which the Supper celebrates. Our accountability to God is made concrete in the form of a specific summons to appear, not at a tribunal, but at 'a rich feast . . . [where] there lacketh nothing but the guests to sit down'. The test of our seriousness is our willingness to sit in company with each other at 'God's Board', and judgement rests on us if we 'separate from your brethren who come to feed on the banquet of that most heavenly food' — or, in the more vivid words of 1552, 'if ye stand by as gazers and lookers on them that do communicate'. And if we doubt our worthiness to belong in this company, then, as the first Exhortation has told us, we know what to do about it: it is in *our* hands to repair the breaches of justice and charity which have made us unworthy.

This is not moralism, but a tightly argued morality of worship, a moral discourse informed at every term by a vision of a holy and gracious God. Our responsibility for a just commonwealth is the *same* responsibility laid upon us to be partakers of this holy Communion. If we are to respond to the invitation of God, we must in will and deed be answerable for our common life. That it is *God* who invites, the holy and sovereign God, must reinforce our sense of the danger to which we are exposed by our collusion in the rapacity and fragmentariness of an unjust commonwealth — 'the great dangers we are in by our unhappy divisions', to quote from a prayer whose original context is political, not ecclesiastical in the limited sense. To repeat and sharpen the point made earlier: the company at the Lord's Table represents a social order; the possibility of sitting together as God's guests is inextricably bound up with the way power and wealth are being used outside the liturgical assembly.

This intensive 'moralizing' of eucharistic participation produced a whole genre of Anglican literature in the shape of manuals for self-examination and preparation for the sacrament. The doubly paradoxical effect of this was the steady decline through the seventeenth and eighteenth centuries of the regular celebration of the Lord's Supper, and the literary definition of Anglican piety as the preserve of the literate and more or less leisured classes, those whose social status gave them the skills and the time to wrestle with the heavy demands of Bishop Lewis Bayly[5] in the seventeenth century, and other writers of his kind. In the middle distance is the spectre of the urban Victorian congregation, divided sharply between the leisured attenders of Morning Service and the unleisured and unmonied who were confined to Evensong — a very dramatic inversion of what the policies of the Prayer Book envisage. But if we can see this moralizing process without these unhappy effects for a moment, we may catch a glimpse of a theologically crucial insight which liturgy readily loses sight of.

The Church of God is the anticipation of a redeemed humanity; and this means that the relationships required by life in the Body of Christ are to be the touchstone for human community at large — and specifically for the communities that any one congregation of Christ's people may be involved in at a particular time, in a particular place. Thus the worshipping language of a congregation ought to find some way of articulating this connection, this taking responsibility for and bringing to judgement of a 'commonwealth'. Tudor and Stuart England resolved this, for the most part, by a crude and ideological identification of the social hierarchy, culminating in the figure of the sacralized monarch, with the form of Christian unity; hence the political content of the prayer for unity quoted in the preceding paragraph but one. 'One Lord, one faith, one baptism, one God and Father of us all' becomes a legitimation for the political principle of religious conformity and centralized authority (read the prayer with the Catholic martyrs of Elizabeth's reign in mind, or dissenting ministers who were ejected from their livings after 1662, or John Bunyan or George Fox, and you will understand its moral ambivalence). And this perhaps has something to do with at least two factors: the mediaeval heritage of conceiving the Church's unity as a legally enforceable uniformity (enforceable, that is, by the sanctions of canon law as promulgated by a single supreme magistracy in Rome), and an undialectical understanding of the nature of divine sovereignty (as the extremest possible projection of the absolute right of the monarch in the Renaissance state). And yet, having taken full cognizance of this, the theological point and the theological challenge remain.

Anglicanism, out of all the Churches of the Reformation, linked its fortunes with *one* nation-state in its formative years.[6] German Lutheranism bound itself to a variety of states, Scandinavian Lutheranism to the nation-states of its region, but theological commitments in these cases extended across political boundaries. The same — eventually — proved true for the Reformed Church in Scotland. But the rationale of the Reformed Church in England was *bound* to locality. The theme that has been deployed in controversy ever since is the affirmation that the Church of England professes no doctrine but that of the 'undivided Church' (i.e. the Church of the early centuries), and claimed simply to be the Catholic Church in *this* place. Its liturgy is, accordingly, designed *for* this place; it does not intend to be a universal form of Christian worship. To put it at its most positive, the first Anglican liturgies refuse to consider the Christian congregation in general or in abstract. This, of course, is why the subsequent history of Anglican liturgy has been such a paradox: devotion to the Prayer Book, irrespective of local culture or need, in international Anglicanism until relatively recently, and the canonizing of the Prayer Book as a 'timeless' model of worship in so much English Anglicanism. The Prayer Books were *meant* to bear the imprint of their time and place, and their authoritative and paradigmatic character is in the way in which they set about constructing a language of worship for a non-abstract congregation.

To sum up so far: the specific Anglican contribution to the theology of liturgical construction and reconstruction has to do with the making of liturgy that connects the catholic pattern of life in the Body of Christ with the patterns of community that prevail in *this* place and time;[7] it is to grasp that part of the task of liturgy is to provide a resource for 'imagining the Kingdom' against the specific social and political background, so that the judgement passed by the structures of Christ's Body on the failed and sinful patterns of an unredeemed or rebellious world may have some chance of being concrete and local. Above all, it assumes that the worshipping congregation is responsible to God for the social patterns in which its members are involved. The genius of the

Prayer Books is to perform this liturgical task in a way which does not become human-centred, but continues to evoke the primacy of God's holiness and generosity.

Paths for the future

If I am right in seeing this as a specifically Anglican perspective of liturgy, what follows for the job of liturgy-making in our own day? *Very* broadly speaking, the Anglican Communion has begun to take on board the question of how to do justice in liturgy to cultural differences, a theme given quite extensive theological treatment in the first report of the International Anglican Theological and Doctrinal Commission and discussed in various contexts at the 1988 Lambeth Conference.[8] But I am interested here in the rather narrower matter of how liturgy is to articulate a sense of the Kingdom vivid and resourceful enough to act as a point of reference for moral language about human community.

Recent English liturgies have been thin in this respect. The Exhortations having long since vanished; where do we look? The Ten Commandments remain as an option, but are not a very happy way of fulfilling this kind of need — especially as they are generally associated now with an *individualistic* moralism rather different from the kind of moral comprehensiveness articulated in the first Exhortation. The invitation to confession and the forms of confession themselves are disappointing. The 'encouraging' reference to God's welcoming love is not balanced by any summons to self-examination; we are exhorted to a 'resolve' to obey the commandments and to 'live in love and peace with all men'. But neither in invitation nor confession is there any help in imagining what specific forms of behaviour impede living in love and peace, thus suggesting that what is in question here is more a matter of disposition, goodwill, than action. We intercede for the 'Church and the world'; experience in more than one parish suggests that prayers for Church-related matters easily swamp the entire intercessory process. This may be inevitable (there's nothing wrong in praying for what is most immediate to you), but the loss of a prayer which wove together the interests of the worshipping community and the community at large, as did the Prayer for the Church Militant, is worth pondering. The introductions to the Peace remind us of the reality of the Body, but treat this as an occasion for exalting to mutual 'upbuilding' rather than any reference to the human community at large.

The Eucharistic Prayers vary in their attention to the themes we have been thinking about. We are reminded that we are a 'people for [God's] own possession'; and that the Church is destined in its unity to be 'a living temple to [God's] glory'; and the third prayer, while it is replete with bizarre theological archaeologisms ('*was seen* on earth', '*revealed* the resurrection'), at least prays that worshippers will be gathered into the Kingdom.[9] Yet despite its use of one of the most potent early Christian images for the universality of Christ's saving work ('he stretched out his arms on the cross'), its prayer for the unity of the Kingdom seems to be restricted to 'all those who share this one bread and this one cup'.

It is easy and unfair (and all too popular a pastime) to list the inadequacies of the Alternative Service Book, while ignoring its strengths: none of what was mentioned in the previous paragraph would be seriously worrying in itself, perhaps, if there were *somewhere* an articulation of what I have suggested was the classical Anglican insight. In some ways, we have returned to a 'mediaeval' liturgy, in which the Church's relation to the world and the Kingdom has become muted in favour of a concern with the Church's internal economy. This is not a failing peculiar to the Church of England's present liturgy; other Anglican and non-Anglican ones suffer in the same way, though some of the often unjustly maligned American Episcopalian orders, official and experimental, show signs of recognizing the problem.[10]

It is not a matter simply of criticizing a particular style of prose or a particular set of assumptions about the structure of worship. These are independent issues (although not completely unconnected). The question is about the theology which informs our understanding of the relation of liturgy to the world which is claimed for Christ's sovereignty by those who worship. Nor is it a matter of tailoring liturgy to the interests or abilities of a mostly non-worshipping public (Prayer Book Mattins as an acceptable cultural activity for the educated unbeliever or half-believer).

The curious accusation that liturgical reform has turned the Church of England into a 'eucharistic' sect and cut it off from the public life of the nation is ironic in the light of the fact that it is the Communion Orders of 1549, 1552 and 1662 that most clearly set out the 'public' and social dimension of belonging in the Body of Christ, since it is precisely at the Lord's Table that the congregation is called to answer for the life of the community. Nor is it a matter of overloading the liturgy with exhortations to good behaviour or social justice at the expense of giving glory to God, but of finding words to express how the pressure of that glory is, concretely, the formation of a community whose corporate life points to the Kingdom, to *God's* world made whole.

I am uncomfortably aware of not being either a liturgiologist or an active composer of liturgies: but this encourages me to indulge in a few irresponsible suggestions which there is little risk of anyone taking too seriously. If one is going to complain in abstruse terms about the shortcomings of liturgy, one is going to be asked, sooner or later, what *ought* to be done. So I venture these reflections on possible ways of doing justice to what I believe to be a central part of the historic Anglican understanding of liturgy.

(i) We need a penitential rite at the Eucharist which will focus our attention on specific offences against the Body of Christ. The 1662 invitation to confession requires a resolve to mutual charity and implies, following the rubric and the Exhortations, a resolve to practical reconciliation. We do not have to hurry. An invitation to confession should be able to put *some* flesh on why we need to confess as we come to the Lord's Supper. I know that primitive eucharistic rites are very short on penitential material, but that's because primitive eucharistic worshippers could take for granted a penitential practice far more draconian than anything we dream of today.[11]

Just as, *de facto*, the Eucharist has become the chief context for expository and doctrinal teaching, so, *de facto*, it is the place where most Christians will learn about their answerability to God. At least for Sundays and major celebrations, we should have a more extended penitential rite, which sets before us positively the requirements of the Kingdom and negatively the particular individual and corporate sins that betray the vision of the Kingdom. Increasingly (outside the world of official liturgies), people are composing good and varied penitential litanies — a form which seems increasingly to recommend itself to contemporary worshippers; a good modern Communion Order might well offer a choice of these.

(ii) The Byzantine liturgy customarily uses the Beatitudes as the third antiphon before the procession of the Book of the Gospels (the 'Little Entrance'), introducing them with the prayer of the Good Thief from St Luke ('Remember me when you come into your kingdom'). This usage of the Beatitudes (from Matthew 5) in liturgy has found a place in the worship of Taizé.[12] Is it feasible to introduce it into our eucharistic worship as part of the evocation of the life of the Kingdom?

(iii) Connected with (ii): can we put some content into what the Eucharistic Prayer says about the Church? As things stand, we have no real *narrative* in the Preface to tell us about the history of the covenant (so that the *'new covenant'* mentioned later is left theologically stranded).

Ever since the first Anglican Prayer Book followed and intensified the Western tradition of curtailing material before the Sanctus, we have been deprived of an opportunity to say something solid about the continuity of God's saving work (compare almost any Eastern rite at this point), specifically about how that work creates a community under God's law and finally the community of the law of Christ; and how the covenant with one group is a sign of hope in speaking of God's promised commitment to the whole human world, and, indeed, the entire creation. We need, in other words, to say more fully what 'a people for your own possession' is supposed to *mean* — not by way of the exposition of an idea, but by putting the notion in a context where it will be more than a rather artificial tag. This is certainly a place where we can say something about the relation of Church and Kingdom, about the *horizon* of the Church's life.

Many traditions recite the elements of the story of God's action with us after the Sanctus, where, as in the Preface, recent English texts are remarkably slight, giving the unmistakable impression that any interesting or worthwhile (worth celebrating) action of God begins with the incarnation (or perhaps even the passion). What has happened to Abraham and Moses? The third and fourth of the Roman Eucharistic Prayers (especially the fourth) do something towards maintaining the narrative element,[13] and thus the universal horizon of our talking about the Church, and so do some of the American drafts, especially the supplementary orders currently (1990) in experimental use. The Church of England and the rest of the Anglican Communion should be taking this to heart. To make this point is not, as sometimes suggested, to cling to the vestiges of an outdated theory of salvation history: simply to recognize that the *raison d'être* of the Church is completely unintelligible without reference to Israel and to the eschatological gathering of all peoples which the election of Israel promises ('a light to the nations'). That is to say, unless we grasp that the characteristic form of God's dealing with us is the formation of a community that manifests the possibility of human healing and justice, and directs the world to the praise of its maker, we shall not see why there is a Eucharist community there at all: the worshipping congregation will be cut off from the pattern of God's 'mission' in the world, and will look like a contingent gathering of individuals who have religious interests. Although 1662 (and its predecessors) have no such material in the Eucharistic Prayer proper, the earlier parts of the rite have made abundantly clear that this assembly is not a 'contingent' gathering of this sort; there is certainly a serious dearth of reference to the first covenant (no provision for an Old Testament lesson), unless we count the Ten Commandments as such, but there is no unclarity at all about the 'communal' effect of the divine act of invitation.

So: somewhere in the 'liturgy of the Eucharist', as we are now, oddly, supposed to call the latter part of the Order, somewhere after the Offertory, we ought to be talking about *covenant* — about the creation of a people by God's act, a people not just baldly 'for his own possession', but called as a sign of promise to the human race. We need words to tell us about God's faithfulness to the divine promise as shown in the history of the Jewish people as well as the history of the Church so that we may confidently look forward to that of which the eucharistic assembly is the foretaste. And perhaps we need, in the concluding section of the Eucharistic Prayer, some fuller petitions about this, a little spelling out

of 'gather into one in your Kingdom' in terms that go beyond the immediate worshipping assembly.

(iv) Why not a re-writing of one or more of the Exhortations? Not
necessarily for public use in the liturgy, since there is an obvious risk in
a didactic interruption or division of the service, evidently rather differently conceived now from what it was in the sixteenth and seventeenth
centuries, but as a general statement setting out the responsibility
entailed in responding to God's gracious invitation. The second Exhortation of 1662, based ultimately on a composition of Peter Martyr's,[14]
has stood the test of time well, and might be worth reworking along
with some material from the first Exhortation; or there might be a
case for a wholly new composition. I realize that this is a very long
shot indeed, but, as I have said, I am simply making irresponsible
suggestions.

(v) My final suggestion is again not necessarily for regular public use,
but might have some ecumenical import as well as some pertinence for
major events in the congregation's life. The post-communion sections
of our liturgies have been abridged almost to vanishing point.[15] It has
been argued that a thanksgiving for communion should be brief and
business-like, since the receiving of communion is itself a sufficient
commissioning and benediction, and should appropriately be left as the
manifest climax of the rite. There is something in this, but the result
has been a quite widespread sense of abruptness or perfunctoriness in
the conclusion of the liturgy. So what about a prayer drawing on something like the Methodist Covenant Service, expressing the *mission* of
individual and community in the world?[16] I know that we already say,
'Send us out in the power of your Spirit to live and work to your praise
and glory'; but once again I should like to see some elucidation of this,
some resourceful imagining what such life and work might mean
within a full story of covenant relationship, leading up to the universal
horizon of Christ's Kingdom.

Conclusion

It might be that, if all these proposals were (by some wild chance)
realized, the resulting liturgy would seem to insist too much on the
wider social or communitarian implications of the life of the Body. But
would it? We are in no danger, on present showing, of any excess of
reference to this dimension, and we need, I believe, a rather strong
corrective to shake us out of the recurrent danger of talking liturgically
as if we were a community of abstract subjects, constituted only by
our identity as worshippers. And the Book of Common Prayer shows
us that it is possible to construct a morally weighty and concretely
anchored liturgical style without compromising the purpose of the

liturgy in giving glory to God. To offer God 'ourselves, our souls and bodies'[17] as our 'liturgy' means primarily, of course, to offer what we have become in Christ; but what we become in Christ is not something existing in a space outside the particular networks and histories of which we are part. Our 'spiritual' or 'reasonable' service to God should not departicularize us, make us discarnate or non-historical.

The Communion Orders of 1549, 1552 and 1662 show clearly how one might try to give glory to the eternal God very consciously *as* citizens of a specific place, as members of *this* historical polity. If we are confident that Anglicanism in general and Anglican liturgy in particular have by the grace of God something to offer in the development of self-discovery of the Catholic Church at large, we should be willing to go on working at our liturgy with these historic attempts in mind. We can see in retrospect how the effort to speak concretely and not abstractly of worshipping persons was disastrously entangled with a set of mediaeval or 'Constantinian' assumptions about unity and authority transferred to the nation-state; we have learned that this is a risky task.

But relating the eucharistic congregation to the history of the covenant community, to the empirical communities which in practice constitute the daily identity of worshippers, and to the eschatological community of all tribes and peoples before God and the Lamb is something in itself quite different from sacralizing the existing order of a nation or the self-sufficient identity of an ethnic group. Along with repenting the ludicrous and tragic chauvinisms of Anglican history, we should be asking what theological edge lies buried and blunted in this muddled story.

The piety of the first Exhortation and what it represents is not something we need to be ashamed of. And, if I can be allowed a concluding more-than-ever-unscientific postscript, I would be inclined to say that a recovery of confidence in the making of Anglican liturgy is imperative, at a time when so much liturgical reconstruction is liable to be bogged down in archaeologism, political horse-trading, and occasional 'hobbitry' (a fascination for the quaint and *folklorique*, on the grounds of supposed antiquity and/or catholicity). Some of this energy is pretty badly needed elsewhere in tackling the question of how Christians are to articulate in praise, repentance and intercession their accountability to the norms of God's Kingdom against the background of the communities in which their human identity is being shaped and tested. After all, no-one else seems interested or equipped to articulate the accountability of political society to something beyond itself.

This essay was originally delivered in Holy Trinity Church, Guildford, on Saturday 16 June 1990, as the second annual Walter Boulton Lecture.

Notes

1 For texts and sources, see F. E. Brightman, *The English Rite II* (London: Rivingtons, 1915), pp. 650ff.

2 See in general G. J. Cuming, *A History of Anglican Liturgy* (London: Macmillan, 1982), pp. 45ff.

3 J. N. Figgis, *Churches in the Modern State* (London: Longmans, 1913), Appendix I.

4 See Rowan Williams, *Resurrection: Interpreting the Easter Gospel* (London: Darton, Longman and Todd, 1982), pp. 110ff.

5 Lewis Bayly published his *Practice of Piety* in its third edition in 1613 (the date of the first edition is not known). It was much read; John Bunyan regarded it as a formative influence on his life.

6 See, for example, Paul Avis, *Anglicanism and the Christian Church* (Edinburgh; T. & T. Clark, 1989), esp. pp. 36ff.

7 See Cuming, op. cit., pp. 191ff., and R. C. D. Jasper, *The Development of the Anglican Liturgy 1662–1980* (London: SPCK, 1989), pp. 342ff.

8 *For the Sake of the Kingdom: God's Church and the New Creation* (Report of the Inter-Anglican Theological and Doctrinal Commission) (London: Anglican Consultative Council, 1986). The writer was a member of this Commission.

9 See *The Alternative Service Book 1980* (London, 1980), Third Eucharistic Prayer, pp. 136ff.

10 See *Book of Common Prayer* (New York: Seabury, 1979), Eucharistic Prayers in Rite II Eucharist.

11 Cf. the optional character of the penitential rite in the *Book of Alternative Services* (Toronto: Anglican Book Centre, 1985), pp. 216ff.

12 The Beatitudes also appear in seventeenth-century Anglican rites such as that of Jeremy Taylor, and the 1689 proposals; see W. J. Grisbrooke, *Anglican Liturgies of the Seventeenth and Eighteenth Centuries* (Alcuin Collections 40; London: SPCK, 1958), pp. 186f., and T. J. Fawcett, *The Liturgy of Comprehension* (Alcuin Collections 54; Southend: Mayhew-McCrimmon, 1973), pp. 101ff. and 235.

13 See *Missale Romanum* (Vatican: Typis Polyglottis, 1971), pp. 456ff.

14 See Cuming, op. cit., p. 73.

15 See discussion of this issue in Kenneth Stevenson, *Accept This Offering: The Eucharist as Sacrifice Today* (London: SPCK, 1989), pp. 80ff.

16 See David H. Tripp, *The Renewal of the Covenant in the Methodist Tradition* (London: Epworth, 1969).

17 See Kenneth Stevenson, *Eucharist and Offering* (New York: Pueblo, 1986), *passim*, esp. on 'story'.

2

Communion, children, and community

David R. Holeton

One of the most remarkable changes in the sacramental practice of the Western Churches over the past several decades is the movement to include all the baptized, regardless of age, as communicants at the Lord's Table. The root causes of this are twofold: once again, Churches are coming to terms with the implications of their own baptismal theology and they are doing so in the context of a new model of the Church. The effect on communities and individuals alike is often little short of revolutionary: they are obliged to re-think their presuppositions about the sacramental life and about the nature of the Church itself.

In the most important multilateral ecumenical document of the last decade the question is put this way:

> If baptism, as incorporation into the body of Christ, points by its very nature to the eucharistic sharing of Christ's body and blood, the question arises as to how a further and separate rite can be interposed between baptism and admission to communion. Those churches which baptize children but refuse them a share in the eucharist before such a rite may wish to ponder whether they have fully appreciated and accepted the consequences of baptism.[1]

The Anglican Communion has not been immune to this change. While there are Provinces which have yet even to discuss the question, there are others where the communion of all the baptized is a common, if not normative, practice. The Church of England sits somewhere in the middle: the issue has been written about and much discussed.[2] Action on the question, however, has been at the unofficial initiative of parents or of local parishes while General Synod has yet to decide on the matter.[3]

Modern discussion of the matter within the Anglican Communion can be dated from Resolution 25 of Lambeth 1968[4] which, in the context of a discussion of the mission and ministry of the Church in the world, asked Provinces to explore the relationship between baptism, communion and confirmation. The resulting provincial reports[5] led to the creation of a number of revised baptismal rites in some of which it was clear that baptism was the sole sacramental act required for admission to the Eucharist and that all those baptized were communicants. Confirmation ceased to be required before admission to communion, although various Provinces have yet to achieve a common mind on the role confirmation should play within the Churches.[6]

While these changes may seem revolutionary to many contemporary Anglicans, the issue has been with us since our Reformation beginnings. The question of why Anglicans are prepared to baptize, but not communicate, infants was posed in the sixteenth century and became a major issue during the theological debates of the next century when infant baptism became an issue of bitter contention.[7] Through the process of this debate Anglican theologians were pressed to clarify their theology of baptism and to admit that there were no theological grounds for the baptism of infants that were not, at the same time, also grounds for their admission to the Eucharist. What, then, kept the Church of England from restoring the communion of all the baptized centuries ago? For, if pressed, most Anglican sacramental and liturgical theologians would admit that there has been an inconsistency in our willingness to baptize people of all ages but then to invoke age or intellectual capacity as grounds for exclusion from the Eucharist. (While the Prayer Book Catechism counts only baptism and the Eucharist as being 'generally (i.e. for all) necessary to salvation' pastoral practice has often insisted on a third, unnecessary 'sacrament', not mentioned in the catechism preparing candidates for its reception, before the second, necessary sacrament can be received.[8]) An answer to this question is to be found more in the operative model of the Church than it is in the theology of initiation.

New models of the Church

Whenever the Church has come to see itself as a small, gathered, eucharistic community, the communion of all the baptized quickly becomes a real question. Conversely, whenever the Church is established and sees itself as including the whole of society there is little concern for including all the baptized in the act of communion.[9] The practice of communicating children and the very young varies directly with the sense of community within the Church. Where the Church sees itself as a community which takes seriously the importance of the individual in the corporate whole, the communion of all the baptized quickly becomes an issue. Where the individual is subsumed in the more important whole, the issue rarely arises. If this thesis is true,[10] there should be little wonder that Churches move at different paces on the question and the Church of England itself is of opposite minds. Any Church which still makes claims based on constitutional establishment

(in which legal arguments about the obligation to baptize are disso-
ciated from any expectation of faithful discipleship within the context
of Christian community) is going to have a very difficult time resolving
the question of the right of all the baptized to the Eucharist, until they
have a clearer understanding of the reality into which baptism admits.
Parishes in which baptism is taken seriously both as admission to the
Christian life and to Christian ministry; in which a wide variety of
people participate in the preparation of candidates for baptism (both of
adults and the parents of infants); in which ongoing Christian nurture
in the context of the parish community is a priority and in which the
ongoing sustenance for the mission and ministry of the parish is found
in the weekly eucharistic gathering, are parishes in which the admission of all the baptized to the Eucharist becomes a natural act. On the
other hand, if baptism remains a private act held at the convenience of
parents and apart from the regular worship of the community; if there is
little or no preparation and what preparation there is involves the parish
priest alone; if the parish has no commitment to nurture either its
adults or children; and if Sunday worship is highly clericalized and
characterized by a collection of isolated individuals, then the communion of all the baptized appears as an artificial act which belies the
life of the whole parish. Here, the question of communicating all the
baptized becomes an indicator of the paradigm under which the Church
is operating. The question which must be posed is: which model is
appropriate for a Church entering the twenty-first century? To me, the
answer seems to be quite obvious but, once we have made the choice,
working out the consequences can be painful. We may be forced to
leave behind many of the trappings of establishment to which we have
strong emotional attachment. Raising the question of the communion
of all the baptized raises some profound questions about the nature of
Christian community itself. It pushes us to examine aspects of our
community life that are often left unquestioned.

Children and the Church

A number of years ago, when I first began to work on the question of the
admission of young children to the Eucharist, I thought of it as something we adults were doing for children. I am no longer capable of thinking of the question in that way. Instead, I have come to realize that the
inclusion of all the baptized has much more to do with what children do
for us adult members of the Church. Having been in pastoral situations
where I have communicated children, including the very young, for
almost twenty years, I have come to see the question in quite a different
light.

As a father and a teacher who spends fair amounts of time with his students' children, I don't think I have many sentimental ideas about children left. With St Augustine, who was a keen observer of children, it did not take long to realize that: 'It is the physical weakness of the infant that makes him seem innocent, not the quality of his inner life.'[11] Everything a child is to become, both good and evil, is present from the earliest days of life. Why, then, does Jesus take a child and set him before the disciples as the model for those who would inherit the Kingdom?[12] For, if we are to take Jesus seriously in this matter, mere, unreconstructed, adults have no hope of entering the Kingdom.[13]

In making a child the model of the inheritor of the Kingdom, Jesus was acting in a fashion that broke with contemporary Jewish thought. For in the tradition which Jesus inherited, children were not important in what they were, but in what they were to become — the promise of a future for Israel. Jesus, however, makes the child important for qualities that are already present, qualities which we tend to unlearn as we grow older, qualities such as a sense of mystery and wonder, a sense of dependence, the unashamed ability to receive, a natural faith or trust, and effervescent joy.

It is impossible to spend very much time with a child without becoming acutely aware that children are often sensitive to the awesome mystery of the divine in a way in which it has become quite casual to us. I am reminded of this repeatedly by looking into the faces of young communicants. As adults, we are only too ready to explain mystery away, taking Christ's self-giving in the Eucharist simply as the natural order of things.

Augustine suggested that the child was the ideal communicant because it images perfectly the helplessness of the human condition. We must come to God with the same helpless abandon as an infant does to its mother.[14] We need to unlearn some of the self-assuredness we have come to assume in our relationship with God.

Just as, I suspect, none of us has encountered a child who is an embarrassed receiver muttering 'Oh, you shouldn't have!', or 'You needn't have bothered!' when being presented with a gift, Christian adults need to learn what it is to be receivers of God's gifts offered freely and unmerited. Children are perfect receivers.

Those who work in early childhood development tell us that children are trusting until they learn not to trust. In a world in which we adults, particularly those of us who live in urban environments, have learned not to trust others, the natural trust of children models for us the true nature of the relationship we are to have with God: a relationship in which our mechanisms for self-defence must be laid aside and our final attitude to God becomes that of trust.

As adults, we spend much time and energy keeping our emotions under control. This is particularly important for those of us who are Anglo-Saxons and for whom a public (or often private) display of emotion is considered unacceptable. As adults, we spend more time controlling the emotions of anger and impatience than the other range of emotions. Children spend more time controlling their emotions of joy.[15] The joy of children is something we have all experienced as infectious; does it not, perhaps, model for us the joy and delight of the saints in God's Kingdom?

Paul tells us that in Christ 'there is no such thing as Jew and Greek, slave and freeman, male and female' (Gal 3.28) for we are all one person in Jesus Christ. I would like to suggest that age and intellectual achievement are also potential human barriers that are also overturned in Christ. For in his Kingdom all the barriers we erect to keep us apart from one another: gender, race, class, social status, age or intellectual achievement are all abolished and we are made one in him. Finding young children receiving communion in our midst is a lively reminder of that reality. Each time I communicate a young child or find an infant receiving from the same cup as I have received from, I am brought up short. I am made to acknowledge that the criteria for participation in the Kingdom are not mine but God's. That often turns my own world on its head. The things which are most important to me — status, intellectual achievement or whatever — are not only relativized but are shown to be false standards for judgement. I am constantly grateful for that reminder each Sunday I am at a Eucharist where children are natural communicants. Having become accustomed to communicating all the baptized, I have a strong sense that something is missing when I am at the Eucharist in Provinces where young children are not communicants.

The message such Provinces seem to be giving is that, somehow, some of us are not good enough or, perhaps, have not learned enough to be welcome at the Table. This message seriously mars who we are as the Body of Christ and does violence to the wholeness we can find only in him. It makes an unacceptable theological statement about the gift of salvation which is freely offered and which cannot be achieved through human merit. In short, I find the theological statement made by excluding children from the Eucharist totally incompatible with what I have come to experience eucharistic community being about: the weekly renewal of the baptismal mystery in which we became one Body and the locus in which we are fed so that we may continue in our baptismal ministry in the world. I reject the idea that ministry is confined to adults and that children can only be receivers. They need nourishment to sustain them in their baptismal ministry too.

I find it increasingly difficult to find any way of explaining why children, whom Jesus held up as the model for those who would enter the Kingdom, should be denied access to the eucharistic meal which is the *antipasto* of that Kingdom. For, surely, it is in the eucharistic assembly that we catch a glimpse of who and what we are called to be as saints in

God's Kingdom. From the gathering of the community itself we learn to live in a truly socialized world in which the barriers of gender, race, class, education *and age* can no longer keep us apart and in which, because of our common birth from the font, we all are equals. It is there that we learn to live in the peaceable kingdom (in which a young child shall lead us — Is 11.6) by sharing a sign of reconciliation and learning the hard lesson of making peace. It is there that we come to know the rich banquet prepared for us by our God in which all are fed, none are sent away empty, none are fed too much but each one has just enough. It is a vision of a world made new in Christ.

Communion, children, and formation

I have written elsewhere[16] of the power of the liturgy to form us as Christians. The liturgy, and the assembly in which it is celebrated, gives us the matrix within which we learn to speak of God, to define our own Christian communities and to construct a paradigm within which we are able to engage the world. We need to ask serious questions about the formation of young children who are excluded or included at the eucharistic meal.

Not so many years ago, when the vestiges of Christendom were still palpable, when urban Sunday schools often numbered in the hundreds, when Christianity was taught in the local schools and society did not know of the religious pluralism that characterizes Western nations, it was fair to assume that simply existing within society provided a basic modicum of Christian nurture. The social values which were publicly proclaimed were given at least a veneer of Christian ethics; daily Bible reading and the recitation of the Lord's Prayer in most of our schools gave children at least a passing familiarity with the great sweep of the biblical story and with prayer. But those days are gone and few of us can imagine that they will ever return. Society will no longer do the Churches' job in their stead. It there is to be Christian nurture it will be found in two places: our homes and our Christian communities.

What are the effects on Christian nurture of excluding some of the baptized from the Eucharist? The post-war confirmation crisis told us a great deal. Confirmands voted with their feet. Adolescents who had been excluded from the Eucharist (and often from the eucharistic assembly by being relegated to Sunday school) dropped out of any Church-related practice in droves — often at the rate of 80 per cent within the first year. This is an interesting comment on the seriousness of their 'mature' profession of faith and their commitment to 'confirm' the baptismal vows taken on their behalf. In many instances, where first communion was to take place on the Sunday after confirmation, parish priests report that as many as half their confirmands did not return for first communion. We should not be surprised by this. Why would adolescents choose to leave the security of their friends and the safety of the Sunday school environment for a Church setting in which they had always been made to feel as unwelcome intruders and in whose central act of worship they had experienced only rejection or, at best, a pat on the head, while all the adults were being fed? To interview those who are still in the Church but who went through the 'traditional' pattern (baptism–confirmation–communion) is often to hear stories of alienation, rejection, growing anxiety as the day of first communion drew near, and contempt for the adults who told them they mattered, but refused to show it in matters that were claimed to be most important to them (reception of the Eucharist).

This sense of alienation and rejection becomes even more serious in communities where, because patterns of church-going have changed, children are a regular presence in the weekly eucharistic assembly. Because the new liturgical texts make claims about eucharistic community which are notably absent from the traditional Prayer Book texts we have made the situation even more difficult. We should not be surprised when a six-year-old girl comments: 'I'm not going to say "We are all one body" again, because we aren't. Me and Ben don't share the bread.' Or to hear a child remark: 'You say Jesus asks us to come to his table, so why do you stop us?'[17] Or, again, to have a child comment: 'Jesus actually *wanted* to have the children come to him, because we are a part of the family of God. We are all God's children — including the adults.'[18] The liturgy has been a primary catechesis for these children and, if we are going to continue to refuse to communicate these children, the catechesis of our actions will certainly overshadow the biblical and sacramental catechesis of the liturgical texts.

To interview those who do not remember a time when they were not welcome at the Lord's Table is a quite different experience.[19] For many, particularly in my own Province, these are the reflected comments of those who are now in their late teens or early twenties and who have been communicants virtually all of their lives. Comments often come in terms of a sense of belonging, equality, and community. One young man commented: 'The church was the only place where, as a child, I felt I counted as an equal.' Another observed: 'Because I always received communion with my family, I always knew I belonged.' A twenty-year-old who does not remember a time when he was not a communicant reflected that as a child he could 'talk to anyone at church (unlike in the rest of life) because everyone was equal at communion'. A seven-year-old who moved from a diocese where he had not been allowed to receive communion into one where the pastoral discipline permitted him to received the sacrament remarked after his first communion: 'For the first time I feel as if I belong to the Church.' A fourteen-year-old girl who has been a communicant since her baptism notes: 'As a child, I always felt discriminated against because of my age, in church I felt like I belonged. Children should be communicants because it makes them feel a part of the community.'[20]

While the sample is not large enough for the claim to be made that comments of this sort are representative of all those who have been young communicants and who continue to live their lives as members of a parish community, it would be fair to observe that the types of comment made by those who have followed the 'traditional' pattern and those who have been communicant for as long as they can remember are qualitatively different.

What is more important, however, is the formation of young Christians in ways that are less easy to articulate. At some point during the teen years, young persons arrive at a point at which they are given an opportunity to decide whether or not they wish to continue to practise their faith. In some cases this happens because parents actually give them the choice, in other cases it happens only when the individual leaves home to continue studies or to begin a job in another part of the country. In the 'no communion-before-confirmation' model the choice with which the individual is faced is made in the decision of whether or not to continue membership in a community in which their dominant memories may be of exclusion or alienation. In the 'communion since baptism' model the decision is made in the context of having to decide to leave a community in which there has always been a sense of acceptance or belonging and a feeling of 'having counted' or 'been equal' that may well have been greater than in any other area of life. For many people I have interviewed, it was this sense of their rejection or belonging that made their decision to continue or cease practising much easier.

The way forward

What are the appropriate steps to be taken by the Anglican Communion on this question? There are three areas in which decisions need to be made. The first is theological, the second ecclesiological and the third is pastoral. I will try to delineate the issues in each.

(a) Theological considerations

Above all, it must be recognized that the question of communicating all the baptized is a theological issue before it is a catechetical or pastoral one. It has been repeatedly demonstrated that there is no theological reason to exclude the baptized from the Eucharist but that there *is* every reason, theological, historical and pastoral, to include all those who are baptized at the Lord's Table. Baptism admits to and is fulfilled in the eucharistic meal both at the time of baptism itself and thereafter.

The withdrawal of communion from the very young is as theologically lamentable as was the withdrawal of the chalice from the laity or the practice of receiving communion only annually. The Reformers were able to redress the latter abuses immediately. The chalice was restored during the earliest days of the English Reformation. Frequent (weekly) communion for all the 'confirmed' has won its way in most Anglican parishes during this century. Refusing to include all the baptized at communion remains the final late-mediaeval abuse to be remedied.

As a step within Anglicanism it is both logical and consistent with the renewal of our baptismal and eucharistic practices which have taken place over the past years. The authenticity of the historical practice has been acknowledged by Anglicans since the early days of the Reformation. The theological legitimacy of the practice has been conceded at every point in our history during which there has been serious discussion of initiation — from the seventeenth-century debates with the antipaedobaptists to the present day. As an Anglican it seems to me very difficult to reject a practice which is deemed consonant with scripture and the historic practice of the Universal Church and when the theological tradition acknowledges that the practice is founded on the self-same principles that legitimate infant baptism. Placed in the context of contemporary Anglican eucharistic practice — the weekly communion at which the whole community is present — it is very difficult to see why we would even consider not admitting all the baptized to the Eucharist. To continue to do so would involve a very un-Anglican disregard for both history and admitted theological truth.

Having relegated baptism to a private (and often domestic) event for so long, it is little wonder that many Anglicans have lost all sense that the Eucharist is the weekly renewal of the covenant made in baptism. We need to work at renewing our baptismal piety so that we have a sense of it as a living reality in our lives. The entire weight of baptismal renewal cannot be allowed to rest on a single act of confirmation. Reaffirmation of baptism is a corporate act of the whole Church, taking place in the weekly celebration of the Eucharist; in the daily living out of the implications of the Gospel; in the participation of faith communities in the baptism of others; and in the use of Lent as a season of preparation for the annual renewal of the baptismal covenant at the Easter Vigil.

Individuals renew their own baptismal covenant by participating in these events as well as on the occasion(s) when they make a particular profession of their baptismal faith in the act traditionally called 'confirmation'. This latter act must be understood in the context of the other acts of baptismal renewal and should not be allowed to take on a pre-eminence in which it risks overshadowing or trivializing the other, ongoing, acts of baptismal renewal, particularly the Eucharist.[21]

(b) Ecclesiological and pastoral considerations

The question of including all the baptized at the Eucharist can serve as a very useful instrument in helping us decide who we are as a Church. Anglicanism, and particularly the Church of England, is at a point where it is being called to make some important decisions about how it sees itself relating to society at large. Most of our actions as a Church are no longer governed by a Christendom model. It is clear to all but the most insulated of Anglicans that we live in a non-believing, or at the very least non-practising, world. Christian nurture, if it is to take place at all, must take place in our Christian communities and in our homes. In sorting out our model of the Church, we are faced with some very basic questions. Who is the Church? What is the relationship of baptism and belonging to the Body of Christ? What are the rights of those who are active members of the Christian community?

The relationship between the model of the Church and our sacramental life is an immediate one in a way in which it wasn't when we operated under a Christendom model. Who we are and who we wish to be as a Christian community is modelled each time we gather together to celebrate the Eucharist. In that sense, the Eucharist is not only a sacrament for the converted, but it is also a converting sacrament. Slowly, and often painfully, we become what we celebrate. This is not unimportant for the young children and infants in our midst. We provide the basic environment for our infants and young children. If we are changed — and in the Eucharist we are changed — then we affect the environment for our children. But, as I suggested earlier, the process works both ways. Communicating children affects us too. As we come to see in them the model Jesus offered of the perfect inheritor of the Kingdom, our own values are challenged and we are continually called to rethink our own lives as we grow in Christ.

Concluding observations

The question of the communion of all the baptized is not going to go away. It is an ongoing agenda item for the Anglican Communion as a whole. In arriving at a point where a decision has to be made to move forward on the issue, it is important to remember that in doing so, Provinces are not only acting on the natural consequences of the renewal of our sacramental life which was promoted by Resolution 25 of Lambeth 1968 but that those actions are consonant with the liturgical and sacramental reforms of the Anglican tradition as a whole. What Cranmer and the Reformers did in reforming the baptismal rite in the first Prayer Books and in their creation of a new, non-initiatory, rite for the renewal of baptismal vows — confirmation — is completely consonant with including all the baptized in the Eucharist.

Until the Church of England acts on that, there will be ongoing dissonance each time the Eucharist is celebrated in the presence of children. Theological dissonance, because it is anomalous to baptize into the Body of Christ but then to refuse all the baptized a share in the Body and Blood of Christ. Dissonance each time we proclaim: 'We who are many are one body, because we all share in the one bread', when that is quite clearly untrue because we do not *all* share in the one bread. Dissonance because we who, quite rightly, wish our children to grow in the Christian life and to continue to follow with us in 'the way' continue to present them with a model in which they are excluded from what is central in our weekly celebration as Christian communities. Dissonance because those who are given to us as models of the ideal inheritors of the Kingdom are excluded from the banquet at which we anticipate that same Kingdom. In a church in which the Eucharist was celebrated infrequently or in which the young were sent off to Sunday school or the nursery this dissonance went unnoticed. In a church in which the Eucharist is celebrated weekly and Christians of all ages are present, the dissonance has become unbearable. Our sacramental theology, ecclesiology and pastoral practice must become consonant once again. To fail in this has serious consequences both for our regular eucharistic assemblies and for those to whom we hope to pass the faith.

Notes

1 'Baptism: Commentary 14 (b)' in *Baptism, Eucharist and Ministry* (Faith and Order Paper 111; Geneva: WCC, 1982), p. 5.
2 Colin Buchanan traces the history to 1981 in 'Infant and child communion in the Church of England' in my *Infant Communion — Then and Now* (Grove Liturgical Study 27; Bramcote: Grove, 1981), pp. 27–31, and brings this up to date in 'Recent Church of England history' in his *Children in Communion* (Grove Worship Series 112; Bramcote: Grove, 1990), pp. 20–2.
3 A minute of the House of Bishops from January 1990 reads:

In 1987 the House of Bishops decided to defer further consideration until after the Lambeth Conference. In view of the Lambeth Conference Resolution 69 asking Provinces to consider this matter and in view of requests from the dioceses for further debate following their deliberation on *Children in the Way* the House expressed the hope and expectation that the subject would be on the agenda of General Synod during 1991.

Quoted in Colin Buchanan, *Children in Communion*, p. 22.

4 The Lambeth Conference 1968, *Resolutions and Reports* (London: SPCK, 1968), pp. 37, 99.

5 I present an overview of these reports in 'Christian initiation in some Anglican Provinces', *Studia Liturgica* 12.2/3 (1977), pp. 129–50.

6 This is partly because of the conflicting theological models of confirmation under which Anglicans have operated since the last century with the rise of the 'two-stage' school which held initiation to be incomplete in baptism without the addition of confirmation. (See Colin Buchanan, *Anglican Confirmation* (Grove Liturgical Study 48; Bramcote: Grove, 1986), pp. 30ff.) This school imposed a Roman sacramental model on Anglicanism and failed to recognize that Cranmer had both reformed the mediaeval baptismal rite and introduced a reformed rite of confirmation which was not a continuation of the second post-baptismal anointing of the mediaeval Roman rite. (See Marion Hatchett, *Commentary on the American Prayer Book* (New York: Seabury Press, 1980), pp. 260–5, and my forthcoming article, 'The beginnings of reformed confirmation' to appear in *Studia Liturgica*.) The 'Boston Statement' on children and communion from the First International Anglican Liturgical Consultation ran into a certain amount of difficulty at Lambeth 1988 not so much for theological reasons but because it (inadvertently) brought into question some confirmation practices — particularly in the Third World — which have more to do with episcopal status and prestige than with the renewal of baptismal vows.

7 I have dealt with this issue in 'Communion of all the baptized in Anglican tradition', *Anglican Theological Review* 59.1 (1987), pp. 13ff.

8 It is important to remind ourselves that the recent rigid observance of the confirmation rubric is an invention of the nineteenth-century evangelical revival, before which it was more observed in the breach than in practice. See J. A. Muller, 'The confirmation rubric', *The Southern Churchman* CGI.47, and Peter Jagger, *Clouded Witness* (Allison Park, PA: Pickwick, 1982), pp. 148ff.

9 At times like this the Church has seen little value in the reception of communion itself. Not communicating all the baptized was tolerated in just the same fashion as was infrequent (usually annual) communion and the withdrawal of the chalice from the laity.

10 I believe I have demonstrated it to be true in the past; see my 'The communion of infants and young children: a sacrament of community' in Geiko Müller-Fahrenholz, . . . *And Do not Hinder Them: An Ecumenical Plea for the Admission of Children to the Eucharist* (Faith and Order Paper 109; Geneva: WCC, 1982), pp. 58ff., and *Infant Communion — Then and Now*, pp. 9ff.

11 *Confessions* I, vii, II.

12 'Truly I tell you: unless you turn round and become like children, you will never enter the kingdom of Heaven': Matthew 18.3 (and parallels).

13 I owe this observation to my colleague the Reverend Professor Eugene Fairweather.

14 Augustine, *Commentary on the Psalms* 54, 24 and *Confessions* IV, i, I.

15 I owe this observation to my colleague the Reverend Dr Philip May.

16 'The formative character of liturgy' in Thomas J. Talley (ed.), *A Kingdom*

of Priests: Liturgical Formation of the People of God (Alcuin/GROW Liturgical Study 5; Bramcote: Grove, 1988), pp. 8ff.

17 Quoted from a survey of children by John M. Sutcliffe, 'Children and Holy Communion' in G. Müller-Fahrenholz, . . . *And Do Not Hinder Them*, p. 25.

18 A comment made to one of my students, Maggie Rose Muldoon-Burr, in a project on the Eucharist with young children.

19 See Kenneth Stevenson, 'A theological reflection on the experience of inclusion/exclusion at the Eucharist', *Anglican Theological Review* 58.3 (1986), pp. 212–21.

20 From interviews I have conducted with long-time communicants.

21 These recommendations are similar to those contained in the *Report of the Confirmation Task Force of the Anglican Church of Canada* (Toronto, 1989), p. 43.

3

The year of grace

Thomas J. Talley

Schemes for the revision of the Christian year in recent decades have frequently begun from the observation that approximately half the year, the time after Pentecost, is unarticulated, as if liturgical development had been inexplicably arrested in mid-course. The unspoken assumption behind that observation would seem to be that in the area of liturgical time we have to do with an annual *curriculum* that presents in an orderly fashion the major scriptural, doctrinal, ascetical and ethical concerns of the Christian community, as means toward more effective communication of those concerns.

From a historical standpoint, however, it is difficult to find any earlier point at which the Church sought to undertake such an articulation of the entire year as a cycle of pedagogical or homiletical themes or topic assignments. One might say that the turning of the seasons marked by times of fast and vigil in the early Roman Embertides represented a concern with the annual cycle as such, but behind those lay the primitive core of the paschal fast and rejoicing for fifty days, the earliest annual observance of the liturgical tradition. The Christian year was not conceived as a complete yearly cycle, but evolved out of the continuing Christian observance of Passover to become a number of festivals that were observed annually, rather than weekly.

New Testament evidences show us only the gathering of the Church for Eucharist on the first day of the week, the day of the resurrection, though some have seen reference to Pascha in the later strata of that literature.[1] In the second century, on the other hand, it is clear that the annual observance of Pascha (Passover) in Asia was on the fourteenth day of the Jewish month of Nisan (or its equivalent) and through the following night, a date fixed without regard to the day of the week. Elsewhere that annual observance had been accommodated to the structure of the week, the fast concluded only on the day of the resurrection. The second century also affords evidence that the paschal festivity was continued for fifty days, the entire period known as 'the pentecost', and some believe that in that same century the Epiphany already marked the beginning of the reading of one or another gospel, a reading climaxed in the passion narrative at Pascha.

Even in the following centuries, evidence for such an evangelical course of reading is lacking in many local churches, and restricted to a shorter period in others. Still other factors would lead to the association of particular dates with significant moments in the gospel narratives, and ecumenical convergence would, by the end of the sixth century, bring all these into a relatively common pattern of feasts and seasons. What is clear, nonetheless, is that these annual festivals were intended to explicate the whole mystery of Christ as presented in the gospels and as celebrated in its entirety on every Sunday.

The annual observance from which this rich development grew was the commemoration of the passion of the Lord on the day of the Preparation of the Passover, and that provided a nexus to the Old Testament that would greatly enrich the thematic content of the paschal liturgy. Detailed evidence for Jewish liturgy is notoriously lacking for the first centuries of our era, but it is patent that the Passover celebrated the exodus from Egypt. There is good reason as well to suppose that the creation of the world as we encounter it in fifth-century hagiopolitan lectionaries for the paschal vigil represents a continuity with Judaism. At Rome in the third century the passion of the Lord was assigned to the date of 25 March, the Julian date on which 14 Nisan fell in the supposed year of the passion, and the following century affords evidence assigning the annunciation to Mary to that same date, quite deliberately. It was both of those, to be sure, but perhaps more pointedly the association of creation with the Passover represented by that date that led Dionysius Exiguus in the sixth century to designate 25 March as the beginning of the year, a calendrical convention preserved in England until 1752. As for the paschal vigil itself, Genesis 1 was the first reading at the vigil almost universally, whether the total number of lessons was four, seven, twelve or fifteen.

By the sixteenth century, however, the paschal vigil was carried out during the daylight hours on Saturday of Holy Week, and its complex ceremonies, especially those connected with the blessing of the font, must have set a stench of superstition in the nostrils of reformers insensitive to non-verbal modes of communication. That vigil, the oldest distinctively annual liturgical observance of the Christian Church, disappeared from Anglican worship in 1549, replaced by provisions for Matins and the Communion of 'Easter Even'. With that, Anglican paschal celebration ceased to reflect any reference to creation.[2]

The absence of that creation motif in the paschal liturgy has had significant impact upon developments in this century. An initiative that was to prove significant for the Church of England had its beginning in the Reformed tradition of the Church of Scotland. There, from 1948, A. Allan McArthur undertook the extended process of research that led to his study of the development of the liturgical year and, later, of lectionary systems together with his presentation of the lectionary devised, tested and established in use in Peterhead Old Parish Church, the 'Muckle Kirk'.[3] In the latter of those studies he revealed his dissatisfaction with the inherited cycle of feasts and seasons that, in fact, covers only about half the year, leaving the time after Pentecost relatively unarticulated. Believing that the liturgical year should be a complete annual cycle celebrating the whole of Christian faith, he noted that the traditional year is primarily a Christological cycle punctuated by the celebration of the gift of the Holy Spirit. He proposed a time before Advent focused on the first article of faith, 'I believe in God the Father Almighty, Maker of heaven and earth'. Also, the time from Pentecost forward should develop all the themes of the final paragraph of the creeds.

McArthur's conception of the liturgical year was, thus, as a program of catechesis, explicating the creeds. Given his earlier study of the evolution of the Christian year, his assumption of such a relationship between the creeds and the year is somewhat surprising, the more so in that he makes no attempt to address these many centuries' failure to take the steps he proposed. He had himself suggested that the time from the Epiphany to Pascha set the temporal frame for the reading of the Fourth Gospel at Ephesus in the second century,[4] and others have supposed the principal lines of the seasonal cycle to reflect the gospels rather than the creeds.[5]

Nonetheless, McArthur proposed a new 'Festival of Creation' on the first Sunday of October, at which point it would coincide with an established 'Harvest Thanksgiving'. Such harvest festivals, however, have a way of falling at different times in different nations — on the fourth Thursday of November in my own country, and on the second Monday of October in Canada. One would think that a festival as important as the beginning of the Christian year should be more universally grounded, and it would be unfortunate if McArthur chose this date for his new festival only for its coincidence with that local harvest feast. In any case, the season it initiates is continued for the five following Sundays, leading into an Advent that runs, in the old Gallican and Milanese fashion, for six Sundays. At the other end of the year, Pentecost initiates a new season that continues through the eighteen following Sundays, and two more are devoted to the Christian hope. Such an understanding of Pentecost as a distinct festival rather than as the conclusion of paschaltide is not without patristic precedent, seeking to find Christian application of Old Testament references to the pilgrim feasts. Nonetheless, it does run counter to what is known now of the earliest Christian use of that term to indicate the period of paschal rejoicing rather than its last day as a pivotal festival in its own right.[6]

Two years after the publication of McArthur's lectionary, Henry de

Candole, then Bishop of Knaresborough, proposed the assignment of Genesis (specifically, Creation, the Fall, and the Call of Abraham) to Advent or, better, to Sundays preceding Advent, and cited the proposal of McArthur.[7] John Gunstone suggests that even earlier the bishop had proposed beginning the Christian year in September, evidently with Creation.[8] That, interestingly, would in some years at least approximate the Jewish custom of beginning the reading of Torah in the synagogue from Simhat Torah, following the Feast of Sukkoth.[9]

It was this pattern focused on beginning with Creation, now on the ninth Sunday before Christmas, that was adopted by the Joint Liturgical Group (JLG) in 1963 as the basis for the two-year lectionary developed by that group and published in 1967.[10] The novelty of those nine Sundays before Christmas was replicated by a canonization of the always anomalous pre-Lent to yield a new designation of Septuagesima as the 'Ninth Sunday before Easter'. This ecumenical group included representatives of the Anglican, Presbyterian, Methodist, Congregational, and Baptist churches, and the Churches of Christ, in England and Scotland, and included an observer from the Roman Catholic Church.

The pattern of the year proposed by McArchur and modified by JLG was fitted with a lectionary system in which the lessons were chosen with regard to a scheme of themes assigned to the various Sundays and festivals, carrying forward the catechetical conception of the Christian year assumed by McArthur. For the time before Advent, it is the Old Testament reading that is the primary locus of that theme, while the gospel controls the theme from Advent to the Ascension, and the New Testament reading is the controlling text for Pentecost and the remainder of the year.

At the urging of the late Dean Ronald Jasper, the JLG calendar and lectionary were, with some emendations, incorporated by the General Synod in the *Alternative Service Book 1980*. By that time, however, a much more conservative revision of the *temporale* as frame for a triennial lectionary had been offered by the Roman Catholic Consilium for the Implementation of the Constitution on the Sacred Liturgy. In a laudable gesture of ecumenical consideration, the Consilium admitted to its deliberations in 1966 six observers from outside the Roman Catholic Church. These observers had neither voice nor vote in the plenary sessions of the Consilium, but could offer opinions in writing and frequently discussed the materials under consideration in informal meetings with members of the Consilium and their consultants. Included among those observers were two Anglicans appointed by the Archbishop of Canterbury: the Reverend Professor Massey H. Shepherd, Jr and the (then) Reverend Canon Ronald C.D. Jasper, Secretary of the JLG.

Although the Consilium's deliberations began a year before the publication of the JLG calendar and lectionary, we must suppose that that scheme was already fully developed. Indeed, on 10 October, in response to a suggestion that for ecumenical reasons it would be desirable to preserve the traditional cycle of readings for one of the three years proposed, Cipriano Vagaggini reported a number of initiatives already taken by particular national Churches or groups of Churches, and the first cited was the proposal in 1965 of the biennial lectionary by the 'London group', the Joint Liturgical Group.[11]

No record known to me preserves any discussions between the two Anglican observers at the deliberations of the Consilium, but the vast difference between them was reflected in 1970 in Prayer Book Studies 19, *The Church Year*, the report of the Drafting Committee on the Calendar, Eucharistic Lectionary, and Collects chaired by the late Massey Shepherd for the Standing Liturgical Commission of the Episcopal Church in the United States.[12] The third section of the first chapter of that report, entitled 'Radical proposals', discusses a number of modern proposals but gives particular attention to the JLG scheme, already adopted in England for experimental use.[13] The following section, 'The meaning of the Church Year', includes this criticism:

> The inherent fallacy in these reconstructions is their approach to the Christian Year on a pedagogical rather than a kerygmatic basis. The Church Year is a Christian Year, an epitome of the Christian era, the 'time of Christ' between his two advents. It proclaims at all times the *mysterium Christi*. It is neither a chronological review of the whole of salvation-history, nor a comprehensive course in all the doctrines of the faith. Its basic framework is the recurrence of Sunday, the day of the Resurrection; and its primary, original season is the great fifty days from Easter to Pentecost, that divides the year roughly into two coordinate periods: the one presents Christ in his earthly life and mission; the other presents him in his reigning life through the Spirit in his Church until his coming again.[14]

So rejecting the JLG approach to the liturgical year a decade before its incorporation into ASB, the Episcopal Church followed the much more conservative reform of the year, with its triennial lectionary pattern, undertaken by the Church of Rome. That was the basis for the calendar and eucharistic lectionary of the American Book of Common Prayer of 1979, a direction taken as well by Lutheran, Methodist, Presbyterian, and other bodies in the United States and Canada, including the Anglican Church of Canada. Through the Consultation on Common Texts, this general approach to calendar and lectionary achieved ecumenical expression as *The Common Lectionary*.[15] In all its forms, this triennial lectionary is focused on the course reading of the three synoptic gospels, the Fourth Gospel being employed in all years. While minor variations persist, especially in the 'neutral zones' following the Epiphany and Pentecost, all this development in North America has amounted to an ecumenical convergence that is truly vast in its extent and its significance. It has enabled truly ecumenical commentaries on and translations of the lectionary that are used by virtually all Christians of any Occidental liturgical tradition on the North American continent.

As concerns the structure of the year itself, the most radical change offered by the Consilium was the removal of the three pre-lenten Sundays that had insinuated themselves, sometimes over vigorous objection, from the fifth to the seventh centuries. More important than that excision of an anomalous growth was a serious commitment to the restoration of the fifty days of paschaltide as a period of unbroken rejoicing. The Rogation Days that had inserted a dysphoric note before the Ascension were removed from the *proprium de tempore*, to be observed as votives at times determined by local episcopal conferences. While the feast of the Ascension is still celebrated on the fortieth day, there is no suggestion that it is the conclusion of the *laetissimum spatium* of paschal rejoicing. The Sundays of this time are not designated as falling *after* Easter as in ASB, but are numbered as Sundays *of* Easter from the second to the seventh. Although Pentecost is so designated, that numbering calls to mind the seventeenth-century suggestion of Hamon L'Estrange that the English expression, 'Whitsunday', derives not from 'white Sunday', but from the French *huit*, being *le huitième dimanche*, the eighth Sunday of Easter.[16] Pentecost is not treated as a distinct festival initiating a new season, but as the conclusion of Eastertide.

The conservatism of the Roman reform, carefully reflecting the best scholarship regarding the calendar, sets the radical novelty of the JLG scheme in even higher relief. We Anglicans have asserted since the days of Charles I that locally variant forms of the Book of Common Prayer are consistent with our unity in Christ, and there is no reason why we cannot tolerate the use of more than one calendar and lectionary. Ecumenical considerations, however, become increasingly poignant with the improvement of communications systems, ease of travel, and the general interweaving of cultures to form a more unified world, phenomena observable around the planet but especially significant in Europe today. When those considerations are added to the theological imperative of ecumenical rapprochement, an 'ecumenically' conceived alternative to the broadly accepted Roman Catholic/Common Lectionary pattern (itself no less ecumenically conceived) might seem called upon to offer something more than a year or two of priority as its *raison d'être*.

The JLG calendar, with its biennial lectionary and thematic scheme, will ultimately be judged, of course, by those who use it, not those who view it from afar. Among those who have published their opinions, the assessment seems mixed. Reference was made above to a highly appreciative presentation of that lectionary by John Gunstone at the Congress of Societas Liturgica meeting in Paris in August 1981.[17] Gunstone expressed his support for the thematic organization of the lectionary while reasserting the importance of allowing the scriptures to speak for themselves. He also expressed gratitude for the ecumenical following accorded the JLG lectionary, although without mention of the even wider ecumenical accord granted to the Roman/Common Lectionary pattern.

Reference has been made above as well to the much more negative assessment of the JLG scheme by Michael Moreton.[18] That publication was revised from a trenchant article by Moreton published in 1973.[19] He was concerned primarily with the theological dislocations connected with the assignment of traditionally paschal Genesis and Exodus themes to the time before Christmas and with the treatment of Pentecost as a distinct festival initiating a new season, rather than as the completion of the paschal mystery, both points that were well taken and forcefully argued. More recently, Martin Dudley, addressing the more practical question, 'Does it work?', answers no less robustly in the negative.[20] Dudley helpfully reminds us of the subdivision of the time after Pentecost in seventh-century Rome by such major festivals of the *sanctorale* as Peter and Paul, St Lawrence, and Michaelmas.

Similarly, *The Promise of His Glory*, a report of the Liturgical Commission in February 1990, speaks of the season before Advent as 'All Saintstide', in what is clearly a reconsideration of the calendar and lectionary of ASB.[21] An alternative triennial lectionary, modelled on the Roman/Common Lectionary pattern, is provided for the time from All Saints to Candlemas. This report and the well-received predecessor to it in 1986, *Lent, Holy Week, Easter: Services and Prayers*, suggest that liturgical authorities in the Church of England are responding creatively to misgivings about the ASB calendar and lectionary.

Two members of the liturgical commission of the Church of England deeply involved in the writing of *The Promise of His Glory* have offered essays that had their beginnings in the deliberations of that commission. Bryan Spinks published in 1987 a survey of the problems faced by that report.[22] There he suggested the lengthening of Advent to its earlier extent of six weeks in view of secular pressures, and also the baptism of Jesus as the central content of Epiphany, instead of the visit of the Magi. The absence of the baptism in Jordan from the Western observance of Epiphany surely merits the attention it is beginning to receive, but it should perhaps be remembered that miming the presentation of gifts by the Magi is as important among Latin populations in Europe as is the giving of presents at Christmas in England. In Rome, serious 'Christmas shopping' does not begin until after 25 December. This could become a significant dimension of the problem with the growing economic interdependence of European nations.

Kenneth Stevenson has considered the role of the feast of the Presentation of Christ in the Temple as turning-point of the incarnational cycle to the paschal cycle.[23] From a historical perspective this point seems well taken, and it has been suggested that the play of the fixed date assigned to this festival against the movable date of Easter may have been a factor in the evident variations in the length of Lent at Jerusalem in the very late fourth century and early fifth. That tension between a feast of fixed date and a movable Easter would still be a problem today, however, and Stevenson does not suggest a Lent of variable length. The desire for such a hinge from incarnational to paschal considerations led the Episcopal Church in the USA to follow the Lutherans in assigning the Transfiguration to the final Sunday after Epiphany, whatever the number of those Sundays, although this does not, as with the Lutherans, replace the feast of 6 August.

A North American liturgist can comment on the work of another Church only with diffidence. One may be allowed the observation, however, that much of the culture of the first decade of the latter half of this century seems, in retrospect, to have been imprudently enamoured of novelty, and novelty is never intended to wear well. That something of the giddiness of that era passed into the Alternative Service Book of 1980 is surely to be understood in the context of ASB's original authorization only to the end of 1990. Certainly, the work of the present English Liturgical Commission, through the sober scholarship exemplified by such studies as those just mentioned, seems to be a welcome corrective to the infatuation with novelty and idiosyncracy that were so characteristic of the sixties in every part of the Church and outside it. Liturgy will always find expressions that are relevant to local and temporary circumstances, but it remains true that the Holy Church is one, and her established patterns of worship will always hunger and thirst for expression of that unity.

Notes

1 This was suggested for the Gospel of John by A. Allan McArthur, *The Evolution of the Christian Year* (London: SCM, 1953), p. 69.
2 Although revision of the office lectionary in 1922 and 1961 did assign Genesis and Exodus from Septuagesima.
3 Published as *The Evolution of the Christian Year* (London: SCM, 1953) and *The Christian Year and Lectionary Reform* (London: SCM, 1958).
4 A.A. McArthur, *The Evolution of the Christian Year*, p. 69.
5 This was suggested in my *Origins of the Liturgical Year* (New York: Pueblo, 1986), esp. pp. 129–34, and has been presented more recently in chapter 9, 'The liturgical year: pattern of proclamation' in T. Talley, *Worship: Reforming Tradition* (Washington, DC: The Pastoral Press, 1990).

6 This point has been made strongly by Michael Moreton in *Theological Principle in the Calendar and Lectionary* (London: Church Literature Association, 1976).

7 Bishop of Knaresborough, 'Can we rationalize the Christian year?', *Theology* 63 (1960), p. 488.

8 John Gunstone, 'Contemporary problems of liturgical time: calendar and lectionary' in Wiebe Vos and Geoffrey Wainwright (eds), *Liturgical Time* (Rotterdam: Liturgical Ecumenical Center Trust, 1982), p. 77.

9 Among many other sources, see Roy A. Rosenberg, *The Concise Guide to Judaism: History, Practice and Faith* (New York: NAL Books, 1990), p. 187. The liturgy on this day celebrates the continuity of the reading of Torah, and the opening verses of Genesis are preceded by the final verses of Deuteronomy.

10 R. C. D. Jasper (ed.), *The Calendar and Lectionary* (Oxford: Oxford University Press, 1967).

11 Annibale Bugnini, *La riforma liturgica (1948-1975)* (Rome: CLV/Edizioni Liturgiche, 1983), p. 411.

12 *The Church Year: The Calendar and the Proper of the Sundays and Other Holy Days throughout the Church Year* (Prayer Book Studies 19; New York: The Church Hymnal Corporation, 1970).

13 *The Calendar and Lessons for the Church's Year* (London: SPCK, 1969).

14 Op. cit., note 9 above, p. 10.

15 *The Common Lectionary* (New York: Church Hymnal Corporation, 1983).

16 Hamon L'Estrange, *The Alliance of Divine Offices*, 4th edn (Oxford: John Henry Parker, 1846), p. 218.

17 Op. cit., note 6 above.

18 Op. cit., note 4 above.

19 Michael Moreton, 'The Calendar and Lectionary: the question of principle', *Theology* 76 (1973), pp. 369-74.

20 Martin Dudley, 'The Lectionary' in Michael Perham (ed.), *Towards Liturgy 2000: Preparing for the Revision of the Alternative Service Book* (London: SPCK for the Alcuin Club, 1989), pp. 35-42.

21 *The Promise of His Glory: Services and Prayers for the Season from All Saints to Candlemas* (GS 907; London: Church House Publishing, 1990), pp. 1-6. Also in *The Promise of His Glory: Services and Prayers for the Season from All Saints to Candlemas* (London: Church House Publishing/Mowbray and Collegeville, MN: Liturgical Press, 1991), pp. 5-7, 370-1.

22 'Revising the Advent-Christmas-Epiphany cycle in the Church of England', *Studia Liturgica* 17 (1987), pp. 166-75.

23 'The origins and development of Candlemas: a struggle for identity and coherence?' in J. Neil Alexander (ed.), *Time and Community* (Washington, DC: The Pastoral Press, 1990), pp. 43-73. This expands an earlier essay in *Ephemerides Liturgicae* 102 (1988), pp. 316-46.

4

The Bible in worship

Martin Kitchen

I. The question to be asked

'What is the place of the Bible in the Church's worship?' is a question which is evidence of a problem. That the Bible has a place in worship is assumed, but beneath the questions which concern what part the Bible should play in worship, and how it should be used, lies the more fundamental issue of how the relationship between the Bible and Christian worship is to be understood. As long as the underlying question of the Bible's place remains unanswered, the more practical consequences will continue to be problematical. All the more reason, then, for asking why this might be so, and attempting a response.

In earlier times this problem would not have existed; the reason for this was simply that the Bible had its origins in worship, and that it belonged there before all other places. The Bible and the liturgy were therefore inextricably linked, and sundering them has had an unfortunate effect upon both worship and the reading of scripture in the present day: liturgists can now express concern about 'the place of the Bible in worship' and wonder how it is to be 'handled'; and the reading of the Bible has become an activity separate from the practice of religion, the preserve either of specialists, or of one particular sector of the Church. The former state of affairs is one in which spirituality can be divorced from its theological roots; and the latter one in which biblical critics can be dismissed along with religious cranks, much as Dean Inge dismissed liturgists along with philatelists.

Both worship and the reading of scripture are proving problematical in the West; the one since our society has lost any communal sense of the numinous, and the other since we have begun the task of critical exegesis. Yet there is no more chance of returning to the imagined Eden of a pre-modern understanding of the world, of society and of our place within them than there is of recovering a pre-critical hermeneutic for the biblical text. We must give thanks for the more or less pleasant places in which the lines have fallen to us, and, just as any other previous age has had to, we must seek an integration which is appropriate for our day.

The divorce between scripture and liturgy goes back at least as far as the Reformation, when 'Bible' was first set against 'tradition' as a basis for authority within the Church. One of the advantages of that divorce was that it eventually enabled critical thinking about both partners. One major disadvantage was that it unduly elevated the importance of 'authority' in the context of human knowledge of God. Another lay in the fact that it enabled the *lex credendi* to take precedence over the *lex orandi*. The 'tradition', which was then viewed as if in opposition to the 'scripture', was primarily a tradition of public worship. Putting it crudely, therefore, one might say that what the Reformers succeeded in doing was to set a theological system over against a way of praying.

On the one hand, the Book of Common Prayer and the Authorized Version of the Bible are the product and symbol of that Reformation in the Western Church and the state of affairs which it brought about. On the other hand, the 1928 Prayer Book, Series II, Series III, the Alternative Service Book, as well as the new Service Books of the other Anglican Churches, along with the superfluity of modern translations of the Bible, are the product and symbol of our present condition. Oddly, the proliferation of neither liturgies nor Bible translations has had the effect of encouraging widespread involvement of people in worship or in knowledge of the sacred scriptures of Western religion.

Yet variety need not produce or symbolize either disorder, or distance from the numinous. Variety was the norm in the worship of the early Church, and the path of the development of the canon of scriptures — along with the evidence of the multiplicity of texts — is testimony to a lively diversity of faith. What is significant is that, in those days, there was no doubt that the Bible and the liturgy belonged together. The letters which St Paul and his imitators wrote were intended to be read to a community of people who were worshipping together. If the insights of form criticism and redaction criticism are to be accepted, then the sayings of Jesus, along with stories about him which were gathered together to form what we have as 'the Gospel according to [each of the Evangelists]', were retold to communities which worshipped, and which made use of traditions about Jesus, or of teaching which was thought to be his word to the Church, for the edification of their faith and the development of their moral life.

II. A starting point

When we consider that the Bible has its origins in those occasions when the early Church met for corporate prayer, it seems all the more strange that our sacred text fares so ill when we meet for worship. In 1970 James D. Smart wrote of the 'strange silence' of the Bible in the Church.[1] What he meant by that was that, after two centuries of biblical criticism, few of the insights of that art had seemed to penetrate the thinking of the Churches. Smart's argument is concerned more with educational than with liturgical uses of the Bible, but it is true that, in the Church's worship, though there is certainly *reading* of scripture, there is hardly much *critical* reading.

Contrary to what many fear, biblical criticism is not an arcane science, designed to confuse the uninitiated, but a recognition that there are complexities within the text which require a kind of elucidation which it is not always possible for conventional piety and systematized theology to supply. The asking of questions about the biblical text of the kind which one might address to other ancient texts may appear to undermine credal and doctrinal statements from the past. However, critical difficulties are raised by the text itself;[2] the question is how to worship — and how to use the Bible in worship — in such a way that complexities and diversities within the text are taken seriously and allowed their rightful place alongside that religious commitment which is a necessary part of any act of worship.[3]

Robert Morgan and John Barton's discussion of biblical interpretation[4] assesses the strengths and shortcomings of the historical-critical method for a religious understanding of the text, and suggests that a way forward out of the impasse that the method has reached may be to take seriously those recent approaches to its interpretation which derive from literary criticism. Such an approach might perhaps be taken a stage further with the recognition that the text of the Bible belongs primarily in worship. It is an historical text, certainly, but it had its origins in worship, and it retains its primary locus there; to recognize that is to see a context which might prove fruitful for further hermeneutical reflection.

The recognition of worship as the context for the Bible and theology underlies the work of Geoffrey Wainwright[5] and Aidan Kavanagh,[6] both of whom recognize and seek to recover the importance for theology of the principle *lex orandi lex credendi*; that is to say, the way in which people pray gives rise to what they believe and how they conceptualize it, and not the other way round.

The practical rejection of the insights of biblical criticism in the life of the Churches is one consequence of that regrettable tendency on the part of many of the Church's ministers to discourage the use of the mind; it is as if church entrances bore a safety warning: 'Soft heads to be worn at all times.' Christians who go to church are worshippers. And they are that primarily. The primary human response to the holy is in worship,[7] and Christians respond to the holy as to the God who has been made known in Jesus, whom they believe to be God's anointed one, God's Christ. Their faith is informed by the act of worship, and their worship is deepened by their faith. Nevertheless, Christians who go to church are also products of the modern world. They think critically, and they require an understanding of faith which is not incompatible with what they know to be true about the world, their life, and the text of the Bible. Their faith must rest upon an approach to worship which does not expect them to leave their minds at the church door

Perhaps one way of establishing links between worship and living, and between worship and thinking, will be the rediscovery that the Church's book has its origins in the Church's worship; the Bible, and the New Testament in particular, was written for the Christian community as it worshipped. It was intended to make worship not only possible but also of life-enhancing significance.

III. Some possible consequences

Clearly what is important is that the Bible be used in such a way that it will help the people to worship, while not expecting them to perform too many tricks of mental gymnastics at the same time. In some traditions the Gospel Book — or copy of the service book from which the gospel is read — is carried into church in procession. At the time of the gospel reading it is ceremoniously taken from its place on the altar and read to an acclamation from the people. Such ceremonial need not be mere form; ritual handling of the book can combine with sensitive handling of the language and symbols which the book contains. The consequences of the discovery of an appropriate relationship between the Bible and the liturgy may be set out briefly under the following five heads:

(a) Quotations

All quotation is necessarily out of context; when a writer said — or wrote — anything, he or she said or wrote it in particular circumstances which no longer pertain. This can create difficulty for the very first hearing of scripture in church; it seems odd to arrive at worship on a Sunday morning and to be greeted by the minister, without introduction, with the words 'Abraham is the Father of all . . .', or 'Stand up, Jerusalem, and look towards the east', or 'Be subject for the Lord's sake to every human institution'.

Now, in some sense it is appropriate that the people of God should be greeted with scripture, since scriptural words are, above all, the language by which the community of faith is constituted. However, they are odd as greetings because they are spoken without preface. Clearly, there has to be some resonance with the tradition, yet bald quotation such as this may suggest an almost magical understanding of scripture. It would be more appropriate for the minister to greet the people directly, and then to introduce them to worship with some words of scripture used more allusively than the method of direct quotation allows. The Canadian *Book of Alternative Services*[8] seems to handle this better, simply putting in statements such as 'says the Lord', so as to highlight the derivative nature of what is said. The new American Book of Common Prayer[9] appears not to allow for an introductory sentence at the Eucharist, but a straightforward greeting such as 'The Lord be with you', or a benediction.

The liturgy also uses quotations as an introduction — and justification — for what is to be done in the service. The Confession in the ASB may begin with a quotation from 1 John, and the Peace with St Paul's words in 1 Corinthians 15. In the Prayer Book of 1662 the words 'Let your light so shine before men, that they may see your good works . . .' amount to an instruction to dig deep into the pocket for the Offertory. The Sanctus is a collocation of quotations, and the Ten Commandments are obviously so.

Anglicans do not believe the scriptures to be immediate and automatic in their effect. Nor are they commited to one particular understanding of the scriptures' inspiration and authority. Care needs to be taken lest any inadvertent use of the Bible which appears to expect the text to operate with 'automatic' effect should allow misconceptions to arise.

(b) Allusions

Quotation is necessarily quotation-out-of-context, and it needs to be recognized as such. Allusion, on the other hand, can take account of subtlety and can fuse horizons as speaker and reader recognize two planes of existence, the biblical and the actual, and bring them together.

The use of the Bible is perhaps most conducive to worship when it is referred to allusively. Examples of this are numerous in the various service books which are in use at the present time, and what follows is only a selection of them.

1. The Invitation to Penitence after the opening Sentence at the Offices in the Book of Common Prayer draws attention to the passage of scripture which has just been read from Ezekiel 18.27, Psalm 51.3, Psalm 51.9, Joel 2.13, Daniel 9.9–10, Jeremiah 10.24 combined with Psalm 6.1, Matthew 3.2, Luke 15.18–19, Psalm 143.2, or 1 John 1.8–11 — and the remaining ten which have not. It refers those familiar with the Bible to such warnings against attempted concealment as are contained in, for example, Joshua 7.11, Proverbs 26.24, Jeremiah 42.20 and Psalm 26.4.

2. The prefaces to the Thanksgivings at Baptism draw the mind to the stories of the creation in Genesis 1 and to the crossing of the Red Sea in Exodus 14. With the address to God's 'most dearly beloved Son', the congregation is reminded of the baptism of Jesus at the beginning of all

four gospels, and the reference to the command to go and make disciples of the nations at the end of St Matthew's gospel sets the rite in the context of the Church's mission to the world.

3. Ordination services include allusions to 'the Son of man' who 'came not to be served, but to serve' (Mark 10.45), to the path of humility chosen by Christ Jesus according to St Paul in Philippians 2, and to the gifts to the Church of office holders according to Ephesians 4.

4. The best Eucharistic Prayers echo biblical language without heavy quotation, and it seems invidious to choose between the better of them; however the suggestive words of the Scottish Liturgy of 1982 come to mind: 'In Christ your Son our life and yours are brought together in a wonderful exchange. He made his home among us that we might for ever dwell in you.' Here themes of John 1 seem to be combined with 2 Corinthians 5.18–21, Galatians 3.6–14 and John 15.

5. Finally, the prayer said by the priest at the close of the Eucharist in the Alternative Service Book ('Father of all . . .') is a fine example of allusive writing. The 'still far off' recalls the story of the prodigal son in Luke 15, so the phrase 'met us in your Son' becomes a play on the word. 'Declaring God's love' has echoes in the atonement language of Romans 5, and 'the gate of glory' reminds the congregation of the story of Jacob at Bethel in Genesis 28. The prayer for the will to share in Christ's risen life, bring life to others and light to the world is an echo of many such passages in the gospels and Pauline epistles, as is the desire to be held firm in hope which is set before us (Colossians 3.1–2, Philippians 1.21–24, Matthew 5.14, Romans 5.2–5, 15.13). Freedom for all the children of God and the praises of the whole earth are the aspiration of Psalmist and apostle (e.g. Romans 8.19–21, Psalms 19, 24, 96, 100).

What seems to be effective in all these instances is the degree to which the compilers of liturgies have allowed the language and tone of the Bible to permeate their minds before they set out to write. This allows a relatively free rein to their creative talent, even though their thought is subject to the discipline of the scriptural text. Allusions tend to serve the purpose, not so much of getting people to do things, but of lifting the imagination to the possibilities of meeting God who acts in grace. What is required, then, is a similar creativity on the part of liturgiologists; they need to fill their minds with biblical imagery and provide words for worship that are appropriate for articulating the religious response of modern people to the world as it evokes their wonder and their terror, their grief and their hope.

(c) Psalmody

Deliberate quotations of sections of the Bible, of value as poetry, and frequently used as versicles and responses, or as canticles, are clearly in a different category of quoted material from that which we have just been considering, and the Psalms are an obvious example of these. Hymn books are important, and can have far-reaching influence on the spirituality and life of a people; the *Methodist Hymn Book* has been a mine of treasure from earliest times for Methodists; their spiritual off-spring, the Salvation Army, values the *Song Book* very highly; and one can immediately spot the tradition of a parish church when one enters and discovers in the pews *Hymns Ancient and Modern*, the *English Hymnal*, or the *Anglican Hymn Book*.

In containing the Book of Psalms within its canon of scripture, the Christian Church has taken over someone else's hymn book. This could be a mark of flattery — one not altogether inappropriate, given the breadth and depth of the material — were it not for the way in which the Church has handled it. There are psalms which voice any conceivable desire to praise, and which speak to every human situation. Here are joy and agony, pain and delight, the humdrum and the extraordinary. There is hardly a human emotion which has not been expressed for us by those ancient poets of Israel.[10] Why then do we start at the beginning of the book and finish at the end? Who would dream of doing that with any other collection of hymns?

A sensitive approach to them would select those which are of use on given occasions and in particular circumstances, and would make clear, much as do those useful publications which help us choose appropriate hymns from the books that are available today,[11] so that our worship might be enhanced by the use of what is fitting in scripture, and not distort its meaning and value by mindless recitation by rote.

(d) Readings: the lectionary

The Bible is not necessarily and automatically 'the Word of the Lord', and it is not appropriate for the Church to pretend that it is. The Word of God is what God speaks; God speaks the fiat which brings all creation into being, and, according to the writer of the Epistle to the Hebrews, he has 'in the last days' spoken his mind in the sending of a Son. For all its divine inspiration, we have warrant in the Bible itself for the view that God does not go into print; our biblical texts are what our forebears, both Jewish and Christian, found it necessary to write and to retain for reading in the community as it worshipped. We do not do it justice as a human book which may be the vehicle of the divine if we insist upon a view of it which is practically monophysite.

There are two families of lectionaries available at the present time: on the one hand that which is to be found in the Alternative Service Book, and which reproduces that of the Joint Liturgical Group;[12] and, on the other, that which emerged from the Roman Catholic lectionary after the Second Vatican Council, and which is found in the American

Book of Common Prayer and the Common Lectionary proposed by the Consultation on Common Texts.

The thematic approach of the JLG/ASB lectionary is not satisfactory, for it tends to distort rather than to enhance scripture. Its lections are too long, and make too much of the prophets and the Fourth Gospel; moreover, its two-year cycle leads to some surprising omissions. Some of these objections have been addressed in the supplementary material issued in later publications, but the basic flaws remain; its four liturgical seasons are theologically rather than liturgically controlled, so it has a too didactic approach to worship.

Martin Dudley proposes quite definite remedies; the lectionary should be conservative in Advent, Christmas, Lent, Easter, so that the central mysteries of the faith might be allowed to unfold 'in the way that tradition has demonstrated is most effective'.[13] During the rest of the year, however, he proposes something more 'adventurous and innovative', with greater emphasis on such contemporary issues such as justice and peace, the option for the poor, solidarity with the oppressed, and the calling and mission of the whole people of God. He calls for a clear theological structure, in which themes are boldly expressed and not merely given a brief and ambiguous title as they are in the ASB. Further, he says, the numerous special Sundays promoted by missionary and other organizations should be replaced by groups exploring certain biblical themes, types and ideas in word and ritual.

There is no doubt that Dudley's aims in all this are admirable, but his enthusiasm runs away with him. Christian people meet together for worship. When they do so they need the mind, heart and affections lifting to the throne of God. As a community and as persons they need healing for their hurts and forgiveness for their shortcomings. 'Contemporary issues' are doubtless of great importance, but their significance is limited in scope and passing in fashion. Furthermore, as a way of approaching the Bible, the selection of 'themes' is precisely what has proven so mistaken in the ASB.

The ancient tradition of uninterrupted reading of the Passion during Holy Week has now been commended by the House of Bishops of the General Synod of the Church of England — in the publication known as *Lent, Holy Week, and Easter*.[14] The effect of the narrative exerts an influence and possesses a religious value which are beyond words and themes. What is more, when the opportunity is taken to read different accounts of the Passion from different Evangelists, the congregation is able to gain some sense of the variety of emphasis in the different gospel accounts, and therefore some sense that each is already an interpretation of the final events in the life of Jesus. The lesson to be learned here is that course reading of scripture is what is effective in that uplifting, for which we have just pleaded, of the hearts, minds and affections of the worshipping people to the throne of God. The Bible needs to be able to speak for itself, without the imposition of form or theme.

The obvious conclusion of this is that a lectionary should be provided which allows for this. If that means the Common Lectionary, then so be it; we do not need to re-invent something which is already available to us.

(e) Preaching

Apart from the appearance here and there of the rubric 'A sermon may be preached', the matter of preaching does not feature greatly in the service books of any of the Churches. It may be as well, then, to allow ourselves a reminder that preaching takes as its starting point the text of the lections for the day, and that it is essentially a liturgical act. It is not primarily an evangelistic, in the sense of a proselytizing medium, nor is it therapeutic, nor educational. Its purpose is to raise the mind, imagination, affections and will of the congregation to worship and serve God. Its primary focus, like that of the Bible itself, is liturgical.

It is the task of the sermon to elucidate the meaning of the biblical text in the context of the enactment of the liturgical text. Certainly, biblical criticism has presented the task of preaching with particular problems; but these are not insurmountable, as long as the laity are regarded as intelligent. With honesty in the pulpit about the nature of the whole biblical text, and the particular biblical text under discussion in that particular service, they will grow in appreciation of the religious value of the scriptures.

This is not a call either for biblicism, or for an understanding of the rôle of preaching which ignores the realities of the present world. Rather it is a plea, both for sound, critical exegesis of the text of the Bible, and for hard work at the hermeneutical problems it raises in the context of modern life.

Is it too much to suggest that, just as the introductions to our service books now give advice about the reverence with which worship is to be conducted, and the care which should go into its preparation, there might also be some advice that the sermon should, as far as possible, elucidate carefully one or more of the readings, drawing particular attention to their implications for the worship of God and for the under-standing and living of Christian faith in the present age and at the present season of the Church's year?

IV. Worship and the world

All these matters may seem a far cry from the questions which pre-occupy the clergy, 'What shall I preach on?', or 'Shall I say all of the

Comfortable Words?', or even 'How shall I best prepare myself for worship in the morning?' Nevertheless, the constant need, both to find appropriate portions of the Bible for use in the liturgy, and to allow its echoes to reverberate through our worship, calls for deep thought about what is being done to the text, and why it is being done. In this sense, the Bible is 'strangely silent' — in spite of the critical work which has been carried out in the exposition of its meaning, and in spite of the many translations which are currently available.

The Church exists in history and is bound, to some degree, by it. Different parts of the Anglican Communion therefore relate in different ways to their surrounding culture; folk religion (or 'implicit religion') is a powerful force in many places, and most Churches which are aware of this are keen to build upon it and lead people and communities to a more articulate Christian faith. The English context is complex; there might be misgivings about the establishment, there may have been considerable advances that have been made in recent years in ecumenism, and British society may now be pluriform in religion, but the Church of England is the church of the nation. Residents in a parish are entitled to have to their children baptized in their parish church, and the Church's ministers enjoy relatively easy access to many places and institutions which is denied to representatives of other denominations and religions. For a variety of reasons, much of the implicit religion of British people is imbued with Anglicanism. This may be worth bearing in mind as the Church of England prepares for the revision of its Alternative Service Book at the same time as the whole Anglican Communion embarks upon a Decade of Evangelism.

Any Church which takes seriously its public and social role might do well to ponder its privilege and vocation to be, in some sense, the nation or society at prayer. One of the best forms of evangelism is good worship; it offers a sense of the numinous which engages people at the point of their need, and it gives appropriate expression to their religious concerns. Few would doubt that worship is symbolic; it has to do with the functioning of symbols as a way of relating to the holy, which most people experience, in one form or another. We need to recognize that scripture, also, is symbolic.

Liturgical symbols bring together the response of a people to God. They meet, for God has called them together. They listen, for God speaks. They give, for God has given and continues to give. They offer, for God is all loving and delights to receive. They take and eat, for God graciously gives and feeds. The Bible as symbol is, first, that compendium of symbols which assures the worshippers that God is, indeed, thus, and that their worship is therefore appropriate. It is also, second, a symbol in itself of God's fundamental address to humanity. This is contained in those statements and questions which God addresses to representative people in various Bible stories; 'Where are you?', 'You shall be my people', 'I will never again destroy the earth', 'Behold my elect, in whom my soul delights', 'By his knowledge shall my righteous servant justify many', 'This is my beloved Son'. It is, thirdly, a symbol of human response to God, for — and the extent and significance of this is the theological contribution to Christendom of the Western Church — its authors were human, and it rewards the application of critical study.

Of those who do believe in God, many find Christian faith difficult to embrace. They nevertheless like to have their children given a religious start in life by baptism. Many like to be married in church, and expect to be buried by the Church's ministers. They like the Church both to affirm society and all that is good in it, and to show itself to be against sin — however that is understood. They are delighted when, once in a while, they discover a member of the clergy who is prepared to mourn their griefs and celebrate their joys with them, in their own style, and on their own terms.

Recent theology has discovered the primacy of narrative, of story, in Christian ways of thinking about God.[15] While this has proved of great significance, it is clear that not all theology can be comprised under this heading; there is not only narrative in the Bible, but also reflection, and poetry, and moral exhortation. Nevertheless, narrative does provide a link with people inside and outside the Church; they can understand their lives as a story unfolding; moreover, they are aware — though they might not express it thus — of moments of creation and of redemption, of passion and of resurrection.

Whether or not they are regular worshippers, all who hear the text of the Bible in church are on a journey of faith. The rite and the reading should accompany them on the way. This would suggest that the Church needs to be able to relate the religious understanding, experience and desires of the people to its own stories, rites and ceremonies. Such 'understanding, experience and desires' find their chief focus and expression in worship. When the liturgy 'works', the people are uplifted, inspired and informed.

The Church claims to have a universal gospel, which speaks to the condition of all. When celebration is genuine, when it speaks to the hearts of the people, then the Church's worship, with its own peculiar symbols, is able to converse with the profundities of the otherwise inexpressible realities of human living, which are the stuff of both life and religion. Those who have attempted a theological understanding of the biblical text have consistently found themselves drawn to make the analogy with the incarnation,[16] which is itself a symbol of how God remains God while becoming human, and how humanity remains human while being taken up into God. Neither is diminished: both are enhanced; the one by the grace of condescension, the other by the glory of divinization. A symbolic understanding of the nature of the Bible has the advantage of preserving the subtlety of this relationship, and thus relieves the text of the 'flatness'[17] of a less symbolic and more fundamentalist understanding of its inspiration and authority.

Geoffrey Wainwright has demonstrated[18] that systematic theology can no longer ignore the dimension of worship; and that gives to the task of theology a particular slant. This essay has argued that that view needs also to be taken into account in the understanding of scripture within the liturgy. The literary critic George Steiner has expressed the view[19] that the primary interpretation is performance. Liturgy is interpretation, therefore, in the sense that a text is provided, and the worshippers make use of it. The hearing, reading and consideration of the biblical text, within the context of the interpretation of the liturgical text, is the first duty of the Christian congregation. Liturgy must therefore allow the Bible properly to be heard.

As the Church undertakes the interpretation of the liturgical text at the same time as the reading of the biblical text, both of them may shed their mutual, natural and gracious light upon the other. Moreover, as it takes seriously the elaboration of rites appropriate to our age for celebrating life and death, love and fear, suffering and redemption,[20] the Church may also discover appropriate ways of handling the Bible in worship. The substantive, theological, question posed at the beginning of this essay must be taken seriously if the other questions, the practical ones, are to be properly resolved.

The place of the Bible in the Church's worship is the one which will give to it its proper status as the treasury of stories, symbols and earliest memories which first encapsulated and fostered faith, and which has continued, over the centuries, to inspire all God's people to worship, to the study of the Bible, to prayer, and to good works.

Notes

1 James D. Smart, *The Strange Silence of the Bible in the Church* (London: SCM, 1970).

2 Cf. the difficulties of harmonizing the gospel accounts of, most notoriously, the resurrection traditions. How many women went to the tomb? What was the reason for their going? What happened as they arrived? How many men (or were they angels?) did they see? And so on.

3 Though cf. T. G. A. Baker, *Questioning Worship* (London: SCM, 1977), p. 20, where the author comments upon the tension between biblical criticism and the conservative tendency of most public liturgy.

4 Robert Morgan and John Barton, *Biblical Interpretation* (The Oxford Bible Series; Oxford: Oxford University Press, 1988).

5 Geoffrey Wainwright, *Doxology: The Praise of God in Worship, Doctrine and Life* (London: Epworth, 1980).

6 Aidan Kavanagh, *On Liturgical Theology* (New York: Pueblo, 1984).

7 The point made, as is well known, by Rudolf Otto, *The Idea of the Holy* (London: Oxford University Press, 1958).

8 *The Book of Alternative Services of the Anglican Church of Canada* (Toronto: Anglican Book Centre, 1985).

9 *The Book of Common Prayer and Administration of the Sacraments* (New York: Church Hymnal Corporation/Seabury Press, 1979).

10 For an excellent discussion of the place of the Psalms in worship, see J. A. Lamb, *The Psalms in Christian Worship* (London: Faith Press, 1962).

11 Such as, say, Robin Leaver (ed.), *Hymns with the New Lectionary* (Bramcote: Grove, 1980). Some hymn books include suggestions for hymns appropriate to particular Sundays of the liturgical year.

12 On this lectionary, see Donald Gray (ed.), *The Word in Season* (Norwich: Canterbury Press, 1988).

13 See Martin Dudley, 'The Lectionary' in Michael Perham (ed.), *Towards Liturgy 2000* (Alcuin Club Collections 69; London: SPCK, 1989), p. 41.

14 See *Lent, Holy Week, and Easter: Services and Prayers* (London: Church House Publishing, 1984).

15 Cf., for an introduction to this, and a discussion of its value, George W. Stroup, *The Promise of Narrative Theology* (London: SCM, 1984).

16 As does, for example, John Muddiman, in his article commemorating the centenary of the publishing of *Lux Mundi*, 'The Holy Spirit and inspiration' in Robert Morgan (ed.), *The Religion of the Incarnation* (Bristol: Classical Press, 1989), pp. 119–35.

17 Cf. Graham Ward, 'To be a Reader', *Literature and Theology* 4 (1990); cf. also George Steiner's insistence on the importance of *meaning* in *Real Presences* (London: Faber, 1989).

18 See above, note 5.

19 Steiner, op. cit., p. 8 and *passim*.

20 Modern service books and collections of supplementary material have already contributed much towards this development; cf. the admirable work of the Church of England Liturgical Commission in *Patterns for Worship: A Report by the Liturgical Commission of the Church of England* (London: Church House Publishing, 1989).

5

Eucharistic theology

Christopher J. Cocksworth

I. Introduction

It might be said that there is no such thing as *Anglican eucharistic theology*. This appears to be quite true on an empirical level. Anglicanism is an amorphous phenomenon. Even in its English form, Anglicanism has always contained a wide spectrum of eucharistic views — most of which have justified themselves from the Articles and the Prayer Book. When one considers the breadth of country and culture which worldwide Anglicanism spans, it is hardly surprising that, in the absence of an authoritative magisterium, multiformity rather than uniformity is the name of the theological as well as the liturgical game. When the 1958 Lambeth Conference abandoned 1662 as a doctrinal norm for liturgical form, it was not actually suggesting a new theological departure, it was merely catching up with the reality of the situation: Anglicanism was simply too heterogeneous for the idea that its liturgical life was united around the doctrine of 1662 to make any real sense.

The claim that there is no such thing as a *specifically Anglican* eucharistic theology also appears quite true on an ideological level. Anglicanism has never seen itself as a self-sufficient unit isolated from the wider Church. Whether through a Protestant eye (as an expression of the Reformation faith) or through a Catholic eye (as a branch of the Church Catholic) or through both eyes (as Reformed Catholicism), Anglicanism has always seen itself as part of a bigger whole. Because of this it is reticent about claiming a distinctive theological content in regard to anything. The most which it has been willing to admit to is a distinctive theological method by which it interprets Reformation truth and Catholic faith.

However, as significant students and statesmen of Anglicanism have argued in recent years, there are dangers in being too vague and self-effacing about Anglican identity. Two years before his retirement as Archbishop of Canterbury, Robert Runcie challenged English Evangelicals to develop an ecclesiology which would be able to place their presence in the Church of England on a firmer footing than pragmatic convenience ('the best boat to fish from' and all that[1]). If Evangelicals have often sat lightly to the Catholic character of Anglicanism and have felt a strong pull towards their Reformed brethren in other denominations, Catholics have often sat equally lightly to the Reformation inheritance of Anglicanism and have felt a strong pull towards their brethren in the Church of Rome. In his study of Anglican identity Paul Avis detects a failure amongst some Tractarians to view the Reformation accurately and to take it seriously. He argues that this was not just out of line with previous Anglican self-understanding but also bequeathed a legacy of problems for Anglicanism's contribution to the ecumenical cause.[2] The liberal character of Anglican life has not escaped comment either. In his study of the integrity of Anglican theological life, Stephen Sykes not only criticizes the reductionalist tendency in Anglican theology but attempts to explode the Anglican preference for method over doctrinal content by lighting an epistemological bomb under its basic assumptions. He claims that as our understanding of how we gain knowledge of God (method) is determined by prior theological beliefs (doctrinal content), it is meaningless to talk of a method without a content.[3]

All three voices are calling for a consciously Anglican systematic approach to theology — not in the sense of ghetto dogmatics but in the sense of naming and developing the distinctive contribution to ecumenical theology which Anglicanism is able to make. This distinctive contribution is born out of the peculiarities of its history. The Protestant–Catholic spectrum within Anglicanism clearly has great potential for the definition of doctrine in ways which maintain and express the essential concerns of both historic traditions. And the liberal mind of Anglicanism, with its openness to the truth from all sources and its critique of traditional formulations, has its own creative part to play by moving the ground on which each has faithfully stood and in so doing often bringing them closer together. The development and definition of an inclusive theology may be done dialectically by holding together competing but ultimately complementary theological concerns, or it may be done through the ways of consensus, by identifying the doctrinal core to which we are all committed. It is the latter which has not only become the method of ecumenical dialogue but is also deeply embedded in the Anglican consciousness.

This essay will follow the consensus route and will seek to show how a number of *unitive categories* have developed within Anglican eucharistic theology which form a significant core of doctrinal content and which in turn should not only continue to shape Anglican eucharistic thought but are also part of our contribution to the ongoing ecumenical debate. They are what we might call the *deep structures* of Anglican eucharistic theology.

This is not to say that the unitive categories leave nothing else to be said about the Eucharist, neither is it even to say that the unitive categories are fully formed, it is rather to remind ourselves of the truism that there is both within and beyond Anglicanism more that unites than divides us. In line with other contemporary studies our analysis will consider the Eucharist under the three classic themes of sacrament, sacrifice and presence.

II. The Eucharist as sacrament

In this section we will be considering the role the sacramental action and specifically the sacramental media play in fulfilling the purposes of God in the eucharistic event. It is an issue which brings to light fundamental differences between the classic systems of Catholic and Protestant sacramental theology. The whole question can be focused by analysing the significance either side of the sixteenth-century debate attached to the liturgical use of the interpretative words in the Institution Narrative.

In Catholic theology the interpretative words were seen as *effecting* a change in the substantial identity of the elements whereby from being bread and wine they become the body and blood of Christ. As a result, the eucharistic gift of Christ's presence is really received by those who communicate in the bread and the wine. In Reformed theology, the words were seen as *affecting* the spirituality of the participants; in Calvin's words they are 'living preaching which edifies its hearers, penetrates into their minds, impresses itself upon their hearts and settles there'.[4] The result, it is hoped, is that the individual's faith will be so stirred that he will believe in Christ and accept him in a new degree of depth. At the risk of oversimplifying the issues, whereas Catholic theology claimed that Christ's presence was communicated *in* the consecrated elements, Reformed theology claimed that his presence could be communicated *with* the eucharistic elements.

Reformed theology accused the Catholic system of undermining the Gospel of grace by suggesting that the person of Christ is present, given and received independently of an authentic faith in his saving work. In its turn, Catholic theology accused the Reformation of so subjectivizing the eucharistic action that the sacramental media were rendered ultimately superfluous — after all, did not even Luther say that he 'could have Mass daily, indeed every hour'[5] by feeding on the words of Christ?

Cranmer's liturgical and doctrinal work placed Anglicanism firmly on the Reformed side of the debate. However, as subsequent Anglican history interpreted the legacy left to it by the Reformation, it very soon developed a way of explaining the relation between the eucharistic elements and the eucharistic gift in a manner which was both acceptable within the framework of the doctrine of justification by faith and, at the same time, accommodating towards certain concerns and features of traditional sacramental theology and spirituality. The *unifying category* was simply that rather than *in* or *with* the eucharistic elements, the eucharistic gift was communicated *through* them. In other words, fairly rapidly Anglicanism recovered the notion of the instrumental function of the Eucharist together with a belief in an objective consecration as an essential part of the eucharistic action.

For example, as early as 1573 John Johnson was chastised for his belief that the dominical words were directed solely towards the worshippers and had no objective relation to the elements. About the same time John Jewel worked hard to persuade the Catholic proponent Thomas Harding that the Church of England did believe in, and its rite contain, a valid consecration of the elements so that 'by them Christ himself, being the true bread of eternal life, is so presently given us that by faith we verily receive his body and his blood'.[6] Later, Richard Hooker went on to develop the instrumental function of the elements and the belief in the objective consecration in more explicit ways claiming that by the 'solemn benediction' these 'mysteries . . . serve as conducts and conveyances of [Christ's] body and blood'.[7]

Simultaneously, Puritanism both inside and outside Anglicanism felt dissatisfied with the absence of a consecratory petition in the Reformed rites and began to re-establish one. However, as Anglicans and Puritans evolved clearer definitions of themselves and as they were eventually forced apart in the seventeenth century, the emphasis on the instrumental function of the Eucharist developed more fully in the Anglican system. To be sure, Calvin was quite happy to describe the Eucharist in instrumental terms.[8] But in the last analysis, for him as well as for Cranmer, the grace was *separate* from the elements even though potentially running parallel with them. In Hooker and the Anglican tradition which developed around and after him, the grace was *tied* to the elements because they were seen to be designated by God to communicate that grace. Whereas in the Reformed tradition the elements were instrumental in the sense that they faced the individual with the reality of the Gospel and thereby encouraged him to *meditate* on its life-giving significance, in the Anglican tradition they were instrumental in the sense that they *mediated* that reality to the receiving faith of the individual.[9]

Anglicanism's insistence that the eucharistic gift of Christ's presence cannot be isolated from the eucharistic elements cut both ways. As well as saying to the Reformed tradition that the appointed media had a real role to play in the gift of Christ's presence, it was saying to the Roman tradition that his gift is given precisely, as Charles Gore liked to say, for the purposes of communion.[10] The relation which Christ's presence has with the eucharistic elements is for the renewal of his relation with the believers and thus for the reconstitution of the Church as it gathers around the Lord's Table. In this sense, the Reformed tradition was quite right in directing the dominical words to the worshippers (as are later Anglican rites in relating the epiclesis as much to the people as to the elements) because it is to them that the gift of Christ's presence is being given — and being given to be received. And the Reformed tradition was right to stress the importance of faith in the eucharistic event because it is only as the gift is received by *evangelical* faith, that is, active faith in the Gospel, that the gift which is really given can be really received and the Christ who offers himself through the appointed media dwell in our hearts. However, Robert Wilberforce was equally right and fully in line with Anglican theology when he warned the Reformed tradition that it always stood in danger of forcing the sacrament into practical redundancy by failing to make the eucharistic action and the eucharistic material intrinsic to the receiving of the eucharistic gift. He regarded the concept of consecration as the key element in eucharistic theology because it ensured that the elements were the *means* for the giving of the gift.[11]

The instrumental function of the Eucharist with its liturgical corollary of an objective consecration (however this is believed to be effected) and its implications for the faith relationship between the Giver and the receiver, has the capacity to unite Reformed and Roman traditions in what they would regard as central to the core of the eucharistic reality. The ARCIC Report provides a neat example:

> In the whole action of the eucharist, and in and by his sacramental presence given through bread and wine, the crucified and risen Lord, according to his promise, offers himself to his people.
> When this offering is met by faith, a lifegiving encounter results. Through faith Christ's presence — which does not depend on the individual's faith to be the Lord's real gift of himself to his Church — becomes no longer just a presence *for* the believer, but also a presence *with* him.[12]

III. The Eucharist as presence

It is very easy for discussion on the eucharistic presence of Christ to begin by identifying those areas of disagreement and so obscure those areas where there is genuine agreement. Following Hooker's example, Anglican tradition has sought to short-circuit this tendency by directing all traditions to the obvious priority and the common experience:

> I can see on all sides at the length to a general agreement concerning that which alone is material, namely the *real participation* of Christ and life in his body and blood *by means of this sacrament*.[13]

The '*real participation* of Christ and life in his body and blood *by means* of this sacrament' is clearly the biblical heart of the eucharistic experience: 'The cup of blessing which we bless, is it not a participation in the blood of Christ? The bread which we break, is it not a participation in the body of Christ?' (1 Cor 10.16). 'Real participation of Christ' as the defined purpose of the eucharistic reality is also a deeply *unitive category*. It expresses the essence of both the Reformed objections to the doctrine of transubstantiation and the truth which Catholic theology sought to express by the doctrine. As far as the Reformers were concerned, the problem with the doctrine was that it so focused on the secondary question of the relationship between the presence of Christ and the elements that it obscured the primary question, which in Calvin's words is 'How do we possess the whole Christ crucified and became partakers of all his blessings?'[14] However, behind all the complexities of the doctrine of transubstantiation was simply the desire to affirm, even guarantee, the reality of Christ's gift of himself to his faithful people in the Eucharist. In fact modern Roman Catholic theologians have become dissatisfied with the traditional formulation of the doctrine precisely because, in the present philosophical world, it does not express this truth clearly enough. They argue that the traditional categories describe the eucharistic presence in a far too static way and so too easily isolate Christ's presence from the interpersonal dimension in which it finds its meaning. Hence, according to Schillebeeckx, Roman Catholic theologians 'no longer say "Christ is there", without saying for whom he is present'.[15]

All this means that there is nothing peculiarly Anglican about the doctrine of our participation in Christ through the Eucharist. Nevertheless, Anglican theology has had a reasonably faithful history in trying to keep the discussion of the eucharistic presence focused on the central Christological and soteriological issues of union with Christ and participation in his life — as Cranmer's prayer says, 'that we may evermore dwell in him and he in us'. It might be said that this focus was shifted in the nineteenth century with the rise of Tractarian and then Anglo-Catholic theology. Indeed, part of the Evangelical criticism of Tractarianism was that the Tractarians were taking the Church back to mediaeval preoccupations with establishing the objective presence of Christ's body and blood in relation to the elements and in isolation from the faith relationship with the believers. However, this is not entirely fair. Their overriding concern was, in Pusey's words, to prove 'the *reality* of the communication of Christ's Body and Blood through the Holy Eucharist'.[16] As we have already shown, this can be seen very clearly in Wilberforce's work. His main interest was in demonstrating that through the consecrated elements we are united with Christ's humanity and thereby given a real participation in his divine life.

Charles Gore set himself the task of presenting the essence of

Catholic theology as it found expression in the Fathers in such a way that it could be seen to be consistent with the mind of Anglicanism as expressed in the formularies. In a way similar to Hooker, he sought to move the debate on from its polarization between objective and subjective emphases, by directing attention again to the heart of the matter:

> that is to say the gift of Christ Himself, in His whole person, given to us for the sanctification of our whole persons, that He may dwell in us and we in Him.[17]

In so doing he maintained a close relationship between the presence of Christ and the reception of Christ, emphasizing continually that the purpose of the Eucharist is to give us a real participation in the glorified body and blood of Christ.

The outward signs of this inner theological concern to concentrate on the reality of our participation in Christ through the Eucharist can be seen in the emphasis placed on *communion* in traditional Anglican spirituality. For example, the very fact that 'Holy Communion' has been the traditional Anglican title for the sacrament and that it is still deeply embedded in much popular piety as the preferred name, speaks volumes of how generations of Anglican worshippers have described and defined their understanding of the sacrament. Similarly, Anglican liturgy has always related the Communion to the rest of the sacramental action and has not tried to isolate it as a separate rite within the Eucharist. This is seen most clearly in the 1662 form where the Communion is in a sense the anamnesis itself, but it still holds true for revised rites which have restored a more traditional structure.

The long history of devotional manuals of which Anglicanism can boast is a further testimony to the Anglican emphasis on communion with Christ in the Eucharist. Whether coming from the Puritan or High Anglican stables of the seventeenth century, from the Evangelical revival of the eighteenth or the Catholic renewal of the nineteenth, they were united in their desire to encourage the sort of expectant spirituality which is ready to receive the fullness of the eucharistic gift and so participate in new degrees of depth in the life of Christ.

The late nineteenth and early twentieth centuries saw the traditional Anglican emphasis on communion disrupted by the emerging non-communicating High Masses. With its slogan 'The Lord's People at the Lord's Table on the Lord's Day', the Parish Communion movement not only sought to restore the fullness of the eucharistic event but also to establish that for which the Reformers, the Puritans, the High Church tradition, the early Evangelicals and the early Tractarians had yearned: the communion of the people as part of the weekly cycle of Anglican life.

Perhaps an extension of the Parish Communion's vision has been the growing call for baptized children to receive communion. In the Boston Statement of 1985, Anglican liturgical theologians recognized that child communion already happens in some Provinces and recommended that the practice should become the norm throughout the Communion.[18] The issues were discussed at the ACC in 1987 and, on the advice of the 1988 Lambeth Conference they should now be under discussion in each of the Provinces. Finally, the pleas for lay presidency from the Southern Cone derive at least in part from a desire to maintain the unity of the Eucharist and to ensure that the experience of communion is part of the life of its new and developing congregations.

There is much that needs to be said on a theological level about the characteristics of our participation in Christ through the Eucharist. For example, we need to say that our participation is with Christ's fully *human* life, that it is with the *ascended* life of the one whose body was given and whose blood was shed, and that our participation with Christ takes place through the power and presence of the Holy *Spirit*. The ecclesiological dimension of our participation in Christ also needs clear expression. The Eucharist is the experience of being united, as Luther liked to say, 'with Christ and all his saints'. It is the event by which the Church realizes and renews its life and identity. These are all themes around which Anglican eucharistic theology has revolved — sometimes correcting tendencies to underplay them both inside and outside its own life. There is not the space to develop these characteristics in any sort of systematic or ecumenical way here. However, the task needs to be done. Creative Anglican theology on the eucharistic presence has become somewhat of a rarity at this stage of the twentieth century — indeed in some ways throughout this century, which on the whole has shown more interest in the theological issues surrounding the eucharistic sacrifice than the presence. The task will find much to draw upon in the Anglican tradition both in terms of theology and piety. It will also find many resources to develop its own richness in both the contemporary High Calvinist and Orthodox theologies which have an uncanny knack of saying very similar things. They both stress the soteriological significance of Christ's humanity. They both refer the eucharistic mystery to our participation in the ascended life of Christ as we lift up our hearts and experience our share in the eschatological life. They both emphasize the role of the Spirit as the one who brings us into communion with the Son and the Father. They both set the Eucharist in the breadth of its corporate setting.

IV. The Eucharist as sacrifice

We have just said that the question of the sacrificial dimension of the Eucharist has received much more attention this century than other areas of eucharistic theology. It is a disproportion (inevitably repeated in this essay as it tries to reflect the interests of Anglican theology) which is partly due to the fact that the issues it raises affect more directly the understanding of the Gospel than those surrounding the eucharistic presence. For example, the Lutheran and Reformed strands of the Reformation showed it was possible to disagree over the nature of the presence whilst being agreed over the characteristics of the Gospel and in consequence convinced about the dangers of defining the Eucharist in sacrificial terms. The preoccupation with the eucharistic sacrifice has also been partly caused by the fact that it affects liturgical language in a more contentious way than does the presence. For example, it is possible for different interpretations of the eucharistic presence to be equally happy about the use of a given liturgical text. Some may want to link the presence directly and explicitly to reception:

Send your Holy Spirit that these gifts . . . which we receive may be to us the body and blood of Christ.

(New Zealand, 1989)[19]

Some may prefer to express the objectivity of Christ's eucharistic presence independently of the moment of reception:

Sanctify them by your Holy Spirit to be the body and blood of Jesus Christ our Lord.

(USA, 1979)[20]

All, however, have to work within the language set by the biblical witness which on the one hand describes the bread and the wine as the body and blood and on the other, directs that they should be eaten and drunk.

The matter is quite different over the eucharistic sacrifice, where the Church has found itself with much more room for liturgical manoeuvre. In short, although 'This is my body' does not solve the theological problem of the sense in which it is the body of Christ, it does give a certain non-negotiability to the liturgical form, whereas 'Do this in remembrance of me'[21] gives a command but leaves little information on exactly how it should be fulfilled. There have been two classic interpretations of the command. One (broadly Reformed) relates it directly to the informed eating and drinking: 'Take and eat this in remembrance that Christ died for you.' The other (broadly Catholic) relates the command to words and actions addressed to God which seek to unite the liturgical moment with the great salvific events in one oblationary movement: 'Wherefore . . . we thy humble servants do celebrate and make here before thy Divine Majesty, with these thy holy gifts, which we offer unto thee, the memorial thy Son hath commanded us to make.'[22]

As we can see from these two snippets from 1552/1662 and the Scottish Liturgy of 1764 (with its roots in 1549), both understandings have had a place in Anglican liturgy. In his 1552 rite Cranmer shifted a whole lot of petitionary and oblationary material to the post-communion position, thus making the communion itself the fulfilment of the Lord's command and in so doing identifying himself and the English rite with the Reformed view. However, as Kenneth Stevenson has recently shown, the theme of offering has an extraordinary persistence. It does not conveniently go away even when an axe is laid to its root. It appears to exert an almost irresistible pressure, managing to find its way back first into the practice and then the words of the liturgy.[23]

This can be seen even within the Evangelical Anglican tradition where, at times, attempts have been made to articulate a fuller content to the anamnesis than the Reformation provided. Bryan Spinks has shown how Puritans inside and outside the Church of England during the seventeenth century threw increasing liturgical and theological emphasis on the fraction (and libation). He concludes that whereas

> in the 1552 Communion service, Cranmer seems to have interpreted 'remembrance' as the actual eating and drinking of the elements ... The Puritan tradition seems to have centred the 'remembrance' on the visible breaking of the bread and the pouring of the wine.[24]

As is well known, in the eighteenth century John and Charles Wesley were quite happy to use sacrificial imagery in eucharistic theology and hymnody:

> Do as Jesus bids us do,
> Signify his Flesh and Blood,
> Him in memorial shew,
> Offer up the Lamb to God.[25]

It is less well known but also true that many Evangelical leaders in the early nineteenth century described the sacrament with a richness which drew on various sacrificial themes: it is 'our Eucharist, our festival of praise and triumph',[26] 'a prevailing means of pleading merits before God'[27] and an opportunity (usually defined as the moment of communion itself) 'to give up your soul to God'.[28]

Within other Anglican traditions there have been more conscious and explicit attempts to recover some traditional sacrificial motifs and to experiment with new ones. The Offertory, the commemoration, the eternal dimension of Christ's sacrifice have all been explored as ways of giving some sort of sacrificial content to the Eucharist whilst affirming at the same time the sufficiency and historicity of Calvary.

This came to its clearest liturgical form through the Non-Jurors' rite of 1718 and through them the Scottish rite of 1764. The ways the '1718–64 tradition' handled the anamnesis and epiclesis, drawing as they did from 1549 and from Eastern forms,[29] have become models for other Eucharistic Prayers in the Anglican Communion even to this day, particularly finding expression in the American *Book of Common Prayer* (1979) and the Canadian *Book of Alternative Services* (1985).

The fact that both understandings of the anamnesis (to receive or to offer) have existed within Anglicanism for centuries was noted by Massey Shepherd in his address to the Anglican Congress in 1954 when he said that Anglicanism has held within itself 'two types of liturgy' which are 'expressions of two approaches to the problem'. He went on to say that although it had proved possible to live with the tension, 'sooner or later . . . it must be resolved'.[30] Back in 1947 Stephen Neill identified the same tension but gave no hope as to its resolution:

> It is impossible to pretend that these two views, even stated moderately, are ultimately reconcilable, as different emphases within a common understanding. They do depend on very deep differences in belief . . . .[31]

An enormous amount of liturgical change has happened in Anglicanism since Neill and Shepherd addressed the issue. Through the sheer quantity of prayers now in use the starkness of the contrast which they identified has been reduced. Nevertheless, when surveying the latest round of change, Colin Buchanan concluded that there are still very different approaches to the anamnesis and suggested that the wording in many prayers would be unacceptable to Evangelical ears.

Despite this, it is possible to detect the emergence of some common forms which, on the one hand, give a fuller content to the anamnesis than Cranmer allowed (i.e. they *say* something about what we are doing in the presence of God) but, on the other hand, do not go so far as 1764 went (i.e. they do not necessarily offer the elements). Broadly speaking they follow a 1549 pattern in which *we celebrate* the saving events *with this bread and this cup*. This is not to imply that there is complete unanimity. Many prayers have an anamnesis which is quite vacuous, whilst others do actually offer the elements or talk of an association between Christ's sacrifice and the self-oblation of the believers in a way which others would regard as far too close and confusing. Indeed, it cannot be doubted that behind the liturgical forms which Anglicans are using in common, there are different theological understandings of their meaning. However, the presence of some common forms of language is still significant — particularly so if it can be shown that there are genuinely *unitive categories* at work which either have helped the movement to a rapprochement or may increase the possibility of a deeper resolution in the future. Of course, to identify and develop such *unitive categories* is an enormous task which we cannot complete here. All we can do is point to some categories in classic and contemporary Anglicanism which have a unitive potential.

The first of these is the category of *proclamation*. As they interpreted the legacy passed on by the Reformation, various Anglican theologians sought both to acknowledge the once-for-all character of Calvary with its complete efficacy *and* to affirm a real role for the Eucharist as an objective commemoration before men and before God. For example, Lancelot Andrewes said that in the Eucharist we repeat the memory of Calvary and as we do so Christ in 'the very act of his offering is made present to us'.[32] Laud, Morton, Taylor and others developed the objective character of the commemoration in a more Godward direction. They saw the commemoration of Christ's complete sacrifice being made before God and in some sense offered to him as an interactive, intercessory, impetratory gesture. We have already seen how the idea of offering the memorial to God appeared in Wesleyan theology and hymnody. The Wesleys believed that in the Eucharist the completed and accepted sacrifice is shown to the Father so that its saving reality might be claimed for us and applied to us.

The objective character of the commemoration has received considerable attention in twentieth-century Anglicanism. This is partly due of course to the work of Gregory Dix, who defined the Eucharist as the 'recalling before God of the one sacrifice of Christ in all its accomplished and effectual fullness so that it is here and now operative by its effects'.[33] It has to be said that Evangelicals have been quite uncomfortable with the full-blown form of Dix's theology which, drawing on the mystery theology of Casel, describes the presence of Christ's sacrifice in much more ontological terms than he appears to do here — not just the presence of the effects but the presence of the event itself. However, the form in which it has filtered into the ecumenical dialogue has been generally of the softer, functional type and this has proved a genuinely *unitive category* as the words of the ARCIC Report show:

> God has given the eucharist to the Church as a means through which the work of Christ on the cross is proclaimed and made effective in the life of the Church.[34]

In his structural survey of the liturgical language of offering to which we have already referred, Kenneth Stevenson identifies *story* as one of the deep structures of the Eucharist. He argues the story is told in such a way as to show that it has a claim on us. It is not a neutral narrative. It is a story which we believe and to which we desire to commit ourselves. The Eucharist, he argues, is a 'sacrifice of proclamation before God'.[35]

Categories of story and proclamation cohere well with the central sacramental concerns of the Reformers. They wanted to relate the

Eucharist to the Word so that through the sacrament the Gospel would be made known in a visible as well as audible way. Of course, it is people and not God who need to see and hear the Gospel. But they also need to believe and receive the Gospel. They need to be able to say before God that they are saved by his grace; they need to acknowledge before God that they are redeemed by Christ's blood; they need to tell God, not for his benefit, but for their own, that they believe this story and want to enter more deeply into the new life it offers. In the Eucharist we proclaim the saving reality of Christ crucified and in so doing say 'Yes, Lord, we believe'.

Quite how this should be expressed in liturgical word and action is another question. However, it is worth giving two South Pacific examples from rites which can hardly be described as a sell-out to Catholic causes:

> With this bread and this cup
> we show forth Christ's death
> until he comes in glory.
>
> (Congregational response at the anamnesis. Australia, 1978)[36]
>
> We lift up the cup of salvation
> and call upon your name.
> Here and now, with this bread and wine,
> we celebrate your great acts of liberation,
> ever present and living in Jesus Christ.
>
> (New Zealand, 1989)[37]

The second *unitive category* follows on naturally from the sacrifice of proclamation: it is the *sacrifice of praise*. With its concentration on the Church's earliest forms, liturgical scholarship over the last century has uncovered the truly eucharistic dimension of the Church's formative sacramental life. Anglican scholars, who have made their own notable contribution to the work, have argued that traditional Anglican liturgy, particularly in its 1662 form, sounded significantly out of tune with the eucharistic song of the early Church. The substance of the charge could not be resisted by Evangelicals who for all sorts of reasons were very wary of any movement away from 1662. Indeed, in time they began to welcome the recovery of the eucharistic dimension of the sacrament, and admitted that 1662 simply did not give sufficient expression to the deep sense of thanksgiving for the redeeming work of God in Christ which is at the heart of Reformation faith and authentically Evangelical experience. Charismatic spirituality, with its inherent emphasis on thanksgiving and praise and its use of sacrificial motifs and language in its words and songs of worship, helped the movement from the solemn tones of the 'Consecration Prayer' to the celebratory joy of the

'Eucharistic Prayer', which we see throughout the Communion, to be received from the section of the Church which was most reticent about structural and theological change. As we said earlier, Anglican Eucharistic Prayers of all persuasions are quite happy to say that in the Eucharist we are celebrating the reality of our salvation in Christ and that we are doing so not just in word but in action and form. Just as the proclamation of our salvation focuses on the bread and wine, so does the praise for our salvation:

> We celebrate with this bread and this cup
> his one perfect sacrifice.
> Accept through him, our great high priest,
> this our sacrifice of thanks and praise.

(England, 1980)[38]

Again this is not to deny that there may be very different interpretations of what it means to 'celebrate with this bread and this cup' and of what it means to offer the sacrifice of praise. Nevertheless, the renewed emphasis on the eucharistic dimension of the sacrament has helped to widen the terms of reference for the two classic understandings of the anamnesis which we mentioned earlier. It reminds the Reformed emphasis on *receiving* of the need to articulate why we are eating and drinking, thus calling for an expression of our thanks for all we have received and will go on receiving in Christ. It reminds the Catholic emphasis on *offering* that our call is to celebrate the completion of the atoning work and to share in the victory feast. Many years before, Richard Hooker brought the two neatly together when he said that the bread and the wine 'serveth as well for a medicine to heal our infirmities and purge our sins as for a sacrifice of thanksgiving'.[39]

The third and final *unitive category* which we will consider revolves around the very contentious area of the relationship beween the self-offering of the Church and the self-offering of Christ. Disagreements over how this relationship should be expressed were at the very centre of the Reformation debate and have continued to dominate discussion on the Eucharist to this day. For example, Anglican Evangelicals have been very critical of the words in the ARCIC Report which say that in the Eucharist we 'enter into the movement of [Christ's] self-offering',[40] arguing that they fail to preserve the distinction between the eucharistic *response* of the Church and the atoning *action* of Christ.[41] For the same reason, many Evangelicals would be unhappy with the introduction to the Canadian eucharistic rites which first accuses Cranmer of failing to give 'adequate expression to the unity between the Church's offering and the offering of Christ' and then goes on to say that the new Canadian prayers have deliberately sought to recover such notions. Similarly, the formula found in the new Scottish prayers, 'Made one with him, we offer you these gifts and with them ourselves, a single, holy, living sacrifice',[42] has not escaped Evangelical criticism.

Clearly, then, we cannot imply that Anglicanism has succeeded even within its own life to express the relationship between the Church's offering and Christ's, in a way which is sufficiently inclusive for Catholics and sufficiently exclusive for Evangelicals. But this is not to say that all attempts to do so are doomed to failure. Indeed, we would suggest that the category of the *perfection of Christ's obedience* provides a unifying potential which is still to be fully realized.

In the 1950s C. F. D. Moule experimented with the notion of Christ's obedience as a way of providing a point of connection between the Church's self-offering and Christ's redemptive work. He argued that by virtue of our fellowship with Christ and our participation in him, our own imperfect obedience is offered to God in union with his perfect obedience so that *'in Christ, our offering becomes a part of his'*.[43] Although such ideas were gaining currency in liberal Evangelical circles at the time, Moule did not convince his more conservative colleagues — particularly as they saw some of his themes expressed and developed without his safeguards in the 1958 Lambeth Report and the 1963 Conversations between the Church of England and the Methodist Church.

Evangelicals were very uncomfortable with the category of Christ's obedience being used as a way of defining his atoning work. They argued that it did not give sufficient expression to the aspect of vicarious sin-bearing which Evangelicals regard as the central feature of the biblical understanding of Christ's death.[44] In traditional terms, the emphasis on Christ's obedience scored high marks in describing him as the Priest (offering to God the perfect human response) but low marks in defining him as the Victim (who bore the judgement of God on sin).

There is a real danger — to which twentieth-century theology has been prone — of so spiritualizing theological categories that they are divorced not only from their historical meaning but also from their relationship to historical event. For example, it is easy to so stress the moral and spiritual dimension of Christ's sacrifice that we forget that what actually happened was very physical and very crude. We must remember that Christ came ready to do God's will precisely by preparing his body to be sacrificed. By holding together the *attitude* in which Christ died with the *event* of his death, the category of Christ's obedience becomes a more acceptable one for Evangelical thought. We see this sort of approach developed in the theology of Karl Barth.[45] He makes Christ's obedience the constitutive element in the atoning action, but only in so far as it is united with the event of his death as the experience of God's judgement. Christ's death is the setting for his obedience, because the perfection of his obedience is demonstrated not so much by his offering all that is best in mankind but by acknowledging all that is worst. He is willing to go to the cross because he is able to confess God's rightness in judging sin, and in so doing not only says so with his lips but accepts and experiences God's judgement on sin in his own being.

Christ's sacrifice is therefore exclusive: it was done *for us*, in our place; as Barth says, it was his blood and not a drop of ours which was shed,[46] and as Cyril of Jerusalem says, when describing the baptismal incorporation in Christ's death — 'we did not really die, we were not really buried, we were not really crucified and raised again'. But it is also inclusive in that, as Cyril goes on to say, while 'our imitation was but in a figure ... our salvation is in reality'; although 'Christ received the nails in His undefiled hands and feet, and endured anguish', to us 'without suffering or toil, by the fellowship of His pain He vouchsafes salvation'.[47] Christ's death is inclusive therefore in the sense that the death he died was our death. It is inclusive in the sense that Christ's attitude of obedience is to be echoed by him in us. It is inclusive in the sense that through this event, followed as it is by the resurrection and ascension, we are adopted into the trinitarian relationship — 'God has sent the Spirit of his Son into our hearts, crying, "Abba!, Father!"' (Gal 4.6).

The reality of our union with Christ and our participation in the eternal life of God, so dear to the heart of Catholic theology, must be given some form of expression in our eucharistic liturgy in a way which stands with the corresponding Evangelical concern that what Christ did *then* needs to be distinguished from what we are doing *now* and indeed from what he is doing *now*. It is a case of making clear that our obedience can be neither *separated* from his perfect obedience, in that ours has no independent validity, nor *confused* with it, in that ours has no atoning efficacy. In a similar way the same may be said of the relationship between Christ's death and his ascended life. In the language of the epistle to the Hebrews, the two cannot be *separated* because it is only on the basis of his death that he is able to enter the heavenly sanctuary, and they cannot be *confused*, because his work is not now to 'offer himself again and again' as a sacrifice for sin, but to 'bring salvation to those who are waiting for him' (Heb 9.25, 28). Our task in the Eucharist is to proclaim that we have been included in the *event* of Christ's obedient self-offering unto death because he died both for us and as one of us; it is to show that we identify with the *attitude* of Christ's obedient self-offering unto death by our repentance and faith; it is to rejoice that we participate in Christ's eternal *life* of obedient self-offering in praise and prayer to the Father.

V. Conclusion

The method followed in this essay has been to identify categories which have the potential to unite key emphases on either side of the

Evangelical–Catholic debate. The outcome has been inevitably selective. There are many other categories than those discussed here which have had a fundamental place in Anglican theology. On the sacramental theme, we could have referred to the Anglican appeal to the mystery of the Eucharist which acknowledges the reality of the event without dissecting its inner workings. On the theme of the presence, we could have referred to the Anglican appeal to the Eucharist as an 'effectual sign' of Christ's presence in a way which prefigured much contemporary Roman Catholic interest in the theology of signification, valuation and finalization. On the theme of sacrifice, we could have referred to the Anglican appeal to the pleading of Christ's sacrifice which appears in various sources including Cosin, Wesley, Bickersteth, Pusey, Gore and is found both in the reply to Leo XIII's Bull condemning Anglican Orders by the Archbishops of Canterbury and York in 1897, and nearly one hundred years later, in one of the Eucharistic Prayers suggested by the Church of England's Liturgical Commission in its recent publication *Patterns for Worship*.[48] The outcome of the method we have followed has also been inevitably Western and scholastic. It may be justifiably said that this is exactly the strait-jacket from which eucharistic theology needs to be released. To do so would involve developing the eschatologial, ecclesiological and pneumatological dimensions of the Eucharist which have been significantly present in Anglican eucharistic theology and which figure prominently in the Orthodox tradition and in much ecumenical scholarship, but which we have been able to mention only in passing. However, both the existence of more *unitive categories* in Anglican eucharistic theology than we have identified, and the resources within our tradition for developing new ways of looking at the Eucharist only go to prove the central argument of this essay, which is that Anglicanism has a rich *content* of eucharistic theology which has already given much to and can give more to the eucharistic life and thought of the 'one holy *catholic* and *apostolic* Church'.

Notes

1 The Archbishop's Address at the Third National Evangelical Anglican Congress in Caister, 1988.
2 Paul Avis, *Anglicanism and the Christian Church* (Edinburgh: T. & T. Clark, 1989), esp. pp. 271–311.
3 Stephen W. Sykes, *The Integrity of Anglicanism* (London: Mowbray, 1978).
4 *Institutes of the Christian Religion* 2, ed. John T. McNeill (Library of Christian Classics XXI; Philadelphia: The Westminster Press, 1960), IV.xvii.39.

5 'Treatise on the New Testament, 1520' in *Luther's Works: Word and Sacrament I*, ed. E.T. Bachmann and H.T. Lehmann (Philadelphia: Muhlenberg Press, 1960), XXXV, pp. 75–112 (p. 99).

6 *Apology*, quoted by Richard Buxton in *Eucharist and Institution Narrative* (Alcuin Club Collections 58; Great Wakering: Mayhew-McCrimmon, 1978).

7 *Ecclesiastical Polity* (Everyman's Edition II; London: J.M. Dent, 1940), V.lxvii.4, p. 222.

8 See Paul Romer, *Calvin and Bullinger on the Lord's Supper* (Alcuin/GROW Liturgical Study 12; Bramcote: Grove, 1989).

9 For a fuller discussion of this particular issue and of Reformed and Evangelical eucharistic thought generally, see Christopher J. Cocksworth, 'A study of evangelical eucharistic thought in the Church of England with special reference to the period c.1960–c.1980' (PhD thesis: University of Manchester, 1989); due to be published by Cambridge University Press.

10 Charles Gore, *The Body of Christ* (London: John Murray, 1907).

11 Robert Wilberforce, *The Doctrine of the Holy Eucharist* (London: John and Charles Mozley, 1854).

12 Anglican–Roman Catholic International Commission, *The Final Report* (London: CTS/SPCK, 1982), Statement on the Eucharist, paras 3 and 8, pp. 12f., 15.

13 *Ecclesiastical Polity*, v.lxvii.2, p. 320.

14 *Institutes*, IV.xvii.32.

15 Edward Schillebeeckx, *The Eucharist* (London: Sheed and Ward, 1968), p. 104.

16 E.B. Pusey, *Letter on the Tendency to Romanism*, 4th edn (Oxford and London, 1840), p. 144.

17 *The Body of Christ*, pp. 65–6.

18 'The Boston statement: Children and Communion' in Colin Buchanan (ed.), *Nurturing Children in Communion* (Grove Liturgical Study 44; Bramcote: Grove, 1985), pp. 42–9.

19 From the rite 'Thanksgiving of the People of God' in *A New Zealand Prayer Book, 1989* (Auckland and London: Collins, 1989), p. 423.

20 From 'Amer 2-2 (c), Rite Two from the American Book of Common Prayer (1977)' in Colin Buchanan (ed.), *Latest Anglican Liturgies* (London: SPCK, 1985), p. 148.
   For ease of reference here and in later citations from Anglican liturgies authorized in the period 1976–84, the Eucharistic Prayers are referred to according to the method used by Colin Buchanan in *Latest Anglican Liturgies* (LAL) with appropriate page numbers to where they can be found in LAL.

21 From the 1552 words of administration — to which, in 1662, the 1549 words were added.

22 From the anamnesis of the Scottish Liturgy 1764, in Bernard Wigan (ed.), *The Liturgy in English* (London: Oxford University Press, 1962), p. 44.

23 See Kenneth Stevenson, *Eucharist and Offering* (New York: Pueblo, 1986).

24 Bryan D. Spinks, *Freedom or Order?: The Eucharistic Liturgy in English Congregationalism 1645–1980* (Allison Park, PA: Pickwick, 1984), p. 63.

25 'Hymns of the Lord's Supper 118' in J. E. Rattenbury, *The Eucharistic Hymns of John and Charles Wesley* (London: Epworth, 1948).

26 Daniel Wilson, 'A practical address' in *Sermons and Tracts*, 7th edn (London: George Wilson, 1825), II, p. 384.

27 Edward Bickersteth, *A Treatise on the Lord's Supper* (London: L. B. Seeley, 1824), p. 61.

28 Thomas Haweis, *The Communicant's Spiritual Companion* (London: Samuel Swift, 1812), p. 48.

29 The '1718–64 tradition' is so named by Richard Buxton, *Eucharist and Institution Narrative* and is analysed by him and compared with the '1662 tradition', op. cit., pp. 159–93.

30 See 'The Eucharistic Sacrifice' in *The Lambeth Conference 1958* (London: SPCK, 1958), pp. 283–5.

31 Stephen Neill, 'The Holy Communion in the Anglican Church' in H. Martin (ed.), *The Holy Communion* (London: SCM, 1947), pp. 65–6.

32 Lancelot Andrewes, *Sermons II* in Library of Anglo-Catholic Theology (Oxford: John Henry Parker, 1841), p. 301.

33 Gregory Dix, *The Shape of the Liturgy* (London: A. & C. Black, 1945), p. 243.

34 Statement on the Eucharist in *The Final Report*, para. 25.

35 Stevenson, *Eucharist and Offering*, pp. 235–6.

36 From 'Aus 5: The Second Order: An Australian Prayer Book (1978)', second, third, and fourth alternatives, LAL, pp. 233–6.

37 From the rite: 'Thanksgiving for Creation and Redemption' in *A New Zealand Prayer Book, 1989*, p. 469.

38 From 'Eng. A: The Church of England Rite A Liturgy (1980)', first Eucharistic Prayer, LAL, p. 10.

39 *Ecclesiastical Polity*, v.lxvii.12, p. 331.

40 Statement on the Eucharist in *The Final Report*, para. 5.

41 For example: *ARCIC: An Evangelical Open Letter to the Anglican Episcopate 1988* (Bramcote: Grove, 1988), sec.B.I.3–4, pp. 4–5.

42 From 'Scot2: The Episcopal Church of Scotland "Scottish Liturgy" (1982)', LAL, p. 58; see also alternative Eucharistic Prayers II–IV in *Scottish Liturgy: The Eucharist* (Edinburgh: General Synod of the Episcopal Church, 1990).

   The formula draws on Augustine's observation that 'if you then are the body and members of Christ, the mystery of yourselves is laid upon the table of the Lord' (Sermon 272). This rich association of ideas which emphasizes the corporate and mystical character of the body of Christ (in its Christological, ecclesiological and sacramental dimensions), has been an important source for eucharistic theology amongst Catholic Anglicans this century. The idea of the Whole Christ (Head and members) being offered to God in the Eucharist looms large in the thought of Charles Gore (*The Body of Christ*, pp. 237–8, 284, 328–9) and Eric Mascall (*Christ, The Christian and The Church* [London: Longmans, 1946]).

   For Evangelical criticism of the Scottish formula see Colin Buchanan,

Anglican Eucharistic Liturgy 1975–1985 (Grove Liturgical Study 41; Bramcote: Grove, 1985), p. 22.

43 C. F. D. Moule, *The Sacrifice of Christ* (London: Hodder and Stoughton, 1956), p. 57.

44 See J. I. Packer (ed.), *Eucharistic Sacrifice* (London: CBRP, 1962).

45 Karl Barth, *Church Dogmatics IV.1: The Doctrine of Reconciliation*, ed. G. W. Bromiley and T. F. Torrance (Edinburgh: T. & T. Clark, 1956).

46 *Church Dogmatics*, IV.1. p. 320.

47 'Mystagogical catechesis: II.5' in F. L. Cross (ed.), *St Cyril of Jerusalem's Lectures on the Christian Sacraments* (London: SPCK, 1951), pp. 40–80 (p. 61).

48 For a discussion of the concept see Bryan D. Spinks, 'The ascension and the vicarious humanity of Christ: the Christology and soteriology behind the Church of Scotland's anamnesis and epiklesis' in J. Neil Alexander (ed.), *Time and Community* (Washington: Pastoral Press, 1990), pp. 185–201; and Kenneth Stevenson, 'The eucharistic prayers in "Patterns for Worship": a commentary' in *Patterns for Worship: Essays on Eucharistic Prayers*, GS Misc. 333.

6

Daily prayer

Paul F. Bradshaw

The theology of Christian prayer

It has often been customary to justify liturgical revision chiefly on historical grounds, to argue that in our traditions of worship we have wandered far from the practices of the golden age of the early Church as a result of mediaeval distortion and/or Reformation ignorance, and that therefore what we need to do is to retrace our steps and restore the purity of early Christian liturgy. I have discussed the limitations of such an approach elsewhere,[1] but since it has been no less operative in the case of patterns of daily prayer than for other rites, it seems appropriate to begin with some theological rather than historical foundations for a reconsideration of the traditional shape of Anglican daily offices.

Christians are not merely disciples or followers of Jesus: according to Pauline theology, they are 'in Christ'. Through their baptism they participate in the death and resurrection of Christ and so are incorporated into him, not merely as individuals but as members of his body, the Church. Hence, if it is to give true expression to this mystical reality, Christian prayer must also essentially be participation in the prayer of Christ himself and in the prayer of the whole Church: it must have both a *Christological* and an *ecclesiological* dimension.

The prayer of Christ to the Father is the prayer of the great high-priest of the new and eternal covenant (cf. Heb 8 – 9). In this priesthood the whole body of the Church shares. As the Roman Catholic General Instruction on the Liturgy of the Hours puts it, 'The baptized, by regeneration and the anointing of the Holy Spirit, are consecrated into a spiritual house and a holy priesthood. They become capable of taking part in the worship of the New Testament, not thanks to themselves, but to the gift and merits of Christ.'[2] Thus, whenever we pray as Christians, we pray in Christ and through Christ and with Christ, and Christ prays in us and for us and with us, so that, through the work of the Holy Spirit, our prayer becomes Christ's prayer and his prayer becomes our prayer.[3] Daily prayer, therefore, is part of the privilege granted to those who are baptized to share in the continuing priestly ministry of Christ. Hence, the obligation to participate in this prayer springs not from some external rule but from the very nature of our Christian vocation itself; and as such, it belongs equally to all members of the Church — laity and clergy alike.

The fundamental characteristics of priestly prayer are that it centres around the offering of sacrifice and involves intercession. The sacrifice offered by Christ is of course the oblation of his whole life, once for all. The Letter to the Hebrews is emphatic about this, yet it is also able to go on to exhort its readers: 'Through him then let us continually offer up a sacrifice of praise to God, that is, the fruit of lips that acknowledge his name' (Heb 13.15). Thus, one of the principal ways in which Christians continue to participate in Christ's priesthood is through their perpetual offering of praise. Hebrews also speaks of Christ maintaining his priestly activity in his risen and glorified state, 'since he always lives to make intercession' (Heb 7.25), and so Christians too are called to share in that intercessory prayer.

Yet, if this prayer is truly to be priestly, both these activities — the offering of praise and of intercession — must necessarily be done for the sake of others. In order to be a priest, there has always to be someone else on whose behalf one acts: it would be a contradiction in terms to be a priest simply for oneself. Thus, we are called not merely to offer praise and thanksgiving for what God has done for each one of us individually, nor even for the Church collectively, but to render to God the praise that is due from the whole of creation. Similarly, our intercession should be focused primarily not upon ourselves and our own needs, nor even just on that of other Christians, but rather upon the needs of the whole world for which Christ died and which he desires to be saved (see 1 Tim 2.1–2). In this way, Christian prayer also has a strong *eschatological* dimension. It both prays for the coming of the Kingdom of God, and is itself a foretaste of the heavenly praise which will be sung unceasingly before the throne of God and of the Lamb by 'every creature in heaven and on earth and under the earth and in the sea' (Rev 5.13).

The ecclesiological aspect of Christian prayer receives its fullest liturgical expression when believers assemble together to pray, and so manifest the presence both of Christ ('For where two or three are gathered in my name, there am I in the midst of them': Matt 18.20) and also of his Church. Corporate daily prayer, therefore, is not an optional extra for those who like that sort of thing; it is what all Christian prayer is meant to be. There is, strictly speaking, no such thing as private prayer for a Christian. Whenever we pray, we do so as a member of the body of Christ and united by the Spirit with the whole company of earth and heaven. We pray as the Church and with the Church. Nevertheless, there are inevitably times when Christians are unable to join physically with others in the regular worship of God, and so must pray on their own. Here the use of common forms of prayer becomes perhaps even more important than in the liturgical assembly. Through participation in patterns of prayer that are being used by other members of the Church, the individual believers are reminded of the ecclesial character of all Christian praying and are helped to shape their prayers according to the intrinsic spirit of their priestly commission.

The forms of Christian prayer

We have argued that the fundamental elements of authentic Christian prayer are praise and intercession. Yet the Judaeo-Christian tradition has not usually expressed its praise principally by the heaping up of laudatory epithets for God. Rather it has done so through anamnesis, the remembrance of the mighty works wrought by God in history. The Bible itself contains many examples of this way of praying. When, for instance, Abraham's servant succeeds in his mission of finding a wife for his master's son, he says, 'Blessed be the Lord, the God of my master Abraham, who has not forsaken his steadfast love and his faithfulness toward my master. As for me, the Lord has led me in the way to the house of my master's kinsmen' (Gen 24.27). Again, in the New Testament both the Magnificat and the Benedictus (Luke 1.46–55, 68–79) fall into this same category. But how does the act of remembrance bring praise to God?

Firstly, it admits or *confesses* that what has happened is not the result of mere chance nor the product of human skill and ingenuity, but instead the work of God; and thus, by interpreting normal human experience in a religious manner and acknowledging God's hidden activity in the world, it ascribes due credit where it truly belongs. God's deeds are recalled not because God may have forgotten them and need reminding of them, nor again necessarily because we feel particularly glad about them, but simply because we know them to be true. Viewed in this way then, there is little difference between a prayer and a credal affirmation. Indeed, New Testament allusions to confessing Jesus as Lord may well be referring to the inclusion of his name within Jewish prayer-forms rather than to a primitive creed as such.[4]

Secondly, when done in the presence of others, the act of remembrance *proclaims* the faith of the one who is recounting the story, and invites the listeners to share that same vision and give the glory to God by making a response, whether that is simply an 'Amen' at the end of the prayer or involves a more extensive liturgical dialogue. In early Christianity, for example, when believers addressed 'one another in psalms and hymns and spiritual songs' (Eph 5.19) which they had either composed or selected from canonical texts, the community seemingly responded to each verse with 'Alleluia' or some other refrain.[5] Viewed in this way then, there is little difference between prayer and preaching the Gospel. Worship and mission are thus not different things, between which a choice may have to be made. On the contrary, they are the very same activity. To do one is to do the other. To proclaim the Gospel is to offer worship to God, and to recount God's mighty deeds in prayer is to preach the good news. Indeed, calling the first part of a eucharistic prayer the 'preface' did not arise because it preceded what was thought to be the main body of the prayer, but because the Latin word *praefatio* meant proclamation: the preface proclaims the mighty works of God.

In this manner, the offering of praise also sanctifies or *consecrates*. By reminding the worshippers who is the true author and giver of all good things, it restores the material elements of creation and the activities of human beings to their proper relationship to God. Through periodic acts of remembrance during each day, time itself can come to be redeemed and human lives made holy and spent in accordance with God's will. This in turn illuminates the connection between praise and intercession. The praise is not simply an initial attempt to flatter the deity before moving on to the real purpose of the invocation — the request for what we want — but is itself at the heart of what Christian prayer is all about. The intercession merely articulates the desire that God may continue the salvific activity which has been celebrated in the anamnesis, sanctifying those for whom we pray and drawing all things back into a right relationship with God, that the divine will may be done and the heavenly kingdom come. The intercession is thus essentially in subordination to the praise: we may only properly petition God to do things which are in accord with the divine nature revealed in our remembrance.

The Anglican tradition

The forms of Morning and Evening Prayer which emerged in the first Anglican Prayer Book of 1549 and have been substantially retained in all later editions of the book throughout the Anglican Communion are unique creations in the history of Christian liturgy. Morning and evening prayer in the parochial (or, as it is often called, the 'cathedral') tradition of the early Church centred upon praise and prayer — one or more hymns or psalms followed by substantial intercession—with readings from the Bible occurring only in occasional services of the Word and not in these daily assemblies. In the early monastic tradition times of prayer consisted chiefly of the alternation of the recitation of psalms and silent prayer. The Pachomian communities of upper Egypt apparently alternated the reading of other parts of scripture with silent prayer in their daily services, and it was seemingly from here, through the influence of John Cassian, that the custom of including a scriptural reading within the later Western monastic offices came. But such readings were generally very brief, often recited from memory, and usually placed at the conclusion of the main psalmody of the office, prior to the concluding prayers.[6]

Only in the night offices of the Western monastic tradition do we find a substantial use of scripture reading. This might be attached to the end of the main psalmody of the office (as it was in the daytime services) or alternatively a group of lections, usually three in number, would be followed by an equal number of psalms, with this unit perhaps being repeated several times. The alternation of lessons and canticles in the Anglican offices, therefore, was a novel idea, as was the shift in balance to the prescription of a large quantity of lectionary material and a relatively small number of psalms at every service.

On the other hand, while the precise forms of daily worship included in the first Anglican Prayer Book may have been new, the concept behind them certainly was not. As the Preface to the book makes clear, the principal aim was understood to be pedagogical — the formation of a Christian spirit within the worshippers. By the regular, systematic reading of the whole Bible and meditation upon it, the clergy were to be 'stirred up to godliness themselves, and be the more able to exhort others by wholesome doctrine, and to confute them that were adversaries to the truth'. Similarly, it was intended that 'the people (by daily hearing of holy Scripture read in the Church) might continually profit more and more in the knowledge of God, and be the more inflamed with the love of his true religion'.

This was analogous to the spirit behind the development of the patterns and rules of prayer of the fourth-century religious communities in the Egyptian desert. As Alexander Schmemann has commented:

> It is essential to understand that these rules developed not as an ordo of worship, but within what might be called a 'pedagogical' system. They were needed to guide the monk on his way toward 'spiritual freedom' ... The purpose of the liturgical ordo is to make worship the expression of the faith of the Church, to actualize the Church herself; the purpose of the monastic devotional rules is to train the monk in constant prayer, to inculcate in him the work of prayer.[7]

Moreover, for the early monk, as Louis Bouyer has said, the work of prayer did not mean just 'any kind of prayer: it was essentially the continual "meditation" on Scripture, meaning its rumination ... Throughout the whole of his day, he did not cease to recall the sacred words, which he learned by heart as far as possible, beginning with the Psalter.'[8]

Thus, while the compilers of the Prayer Book no doubt sincerely believed that they were returning to the spirit and forms of prayer current in the congregations of the early Church, what they were actually doing was in a large measure restoring the spirituality of the fourth-century desert fathers, a spirituality which was essentially individualistic and non-liturgical, concerned primarily with personal ascetical growth, rather than with praying as the Church for the sake of the world.

Nevertheless, even granted that the Anglican offices were intended to fulfil a somewhat different function from what we have earlier outlined as the principal purpose of Christian praying, can they not still be used as instruments for that prayer? Such a thing is certainly not impossible. Through the recitation of the Psalter and regular reading of scripture which is prescribed in these offices, it can be said that the anamnesis of God's saving activity is made, and through the canticles and prayers that praise and intercession are offered. What is missing, however, in most cases is the worshippers' perception of what they are doing as being participation in the priestly prayer of Christ. Instead, insofar as they have any notion of what the office is supposed to be for, their understanding is likely to be along principally monastic lines: that they are fulfilling a religious duty which is canonically imposed upon them, and that they are intended to derive understanding and spiritual benefit from the reading. The latter is confirmed by the widespread tendency to include substantial periods of reflective silence within the office, and to convert opportunities for intercession at the end of the rite into times of meditation.

This suggests that what we most need is not so much a change in external forms as a renewal of the inner spirituality. The really important differences between 'cathedral' and 'monastic' patterns of daily prayer are not so much matters of external appearance, as many people unfortunately tend to suppose, but of the inner spirit of what is being done. We do not switch from one style of praying to the other merely by putting an end to a *cursus* of psalmody, reducing the quantity of scripture read in the service, and making sure that certain elements feature in it, as for example Psalm 141 in the evening office. It is true that there are marked differences in the outward forms of the fourth-century cathedral and monastic offices, but these are less significant in themselves than they are as evidence of the strikingly different concepts underlying each of them.

On the other hand, it is unlikely that such a transformation of the spirituality of daily prayer can be brought about unless at the same time some modification of the forms themselves is effected. The recent revision of eucharistic rites provides a parallel here. What was of greatest importance with regard to the Eucharist was not the replacement of the 1662 order of service with one that better reflected the shape of the primitive rite, but the effecting of a transformation in the way in which people envisaged and participated in eucharistic worship itself. The Parish Communion movement in England first struggled to do this at the time when there was no prospect of official liturgical revision taking place, but found that it could succeed only up to a point. Its efforts were resisted by the rite itself with all the connotations which traditionally attached to it. Only when the text and rubrics were changed did it really become possible to engender a new eucharistic theology and spirituality.

In the same way, it is desirable that the shape of Anglican orders for daily prayer should also be revised, or new alternatives set alongside the traditional models, in order that the prime purpose of Christian praying may be more clearly set forth and appropriated by those who want to associate themselves with the Church's life of prayer. So far, revised versions throughout the Anglican Communion have generally not done this. They have tended merely to reduce the quantity of psalmody and Bible reading in each office by spreading it more thinly over a longer period, and to increase variety by a wider selection of canticles and seasonal material, but they have not fundamentally disturbed the structure or spirituality of the traditional forms.

The 1985 *Book of Alternative Services* of the Anglican Church of Canada is the only real exception to this rule. It has made a serious attempt to introduce a different approach, not just by alterations in the rubrics and texts, but by the provision of a substantial preface to what it describes as 'The Divine Office' which attempts to explain the rationale behind the forms and makes suggestions as to the way they might be used. Although this preface contains some historical claims that are questionable and needs to go further in explaining the purpose of the various parts of the services, it is at least a public acknowledgement of the fact that it is not self-evident to people what they are doing when they celebrate the office. However, in its orders of Morning and Evening Prayer themselves, the attempt to put forward a new style of worship is hindered by the need at the same time to continue to permit the traditional shape to be retained. The result is inevitably a compromise with a wide variety of alternative choices, which those who understand the rationale can certainly use creatively but which does not clearly set forth a new model of prayer and still has the appearance — at least on paper — of services centred upon a good deal of meditative Bible reading. Even in the new orders for 'Prayer at Mid-day' and the 'Vigil of the Resurrection for Saturday evenings',[9] where the constraints of tradition were not so strong, opportunities to break away from such an emphasis were unfortunately not taken.

Some practical suggestions

There is much valuable material within the Canadian book, which can certainly be utilized by other Provinces as a starting point for their own attempts. Worthy of particular note is the rich variety of intercessory material, of introductory responses and canticles for the seasons of the year, and of forms of thanksgiving for light included in Evening Prayer. What is needed is for this to be set within a structure which better articulates the primary purpose of Christian prayer and to be accompanied by explanation in a variety of forms which attempts to communicate its true inner spirit. I have already made some suggestions elsewhere as to the direction which such a reform might take,[10] but there are two main areas in which Anglicans often have difficulty when it comes to thinking about changing the pattern of their daily offices — the purpose of psalmody and the function and form of lectionaries — and these deserve further consideration.

There is a widespread tendency among Christians to think of all psalms as being fundamentally alike and to use them indifferently. This is particularly so for Anglicans nourished on the Prayer Book usage in which psalms follow one another in their biblical order without any attention being paid to whether they are of praise or lamentation, whether they refer to morning, evening, or night, or whether they are appropriate to the current season of the liturgical year. Even decisions about ways of saying or singing them (antiphonally, responsorially, etc.) are usually made without reference to the nature of the particular psalm itself. However, a distinction needs to be made between different types of psalms, and the different functions which they may exercise within Christian worship.

Some psalms naturally lend themselves to appropriation as the hymns and prayers of the Christian community, and can be used in this way together with other scriptural canticles or non-canonical hymns and prayers. In the fourth-century cathedral office, for example, Psalms 148–150 became the universal nucleus of praise within the daily morning service, often followed by the *Gloria in Excelsis*; and Psalm 51 is also frequently found as the beginning of that service, as an expression of penitential prayer. Some psalms might be considered particularly apposite for use at certain hours of the day, days of the week, or seasons of the liturgical year.

Other psalms, however, are less suitable for the lips of Christians to address to God. Psalm 37, for instance, may contain much that is valuable and true about the human relationship to God, but it is hardly an appropriate vehicle for expressing direct praise or petition. Such psalms can still find a place in Christian worship, but as a part of a ministry of the Word. As we have indicated earlier, this seems to have been the way in which the majority of both canonical and non-canonical compositions were used in early Christianity: individuals sang them to others, who listened and responded — with a corporate refrain in the cathedral tradition[11] or with a period of silent meditation and a concluding vocal prayer in the monastic tradition. In both cases they were thus seen as embodying the word of God addressed to human beings, and it was only with the disappearance of both the refrain and the period of silence between the psalms in later centuries that the understanding tended to be reversed, so that they tended to be seen as the words of human beings addressed to God. However, the common custom of sitting for the psalms is a veiled reminder of their original function. If some psalms are still to be used in this way, it would seem desirable that the verses should be said or sung by one voice alone, so that the rest of the community may listen more easily.

Nevertheless, there is no obligation on Christians to use all of the Psalter or even to give psalms pride of place in their worship. The early Christians, like their Jewish counterparts,[12] seem to have had no particular preference for the canonical psalms over their own liturgical compositions, and it was only in the fourth century that two things happened to change this attitude. The first was a fear, largely occasioned by the Arian controversy, that heretical views might be promoted in non-scriptural material, and this led to a preference for biblical psalms and canticles. Consequently, only a very few well-established hymns — most notably *Gloria in Excelsis* and *Phos hilaron* — survived in later usage from what must formerly have been an enormous wealth of creative contributions, usually termed *psalmi idiotici* by scholars.

The second cause of the change in the place of psalms in Christian worship was the practice of the Egyptian desert fathers, who learned the whole Psalter by heart and recited it as part of their continuous prayer. The esteem given to their spirituality by other Christians led to some imitation of this custom by religious communities and other pious individuals elsewhere. This influence was especially strong in the West, not least as a result of its promotion in the writings of John Cassian, and the recitation of the whole Psalter thus came to dominate monastic worship there, and through that to exercise a decisive effect on the daily offices of the Western Church.

The role of Bible readings within daily prayer also requires some reconsideration. If their purpose is to recall God's saving works in such a way that worshippers are led to offer praise, care needs to be taken in their selection and arrangement. As with the psalms, some parts of the Bible lend themselves more easily to this function than others. A distinction, therefore, needs to be made between reading the scriptures for the purpose of study or meditation on the one hand, and their proclamation as liturgical anamnesis on the other. The whole Bible is obviously suitable for the former, and it is appropriate for the Church to draw up a suggested scheme of readings which would enable this activity to be carried out, though this does not need to be done in direct association with daily prayer. A scriptural passage for liturgical proclamation within a pattern of daily prayer, however, will need to be (a) selected for its suitability for this function and with some consideration of the day of the week and season of the liturgical year, (b) probably quite short in length, and (c) placed before the principal act of praise, which will constitute the response to it.[13]

All of this suggests that an appropriate pattern for the daily office might look something like this:

> Preparatory rites (e.g., act of penitence, invitatory psalm, or
>   evening thanksgiving for light)
> A psalm and/or short scriptural reading
> One or more hymns, canticles, or psalms of praise
> Extensive intercessions for the world
> Concluding rites (e.g., exchange of peace[14] or blessing)

It cannot be stressed too much, however, that shape alone is not enough. Whilst varying according to the changing seasons of the liturgical year, the format must be easily understood and simple to use if it is to commend itself to ordinary churchgoers. Rubrics must be flexible enough to cater for a wide variety of different situations, but should encourage a true liturgical celebration, where possible, involving movement and ceremonial and not merely a sedentary recitation. Texts should include musical settings simple enough to prompt singing in even the smallest of groups. Above all, a process of formation in the spirituality of liturgical praying must accompany the revision if it is to have any chance of becoming what the compilers of the first Anglican Prayer Book intended — the daily prayer of the whole Church.

Notes

1 Paul F. Bradshaw, 'The liturgical use and abuse of patristics' in Kenneth Stevenson (ed.), *Liturgy Reshaped* (London: SPCK, 1982), pp. 134–45.

2 Section 7. See A. M. Roguet (ed.), *The General Instruction on the Liturgy of the Hours* (London: Geoffrey Chapman/Collegeville, MN: Liturgical Press, 1971), pp. 19–20.

3 Cf. Augustine, *Enarr. in Ps.* 85.1: 'When the body of the Son prays, it does not separate its Head from itself; and it is the one saviour of his body, our Lord Jesus Christ, the Son of God, who prays for us, and prays in us, and is prayed to by us. He prays for us as our priest; he prays in us as our head; he is prayed to by us as our God. Let us therefore recognize our words in him and his words in us.'

4 On this point, see further Paul F. Bradshaw, *Daily Prayer in the Early Church* (London: SPCK, 1981/New York: Oxford University Press, 1982), p. 31.

5 See *Apostolic Tradition* 25; Clement of Alexandria, *Strom.* 7.7; Cyprian, *Ep.* 1.16; Tertullian, *Apol.* 39.

6 A very readable introduction to the historical evolution of the daily office is provided by George Guiver, *Company of Voices: Daily Prayer and the*

People of God (London: SPCK/New York: Pueblo, 1988). The standard work, however, is Robert Taft, *The Liturgy of the Hours in East and West* (Collegeville, MN: Liturgical Press, 1986). See also Paul F. Bradshaw, 'Cathedral vs. monastery: the only alternatives for the Liturgy of the Hours?' in J. Neil Alexander (ed.), *Time and Community: Studies in Honor of Thomas Talley* (Washington: Pastoral Press, 1990), pp. 123–36; and, for later development, Paul F. Bradshaw, 'Whatever happened to daily prayer?', *Worship* 64 (1990), pp. 10–23.

7 Alexander Schmemann, *Introduction to Liturgical Theology* (Leighton Buzzard: Faith Press/Crestwood, NY: St Vladimir's Seminary Press, 1966), pp. 107–8.

8 Louis Bouyer, *A History of Christian Spirituality* I (New York: Desclée, 1963), p. 319.

9 This latter service might be even more appropriate, and much more widely observed, if it were made the form of Sunday morning prayer instead.

10 See Paul F. Bradshaw, 'The Daily Office' in Michael Perham (ed.), *Towards Liturgy 2000* (Alcuin Club Collection 69; London: SPCK, 1989), pp. 27–33.

11 The Canadian book contains some interesting examples of biblical material cast in a responsory form.

12 See James W. McKinnon, 'On the question of psalmody in the ancient synagogue', *Early Music History* 6 (1986), pp. 159–91.

13 The main weakness of the Canadian 'Prayer at Mid-day' and 'Vigil of the Resurrection' is that no act of praise follows the reading. It could be solved there by reversing the order of psalm and reading.

14 Tertullian (*De Or.* 18) describes the kiss of peace as constituting 'the seal of prayer'.

7

Christian initiation

Paul J. Roberts

If the huge endeavour of the twentieth century's liturgical renewal led to considerable discussion concerning the theology and practice of the Eucharist, it now appears that initiation may well become the future frontier of high debate concerning liturgical theory and practice. A glance at the changes, textual and practical, in Christian initiation as it happens in any of the major denominations will show that large issues lie under the surface of minor debates, betraying often unspoken concerns about the very nature of the Church and what it is to be a Christian. The Churches of the Anglican Communion are no exception.

Symptomatic issues

Some of these 'symptomatic issues' have been with us for a long time. Most obviously, the debate concerning the nature of confirmation remains on the agenda of many an Anglican synod. Others have arisen from changing circumstances and contexts which affect some areas but not others, whether Province or parish. Such is the nature of initiation, reflecting as it does the self-understanding of Church, individual and society. While it is not possible to take a snapshot view of initiation in the Anglican Communion, certain traits and trends are observable in the last three decades or so of Anglican liturgical revisions.

(i) The liturgical significance of confirmation has diminished. This has been in part a result of modern historical scholarship, which most optimistically sees it as part of the fragmented rite of initiation, which originally held baptism, confirmation and first communion together in one event,[1] less optimistically as a patristic falling-short of a biblical norm, where Christian initiation was complete with baptism,[2] or least optimistically as nothing more liturgically significant than an episcopal dismissal.[3] This historical enquiry has been reflected in the process of liturgical revision, where rites which spoke unequivocally of confirmation as founded upon the incident in Acts 8 (e.g. Scotland, 1929; Canada, 1962) were gradually replaced by books which assigned a role which at most integrated it with baptism as a norm (England, 1980), or even removed it from the central sequence of initiation altogether, allocating it a place as a pastoral office, rather than an initiation service (ECUSA, 1979; Canada, 1985).

(ii) There has been a move away from having infant baptism as the liturgical norm, towards framing the service around a rite designed for adults.[4] Partly this is a result of the normative nature of a reunited sequence of baptism, confirmation and Eucharist, which demands that the candidates be of 'confirmation age' (whatever that might be). It is also indicative of the influence of historical sources, which date from a (patristic) time where (it is often assumed) the majority of candidates were adults. All this is in contrast to the Book of Common Prayer, which had no services for adults until 1662. The case of adults is clearly derivative and regarded as for use in exceptional cases only. The shift in liturgical norm may imply only an incipient change in the Anglican theology of initiation, but one which may have great significance.

(iii) There has been a move towards the concept of 'initiation', as opposed to 'baptism'.[5] Again, this may have arisen from a desire to see baptism and confirmation reunited, whilst retaining the latter, but on the other hand it has opened the door to seeing baptism not as the *context* itself, but as one *element*, albeit a critical one, of a spiritual process through which someone becomes a Christian. This has resulted in a move, not simply beyond the outlook of Cranmer's model, but beyond the original motivation to speak in terms of 'initiation'.

(iv) Closely identified with (ii) and (iii) above is the desire now surfacing in a number of Provinces for a staged catechumenate, modelled on the Roman Catholic Rite of Christian Initiation of Adults (RCIA), and behind that, based upon the catechumenate which we first glimpse in the writings of the third century. This approach sees initiation as a ritualized staging of the process of becoming a Christian, from enquiry through to baptism and communion. The ritual framework encompasses a careful programme of nurture where the candidate's thought, life and actions are brought to face up to the challenge of the Gospel. Here Christian initiation is seen as a process which may or may not come to completion. Baptism and communion form the climax of this process and the rite of passage into full and active Christian membership. Some provinces have already made some liturgical provision for such a catechumenate (e.g. ECUSA, *Book of Occasional Services* (1979)), while others are considering using it.

After such observations must come a degree of interpretation. This step is more hazardous, particularly since the understanding of why something is happening in different parts of the Anglican world demands a comprehensive knowledge of so wide a range of cultures and contexts. Perhaps it is uniquely an Anglican privilege to look at one's partners and to construct hazardous theories based upon what we have in common, as much as where we differ. So, with appropriate caution, we shall proceed to make some more general comments about factors which are shaping the development of initiation in the larger Anglican setting.

Shaping factors

The first concerns the relationship between the tenacity of confirmation and the role of bishops. Here the most influential liturgical example for conservation in revisions has been that set by the Church of England's *Alternative Service Book* (1980), which retains confirmation as a distinct initiation service, albeit in close relation to baptism. On the other hand, ECUSA's 1979 Prayer Book proved to be the pioneer of a more radical approach, which set confirmation on a course to being an optional pastoral office, removed from the context of initiation. It is not unreasonable to surmise that the degree to which confirmation is retained as part of the norm of Christian initiation is controlled in part by the societal role of the bishops in a particular provincial context. Where historical or cultural factors serve to enhance the bishops' societal role, confirmation is more tenacious. A deeper liturgical question related to this is the role of the bishop in the total structure of sacramental initiation: is he (or she) a crucial ingredient without whose physical presence at some stage a person's Christian initiation cannot be completed?

A larger area of enquiry concerns the normative nature of infant baptism. This is the unquestioned norm of the 1662 Prayer Book which forms an important part of the shared inheritance which binds the Churches of the Anglican Communion together. In many parts of the Communion, infant baptism remains the practical norm, if not the theoretical one. In others, the effects of either secularization, pluralist culture or the missionary situation to which the Church has adapted itself, serve to loosen the effects of that historical inheritance. In terms of liturgical revision, the degree to which a 'neat and tidy' sequence of framing the initiation rite around adult candidates[6] (altering as it does the Anglican inherited pattern[7]) affects the understanding of initiation in the parishes will be conditioned by the ecclesiology and understanding of mission which that Church actually has (as opposed to what it says it has, in synodical reports). In an increasing number of contexts, the practice of the Church is evolving into one where infant baptism is no longer the practical norm, yet sometimes it is in these places that the liturgical texts lag behind.

The effects of secularization upon many Western societies has led to tensions in the issue of candidature for infant baptism. For example, do 'baptismal policies' which restrict access to the offspring of parents who make a visible token of church affiliation of some sort make a positive or negative contribution to the Church's response to a society in the process of secularization? Lying behind such questions once again is the challenge which context places upon the ecclesiology and mission of the Church, as well as the residual societal expectation of baptism as a universal rite of passage.[8] For in the above case, a decision has been made as to what constitutes appropriate candidature for baptism, and so membership of the Church. In turn, this decision is affected by ecclesiology (what is the Church?) and mission (what should the Church be doing?).[9] In liturgical terms, the change of norm has been accompanied in many revisions by statements making clear the expectations which the Church has of the candidates, the parents and the godparents or sponsors. It would seem most likely that *lex orandi* (rule of worship) is reflecting rather than affecting ecclesiological *lex credendi* (rule of belief) here. However, future liturgical revision is inevitably going to be the catalyst for a debate which arises from a much larger crisis of identity. This will need to be borne in mind, and prepared for, if the liturgical endeavour is not going to be swamped by what is really a crisis of ecclesiology.

If the questions for ecclesiology raised by the move away from infant baptism as a liturgical norm are significant, the implications arising from the adoption of an adult catechumenate would be enormous if Anglican Provinces followed the example of the Roman Catholics in making such a sequence the norm of initiation. Even though this has yet to happen, the use of such a scheme testifies to another, even more radical, current in the flow of Anglican ecclesiology. In terms of the relationship between Church and society, this amounts to a reversion to a patristic, pre-Constantinian, model in societies where the influence of mediaeval 'Christendom' was once predominant.[10] In parts of Anglicanism arising from the missionary expansion of the last century, such an ecclesiology has long had to work within a liturgical tradition which envisaged the majority of baptisms arising from births rather than conversions. What future shape will initiation take in these Provinces, once the option of a ritualized catechumenate is available?

In this discussion of the issues arising from present practice, the question of an evolving ecclesiology has been dominant. However, there are other theological issues which arise related more specifically to the liturgical context.

The continued existence of the debate concerning the theology of confirmation is in fact associated with the larger question of the theology of baptism, and in turn the relationship between baptism and the whole of Christian initiation. In liturgical scholarship, most of the developments which have happened this century have been influenced by two 'breakthroughs'. The first was the realization that confirmation (if it can still be called that) has its origin in a single rite of initiation, rather than always having a separate existence.[11] The second was the influence of the reconstruction of Hippolytus' *Apostolic Tradition*,[12] which provided a textual model of such a united rite at a stage nearly four hundred years earlier than the next known liturgical text.

The benefits of these works to scholarship have been considerable, but the effect has tended to lodge the insights underlying modern revision firmly in the third century. Many modern texts contain exactly the same sequence as that reflected in Hippolytus, but with comparatively little reflection on the origin, and, behind that, the meaning, of each component of the rite. This situation is now changing. Attention has moved eastward to the Syrian rites of baptism, and a number of studies have shown that this is a source which gives insights into the original meanings of major elements in the rite of initiation, for example, pre- and post-baptismal anointing, and water itself.[13] These studies suggest, for example, that the 'death–resurrection' motif of Romans 6, with its emphasis upon sin and forgiveness, expanded in the ritual development at the expense of the themes of anointing with the Spirit and rebirth, which originally predominated. This may have resulted in the tradition being fatally starved of a Spirit- or charismatic-dimension. Similarly, if Aidan Kavanagh is to be believed, the root of Western confirmation lies in the resurgence of the Spirit motif which attached itself to what was originally merely a liturgical dismissal by the bishop.[14] One of the consequences of these studies for contemporary rites, and the way they are appropriated, is that an overemphasis on 'death–resurrection' (Rom 6) misses out on baptism as 'rebirth' (John 3), which results in a baptismal spirituality that tends to 'stop' at the point of baptism, rather than 'lead on' into a life of rebirth and continual growth. In the light of such studies, questions surrounding the original content of initiation recur once more. For example, is it appropriate any longer to talk exclusively of 'baptism' as the sacrament of Christian initiation,[15] or is the water of baptism merely one part of an amalgam of liturgical ritual and experience which could take place over time?

Talk of a lost doctrine of the Spirit raises an issue here which has not been mentioned previously. Many Anglican Provinces are having to come to terms with increasing numbers of requests for 're-baptism', often from persons who have encountered an experience of personal, Charismatic renewal. Behind these requests lies a complex of reasons: the experience of the filling with the Spirit may have so transformed their experience of Christianity that all previous observance seems less 'real', or there may be an implied protest against an infant baptism which never led to subsequent nurture, or they could have received teaching which is not adequately related to the Anglican sacramental inheritance. Underlying this phenomenon is an existential approach to faith, which predominates in Western society. While there may be weaknesses in the presuppositions of this whole approach ('Do I have to feel it for it to be true?'), it is nevertheless an important part of the cultural context of many Provinces. How should the Church address this issue in its liturgy and sacramental theology?

It is arguable that the present existentialism may be the latest phase in a process which is proving the classical Western sacramental system to be phrased in terms which are philosophically irrelevant. How does one reason in terms of 'outward visible signs' relating to 'inward spiritual graces' with someone who complains that they never 'felt anything like this before'? In the light of scholarship which is showing the Western initiation tradition to be impoverished in its doctrine of the Spirit, and remembering that it was that liturgical tradition which underlay the development of classical Western (and Anglican) sacramental theology, do we have to face the fact that perhaps some major doctrinal restatement is long overdue?

In assessing where the present situation is leading, the wider ecumenical framework needs consideration. *Baptism, Eucharist and Ministry*[16] raises some issues which have already been mentioned. There is a reference to 'apparently indiscriminate baptism', and with regard to the gift of the Spirit: 'Baptism in its full meaning signifies and effects both', but with an acknowledgement of the diversity of ritual form. Yet this is hardly revolutionary thinking, nor does it attempt to tackle common issues facing many Churches' practice of initiation now. Furthermore, modern liturgical scholarship is so ecumenical that differences across Churches often can be identified only by seeing how the fruit of scholarship is applied to a particular tradition or context, as we have seen within Anglicanism in the case of the revival of the catechumenate.

An Anglican way?

In the light of the present state and direction of initiation liturgy, how does Anglicanism relate both to the wider scene and to itself? Perhaps by its very comprehensiveness, Anglicanism is itself a model of how plurality of practice and context in initiation can happen, while at the same time recognizing an essential unity. Every issue raised in this discussion is also an issue for other Churches (allowing for the shift of context in the case of Churches who practise adult baptism only); there is nothing unique about our problems. But it may be that the very fact of Anglicanism's traditional diversity, arising from a common origin, sets it in a unique place to be the testing ground as the wider Church seeks to develop initiation against a background of greater understanding between the Churches.

It is impossible simply to identify a single 'Anglican' ecclesiology: the varieties of approaches to initiation are themselves testimony to that fact. But the issues raised by any one approach set up a tension within Anglicanism's own 'conscience'; whether it is the desire to be inclusive of those who lie on the boundaries of the Church, or the desire to stand visibly as an alternative society to one which embraces material and pagan values as absolute. In any particular context, one or another of these approaches may dominate, yet this aspect of the 'identity of Anglican initiation' can only be discovered in the tension.

Similarly, the difficulties to which existential approaches to faith give rise within a received framework of sacramental theology is an issue which Anglicanism shares with other Churches.[17] Yet here again, the fact of shared traditions in the midst of diversity might also act as both stimulant and controlling factor upon any doctrinal development. The contexts demand the change, the tradition and plurality control it.

What do we do with these questions which the current practice of initiation raises? Is the Anglican Communion simply to allow the situation to 'just develop', with problems being tackled in different ways? Alternatively, should a definitive methodology be found, through which a common, easily identified pattern of Anglican initiation evolves? Perhaps the most realistic approach would be somewhere between these two. Our cultural and traditional diversity may well argue against a single 'methodology', yet with a greater degree of consultation between the different Provinces, solutions to problems arising from the process of revising initiation liturgy may profitably be shared and prove enlightening without being prescriptive. Such a course of action could give rise to a liturgical tradition reflected in all of our future liturgies, which both is culturally rooted in its practical context, and avoids being evanescent and 'parochial' (in the worst sense!). This would not simply answer wistful remarks about a 'shared Prayer Book' (we never had one), but get to the root of a desire that we might all more visibly share an Anglican identity.

It will, indeed, be interesting to see how the recent spate of revisions develop in the future, and to see exactly what sort of shape they take on. Meanwhile, there are two very practical areas, which have acute theological implications, that are coming to the surface. The first relates, once more, to the role of confirmation.[18] The USA (1979) and Canadian (1985) books (and an experimental Australian rite (1990)) propose a way of 'stretching' confirmation, so that the laying-on of hands can be done not just at the public profession of faith, but in two other contexts that are very much part of the world and Church of this century. These are, first, when someone wishes to express a renewal of faith, perhaps after a time of lapse, or else after a special experience of God's power in their lives — the issue touched upon earlier. The second type of occasion is when a person wishes to join the Anglican Church from having been a communicant of another Church. In both these cases, a public rite, at which the bishop is (normally?) the president, with the laying-on of hands, is totally appropriate. But the libretto of the bishop (or presbyter?) while giving that laying-on of hands is *not* appropriately that of the confirmation service. Here is, arguably, an authentic home for a traditional Anglican rite, for the much-changed circumstances of our own century.

The other development concerns symbolism. The Prayer Books, as a necessary counter-reaction to things mediaeval, draw a sharp distinction between primary symbolism (water, laying-on of hands) and secondary symbolism (movement, the position of font and sponsors). We now live more easily with candles, and oils of various kinds, as recent revisions show. Part of our future work is not just to use these *old* symbols as vivid interpretations of the liturgy, but to find *new* symbols as well. But symbolism does not arrive to order. Like much else, it only grows.

Notes

1 Gregory Dix's view was that confirmation as such formed an indispensible part of initiation: see, e.g., *The Theology of Confirmation in Relation to Baptism* (London: Dacre, 1946). The demise in the mediaeval period of the once united rite is illustrated by J.D.C. Fisher, *Christian Initiation: Baptism in the Mediaeval West* (Alcuin Club Collections 47; London: SPCK, 1965).

2 So G.W.H. Lampe, *The Seal of the Spirit* (London: Longmans, 1951) (2nd edn, London: SPCK, 1967); and E.C. Whitaker, *Sacramental Initiation Complete in Baptism* (Grove Liturgical Study 1; Bramcote: Grove, 1975).

3 Aidan Kavanagh, *Confirmation: Origins and Reform* (New York: Pueblo, 1988).

4 England (1980) places a united service at the opening sequence of its initiation services, and adult (i.e. 'vocal') candidates are assumed throughout. Infants have a service specifically framed for them.

5 See P.-M. Gy, 'The idea of "Christian initiation" ', *Studia Liturgica* 12 (1977), pp. 172–5.

6 There is some variation of the degree to which the norm is reflected in revisions: for example, the Anglican Churches in North America have no specific service of infant baptism (infants are catered for within the standard rite of baptism), whereas in England there is a specific provision.

7 This is a point made strongly by Stephen Sykes, ' "Baptisme doth represente unto us oure profession" ' in Margot Johnson (ed.), *Thomas Cranmer: Essays in Commemoration of the 500th Anniversary of his Birth* (Durham: Turnstone Ventures, 1990), pp. 122–43.

8 If baptism is to be regarded as a social rite of passage, some serious questions need to be asked about how the framework of meaning underlying such a rite squares with an acceptable view of what the Church is.

9 Mark Dalby reflects a growing unease in some circles with the implications of revision exemplified by the initiation rites of England (1980): see *Open Baptism* (London: SPCK, 1989).

10 It seems probable that once ancient society had become 'Christianized' with its emperor, the writing was on the wall for the historical catechumenate. Infant baptism became normative, and a form of the earlier ecclesiology only survived in monasticism.

11 See above, note 1.

12 Proposed reconstruction by R. H. Connolly, *The So-called Egyptian Order* (Texts and Studies Contributing to Biblical and Patristic Literature; Cambridge: Cambridge University Press, 1916); first (partial) critical text, G. Dix, *The Apostolic Tradition of Hippolytus* (Church Historical Society; London: SPCK, 1937); full critical edition, B. Botte, *La Tradition Apostolique de Saint Hippolyte* (Liturgiewissenschaftliche Quellen und Forschungen 39; Münster: Aschendorff, 1963) (rev. edn, with additional notes by Albert Gerhards and Sabine Felbecker, 1989).

13 Significant studies include the following: Sebastian Brock, 'Studies in the early history of the Syrian Orthodox baptismal liturgy', *Journal of Theological Studies* 23 (1972), pp. 16–64, and Gabriele Winkler, *Das armenische Initiationsrituale. Entwicklungsgeschichtliche und liturgievergleichende Untersuchung der Quellen des 3. bis 10. Jahrhunderts* (Orientalia Christiana Analecta 217; Rome: Pontifical Institute of Oriental Studies, 1979).

14 See above, note 3.

15 As insists Colin Buchanan, 'Adult initiation in the Anglican Churches' in D. Withey (ed.), *Adult Initiation* (Alcuin/GROW Liturgical Studies 10; Bramcote: Grove, 1988), p. 24.

16 *Baptism, Eucharist and Ministry* (Faith and Order Paper 111; Geneva: WCC, 1982).

17 Even the Eastern tradition of initiation has been more heavily influenced by the same factors as the Western rites than is often allowed for: see C. Argenti, 'Chrismation' in M. Thurian (ed.), *Ecumenical Perspectives on Baptism, Eucharist and Ministry* (Faith and Order Paper 116; Geneva: WCC, 1983), pp. 46–67.

18 See David R. Holeton, 'Confirmation in the 1980s' in *Ecumenical Perspectives on Baptism, Eucharist and Ministry*, pp. 68–89; and David Stancliffe, 'Confirmation and its future' in Michael Perham (ed.), *Liturgy for a New Century* (London: SPCK, 1990), pp. 71–82.

8

The eucharistic prayer

Bryan D. Spinks

The eucharistic prayer or anaphora is the verbal heart of any eucharistic liturgy. It articulates the Church's experience of redemption centred on the sacrifice of Christ,[1] and its eschatological hope, and gives meaning to the whole rite. Here perhaps more than in any other prayer is to be found the 'Engine against th'Almightie, sinners towre, . . . the six-dais world transposing in an houre, . . . Exalted Manna';[2] here is distilled the 'grammar of the overwhelming'.[3] Stimulated by the appearance of new eucharistic prayers in the *Ordo Missae* of the Roman Catholic Church in 1969, the last two decades have seen an unprecedented proliferation of anaphoral composition in the Western Churches. Within this proliferation, the contribution from the Anglican Communion has been far from negligible; indeed with the appearance of a 'Liturgy for Africa' in 1964, and the Church of England Series II in 1965, it can even claim to have anticipated Rome in the quest for restored and new structures. But the resulting diversity which is to be found in more recent Anglican rites has helped intensify questions about the identity of Anglican eucharistic worship.

In the past there seemed to be a sameness or givenness about the Prayer of Consecration which gave an Anglican imprint to a liturgy regardless of its ceremonial dress. A cursory glance through Wigan's *The English Liturgy* shows that from England to the USA, South Africa, Nyasaland and Northern Rhodesia, Korea and even Nippon Seikokai there was to be found a familiar 'Prayer Book' phraseology and pattern. Yet already with the Bombay Liturgy 1920, Ceylon 1938 and then the liturgy of the Church of South India, moves towards new structures and innovative vocabulary can be clearly detected. This trend intensifies through the rites collected by C.O. Buchanan in *Modern Anglican Liturgies 1958–1968* (1968), *Further Anglican Liturgies 1968–1975* (1975), and *Latest Anglican Liturgies 1976–1984* (1985), to a point where it is extremely difficult to speak of a distinctive Anglican pattern to the eucharistic prayer, let alone phraseology.

It is true, of course, that certain rites (England and USA) have been influential in other Provinces. However, at the same time, in the

Church of North India, the Church of South India, and in Sri Lanka and Kenya, we find moves to compose distinctly 'Indian', 'Sri Lankan' and 'Kenyan' eucharistic prayers; inculturation is fast emerging to replace sixteenth- and twentieth-century English (and American) imperialism. Feminist groups in ECUSA have written feminist eucharistic prayers, thrusting the politics of American contextualization into the consciousness of the whole Communion; and New Zealand's gesture to the Maori language and culture reveals a concern for the minority groups. At the same time there is the strange phenomenon of the South African rite including one of the Roman Catholic eucharistic prayers for authorized use in that Province, and an Anglican parish in the USA being received into the Roman Communion but retaining its 'Anglican' liturgy! All these raise the question of whether we can speak any more of a distinctly 'Anglican eucharistic prayer'. Perhaps now we can only speak of 'eucharistic prayers used by Anglicans'.

Since at least the 1958 Lambeth Conference there has been concern to formulate some policy of liturgical standardization to arrest what was a gradual growing away from the historical Prayer Book forms, and in particular, the 1662 Prayer of Consecration. The 1948 Lambeth Conference had still spoken confidently of Anglican authority being 'reflected in our adherence to episcopacy as the source and centre of our order, and the Book of Common Prayer as the standard of our worship'.[4] The 1958 Lambeth Conference subcommittee report entitled 'The Book of Common Prayer' noted that loyalty to the historic liturgy was more evident in some places than in others, and conceded the force of Article 34:

> Every particular or national Church hath authority to ordain, change, and abolish, ceremonies or rites of the Church ordained only by man's authority, so that all things be done to edifying.

Where once this Article had served as an apologia for the Church of England vis à vis Rome, now it was invoked by Provinces to defend their liturgical drift away from the received 1662 forms. The subcommittee report went on to list features in the Books of Common Prayer which could be regarded as essential for safeguarding the unity of the Communion, and those which helped maintain the traditional doctrinal emphasis of its worship and witness. Significantly perhaps, the Prayer of Consecration received no mention. On the contrary, under the suggestions for modification for the recovery of other elements of the worship of the primitive Church, item 6 stated:

> The events for which thanksgiving is made in the Consecration Prayer are not to be confined to Calvary but include thanksgiving for the principal 'mighty works of God', especially the resurrection and the ascension of our Lord, and his return in glory.[5]

This statement conceded that the 1637/1928 type of prayer adopted by some Provinces was perhaps preferable to the 1662 model. Yet at the same time there was in this document a concern for some uniformity. Its opening paragraph suggested that it was possible to work towards a liturgy which would win its way through the Anglican Communion, and it urged the possibility of a basic pattern for the service of Holy Communion.

Such a basic pattern was set out in the 'Pan-Anglican' Document of 1965, and the 'Second Pan-Anglican' Document of 1968 went so far as to give a detailed recommendation on a structure of the eucharistic prayer:

The basic elements and progression of this eucharistic prayer are:
(a) Sursum Corda.
(b) The proclamation and recital of the mighty acts of God in creation, redemption, and sanctification.
(c) The Narrative of the Institution.
(d) The anamnesis of the work of Christ in Death, Resurrection, and the Ascension 'until he come'. It is recognized that this is the most difficult section of the prayer in view of the different doctrinal emphases which are expressed and recognized within the Anglican Communion. The whole concept of anamnesis is, however, so rich in meaning that it should not be impossible to express it in such a way that the needs of everyone are met. Whatever language is adopted should, however, avoid any idea of a propitiatory sacrifice or a repetition of Christ's sacrifice. This 'once for all' character of his work must not be obscured.
(e) The prayer that through the sharing of the bread and wine and through the power of the Holy Spirit we may be made one with our Lord and so renewed in the Body of Christ.
The whole prayer is rightly set in the context of praise, e.g. Sursum Corda and Sanctus.[6]

Although this outline has had some influence on the liturgical revisions of the late 1960s and the 1970s, it has not been completely successful in establishing an absolute norm for the Communion in the 1980s. This fact is reflected in the 1988 Lambeth Conference statements and recommendations on the liturgy which exploit Article 34, encouraging authentic local inculturation of the liturgy and flexibility.[7] The idea of common set forms, rather on the 1662 model, to undergird the Anglican Communion's identity, was rejected.[8]

The concern of some common form or standardization can of course be traced to Cranmer's principle that in place of great diversity there would henceforth be in the realm but one use. However, I would like to argue that quite apart from the implications of Article 34, Cranmer — however unwittingly — has bequeathed a principle of liturgical diversity to Anglicanism, which of course includes the eucharistic prayer.

The eucharistic prayer in the successive Books of Common Prayer had as the original paradigm the single Roman *Canon Missae* which had come to displace or replace all earlier regional Western eucharistic prayers. In spite of his knowledge of the Byzantine anaphoras and his experience of Lutheran forms, it was the Roman Canon which Cranmer recast in 1549, though Catholic doctrine on sacrifice and presence was with great subtlety transposed into a Protestant key. The 1552 rite simply separated and repositioned the material (later to be called 'The Church Militant' Prayer, 'The Prayer of Consecration', and 'Prayer of Oblation') and the phraseology was modified to remove certain ambiguities.

It has become commonplace in Anglicanism to speak of *lex orandi, lex credendi*, suggesting that a firm Anglican principle is that the liturgy gives us our doctrine.[9] However, it is reasonably obvious that Cranmer worked in reverse, and his own *lex credendi* gave rise to the successive Prayer Books. His own theological leanings were influential in forming the 1549 Canon, and its further more obviously Protestant revision in 1552. A prime concern was to remove all ideas of eucharistic sacrifice and of consecration in the sense of a real presence in the elements of bread and wine.[10] A number of theological influences upon him can be detected — Lutheranism, and Swiss and Italian Reformed — but ultimately he held his own carefully nuanced views; he was a 'Cranmerian'. Herein lies part of the theological and liturgical contradiction within Anglicanism. The bishops of the Elizabethan Settlement had a rather different theological agenda from that of Cranmer, and they had been influenced by later reformers such as Calvin and Beza. They were not, and did not attempt to be, a school of 'Cranmerian' theology. They had to defend Elizabethan Anglicanism on the one hand against post-Tridentine Roman attacks, and on the other against the growing Puritan dissent. The *lex credendi* of the Elizabethan bishops was not identical with that of Cranmer. Already in the dispute with Bishop Harding, John Jewel, for example, attributed to the words of institution at the Eucharist rather more than Cranmer did — as Robert Johnson was to find to his regret in 1573. Johnson had run out of wine during the administration of communion, and sent out for a fresh supply which he delivered to the communicants without repeating any words over it. For this he was tried by the Queen's Commissioners. Johnson appealed to Cranmer's rubrics, or lack of them — *lex orandi, lex credendi*; the court appealed to the teaching of St Augustine — *lex credendi, lex orandi*. The use of the words of institution to effect consecration, based upon Augustine's words 'Accedit verbum ad elementum, et fit sacramentum', was enshrined in canon 21 of 1604.[11]

In his Preface to both Books of Common Prayer Cranmer had appealed to the 'decent order of the auncient fathers' and 'to the mynde and purpose of the olde fathers'. Cranmer was well schooled in patristics, but like most theologians of his era, found them useful mainly when they supported his own views. Jewel's Sermon of 1559 made an appeal to the first six centuries of the Church. Later Anglican divines, from Hooker to Taylor and Cosin, took this appeal to the Fathers rather more seriously than Cranmer might have intended. On the question of the Eucharist we begin to see the development of a 'Reformed Patristic' theology of the eucharistic presence and sacrifice, a *lex credendi* which better fitted the *lex orandi* of 1549 than 1552 and 1559. Against the Roman doctrine of transubstantiation, some of these divines could appeal to the Eastern Church and the epiklesis, which they felt that Cranmer had included in 1549.[12] The Scottish rite of 1637, although the work of Scottish bishops, provides a good representation of the *lex orandi* of the Caroline divines' *lex credendi*. The survival of this rite in the 'wee bookies', and later, its influence on the American Church, has meant that as the 1958 report noted, there were always *two* eucharistic liturgies, and eucharistic prayers, in the Anglican Communion, originating from 1549 and 1552. Although Cranmer himself claimed that the 1552 rite was simply the 1549 rite 'explained and made fully perfect', the 1549 forms presented not only a different treatment of the eucharistic prayer, but allowed a rather broader *lex credendi*. It may be true that for a large period of Anglican history the 1549 strain of liturgy was so minor as to be of little importance. Nevertheless it has been like a seed in the desert, awaiting a more favourable climate.

Thus, although for Cranmer the progression from the 1549 revision of the eucharistic prayer to that of 1552, together with his appeal to the Fathers, formed a single coherent theological position, later Anglicans have put asunder what he had joined together and have used the resulting separate components as a wider source of appeal for both *lex orandi* and *lex credendi*.

In subsequent Anglican history it is possible to identify three major approaches to thinking about the eucharistic prayer.

(a) The appeal to the Fathers continued by Jewel and subsequent Anglican divines has had a more direct liturgical application. Already with Andrewes, Cosin, Thorndike and Taylor amongst others we find a concern with early liturgy and the Eastern rites. In the seventeenth and eighteenth centuries a number of Anglican writers were concerned to find some apostolic or primitive eucharistic prayer, and were particularly attracted to the anaphora of *Apostolic Constitutions VIII*.[13] The result of this liturgical research — in part seen in 1637 and the Durham Book — was given textual expression in the liturgical writings of the Non-Jurors. The continuing concern with antiquity and Eastern forms can be seen in the writings of W. H. Frere, and a number of eucharistic prayers which were composed c. 1928, even if the expression of the concern tended to be limited to the anamnesis and epiklesis. But the same approach underlies the work of the 1960s, where composition of eucharistic prayers was greatly inspired by the evidence from Justin Martyr, the anaphora in the *Apostolic Tradition* of Hippolytus, and the pattern of the West Syrian eucharistic prayers.

(b) The Tractarian movement gave rise to a second generation of clergy who looked not to the East for inspiration, but either to pre-Reformation English usages and forms, or to contemporary Roman forms. This resulted in the use of the Roman Missal and the printing of the English Missal, and it directly influenced the form of the eucharistic prayer in the rites of South Africa and Swaziland. This trend looked back to the paradigm which Cranmer had worked from, but without his *lex credendi*.

(c) Much more recently in the 'mission' fields there were those who were aware that both the 1662 forms and the Roman Missal were products of European culture and theological controversy and were not in harmony with the cultural outlooks of Africa and Asia. Winslow and Ratcliff argued that the anaphora of St James was more congenial for India, and the Church of South India, under Protestant influence, felt that a less English Anglican form of liturgy was more suitable for India. Then in 1964 L.W. Brown attempted a 'Liturgy for Africa' with a eucharistic prayer inspired in part by that of the Church of South India, but for Africa. In hindsight this eucharistic prayer was not particularly African, but more an expression of the concerns of Lambeth 1958. (It was no accident that Bishop Brown was also involved in the 'Pan-Anglican' documents which laid down a suggested pattern for the eucharistic prayer.) Appeal could be made to Cranmer's wish for a liturgy which was understood by the people. It was not just a matter of the vernacular, but the very thought forms of a particular culture. This opened the way for a break with sixteenth-century English theological expression and language.

In one sense all present new Anglican eucharistic prayers represent one or a mixture of these approaches. The South African inclusion of a Roman Catholic eucharistic prayer is atypical, but represents a perpetuation of (b), and in a different way the Church of England revisions represent a mixture of (a) and (c), but have continued so far to avoid a post-anamnesis epiklesis, and have retained something of the Western structure of the prayer.[14] The ECUSA and Canadian books have reflected the West Syrian interest (a), but have also attempted to reflect modern Western culture in the 'Star Trek' eucharistic prayer (c).[15] One may argue that all Anglican eucharistic prayers open with thanksgiving for creation and redemption, and include the Sanctus. Some, however, represent a new structure in the sense of combining the themes of creation and redemption before the Sanctus, and then switch to supplication (mainly concerned with consecration) as in the Church of England ASB Rite A eucharistic prayers, or faithfully reflect the West Syrian pattern (though generally without a multiplicity of intercessions for the Church and world). The institution narrative still seems to have an important role in the prayer, undergirded not only by canon 21 of 1604, but also the Chicago–Lambeth Quadrilateral 1886/88. In the Church of England ASB Rite A prayers this is a lengthy composite form, which is identical in all four eucharistic prayers — almost suggesting that for Anglicanism this really is the non-flexible, non-negotiable part of the prayer. The anamnesis either follows a very cautious (some would describe it as ambiguous) phraseology or is bold enough to include a reference to the offering of the bread and wine. Despite great efforts to reach some compromise, the 1549–1637/1552–1662 division over oblation continues. The epiklesis, too, seems to raise some problems for some Provinces, and only a few prayers have developed the eschatological climax to include intercessions.[16] Nearly all the recent eucharistic prayers show a concern to reproduce or emulate the so-called 'classical' pattern of the eucharistic prayer — the format and material or themes which emerged in the written anaphoras of the fourth and fifth centuries.

The above represents an attempt to give a brief sketch of the present situation in the Anglican Communion, and argues that Cranmer himself unwittingly bequeathed to us elements of diversity. But what guidelines or principles, if any, can be suggested for the future?

To begin with it would seem to me to be both a fundamental theological and a liturgical mistake to attempt consciously to compose 'Anglican' eucharistic prayers. The proper object of theology and doxology is Almighty God. To attempt to control eucharistic prayers by an 'Anglican identity' would be a wrong use of *lex credendi*, and would replace God as the object of doxology. Worship and prayer, like all theology, must resist serving the self-interest of a particular denomination or social class, or an intellectual elite. Anglicans should concern themselves with formulating good eucharistic prayers rather than specifically 'Anglican' eucharistic prayers.

Yet if this is conceded, are there particular methods which Anglicans could be expected to follow when writing eucharistic prayers? It may be that the claim that Anglican theological method is a combination of scripture, tradition and reason is an over-simplification of Hooker; nevertheless, these together with D.R.G. Owen's categories of reasonableness, tolerance, and a qualified rationalism open to new knowledge[17] do seem to provide a general description of the Anglican approach to theology. These of course do not act in isolation of one another, but interact. But if this is a fair general description of the Anglican approach to theology, it must, or should, also be true of doxology. If applied directly to the eucharistic prayer, I would urge that future Anglican anaphoral composition will need to take account of different structures, and different images or theologies.

(1) Different structures

Almost in fundamentalist fashion some liturgists have attempted to identify the precise prayers presupposed by the narratives of the institution of the Last Supper — 'Blessed' and 'gave thanks'. The Jewish *berakot* of the Kiddush have been cited, and more recently 'gave thanks' has been linked specifically to the *birkat ha-mazon*. A number of liturgical scholars have put forward very persuasive hypotheses showing how *Didache* 10, the eucharistic prayer of Hippolytus, the Strasbourg Papyrus and St Basil might all have been developed from the model of the *birkat ha-mazon*, with a stress on the twofold thrust of thanksgiving and supplication found in these Christian prayers and the Jewish model.[18]

The lack of methodology in many of these hypotheses has been sharply criticized by Paul Bradshaw.[19] Indeed, however persuasive many of these hypotheses are (and some of them are extremely helpful), they seem to undervalue or ignore a number of important factors. Jesus himself was not always 'orthodox', and may have departed considerably from the 'statutory' meal prayers. The institution of the supper was a new covenant, and new wine demands new skins. But even if Jesus used an identifiable Jewish prayer form, the diversity of early Christian groups, e.g. Aramaic Jews, Hellenistic Jews, priests, Samaritans and *merkavah* groups, as well as a whole variety of Gentile groups, suggests that just as there was a multiplicity of theologies and Christologies, there was also a diversity of doxological forms used at the Lord's Supper.[20] Indeed, J.H. Charlesworth has demonstrated that a multiplicity of Jewish prayers influenced early Christian prayer forms.[21] Geoffrey Cuming showed that the Psalms were also important in the formation of early eucharistic prayers,[22] and shortly before his death had spoken with me, agreeing with my view that the LXX version of Nehemiah 9 had also been a source of inspiration for some early eucharistic prayers.[23] The overall evidence of the pre-Nicene eucharistic prayer (including those found in Gnostic documents, where there is no suggestion that the prayers themselves are unorthodox) shows a diversity of patterns and structures to the eucharistic prayer.

Anglican appeal to tradition, if it is to remain open to new knowledge, must acknowledge the diversity of structures in both the pre-Nicene evidence, and within the various families of the 'classical' anaphoras of the fourth and fifth centuries. Amongst the latter, the Roman family is quite distinct from that of the Gallican and Spanish, which in turn are different from the Egyptian, East Syrian and West Syrian patterns. Cranmer, we have noted, worked from the single pattern of the Roman Canon of the Mass. The Canon is certainly an 'anaphora', but 'eucharistic' is not a term which would readily suggest itself from its overall content. Apart from the proper prefaces, there is practically no thanksgiving at all. Rather, the *Canon Missae* is almost entirely supplicatory in structure, with its petition for God to accept the gifts, to hallow them, together with petition for the Church, the communicants and the departed. Cranmer retained the consecratory/ supplicatory thrust of the Canon in his 1549 reform, and the 1552 rite simply separated out the material. The Church of England eucharistic prayers in ASB Rite A have retained the concern for consecration/ supplication, with the institution narrative sandwiched between a double epiklesis. Other patterns, e.g. West Syrian, have been adopted by some Provinces. Why not other patterns? There is nothing sacrosanct about any one pattern or family, so why not compose prayers reflecting the pattern of other eucharistic prayer families? Why not new patterns, as the Church of England Liturgical Commission has attempted in GS 898, *Patterns for Worship*, published in 1989?[24]As David Power has written:

> The rich diversity of early traditions suggests the possibility of a richer variety in the contemporary liturgical creativity, as well as the continued possibility of drawing on the creativity of the Reformation era.[25]

Tradition and new knowledge also call in question the hitherto almost fundamentalist approach to the institution narrative, which we have observed is most explicit in the Church of England ASB prayers. There is clear evidence to suggest that some early traditions had a shorter narrative, or only a brief reference to the example of Jesus at the supper, or even no narrative at all.[26] Another factor which Anglicanism should also face is that following tradition from at least the third century, the eucharistic prayer is *one* prayer said over the bread and wine. The tradition of *scripture* means that *separate* prayers over the bread and wine cannot be entirely ruled out as a valid option. Perhaps, therefore, Anglican appeal to tradition and new knowledge may result in a move away from the 'Pan-Anglican' structure and a move beyond only certain fourth- and fifth-century structures. Cranmer has bequeathed to us an example of diversity, experimentation and innovation which can be utilized alongside tradition. Anglicans can bring forth treasures and eucharistic prayers new and old.

(2) Different images and theologies

Anglicans have inherited a prayer of consecration in which the words of institution — following Jewel and the Johnson case rather than Cranmer — were regarded as in some sense consecratory.[27] For all his concern for scripture, Cranmer provided a harmonized form of the narrative, just as the Roman Canon had in fact done. This trend is still perpetuated in many Anglican eucharistic prayers. However, the use of a composite form results in the loss of the subtle different theologies between the Pauline–Lucan form and the Marcan–Matthean form. William Crockett points out that in the Pauline–Lucan form there is an allusion to the new covenant in Jeremiah 31.31–34, whereas in the Marcan–Matthean form there is an allusion to the Sinai covenant and its accompanying ceremonies:

> These two covenant traditions are in marked contrast to each other. In the account of the Sinai covenant in Exodus, the elements of sacrifice and of sprinkling with blood are both features of the covenant ceremony. Jeremiah, on the other hand, contrasts the new covenant with the Sinai covenant. Here there is no mention of sacrifice or blood. God accomplishes the renewal of the covenant with the people including the forgiveness of their sins, by means of a direct interior renewal of the heart without external rites. Jeremiah's account of the new covenant belongs to the Old Testament tradition of eschatological prophecy, whereas the account of the Sinai covenant in Exodus belongs to the sphere of the sacrifical cultus.[28]

Thus in the institution narratives themselves there are two different theological evaluations of the death of Jesus, which become lost in a single composite narrative. It is quite possible to write eucharistic prayers which reflect or develop one or other of these theologies.

Elsewhere in the New Testament the death of Christ is interpreted using different images. For example, the Day of Atonement and the intercession of the High Priesthood are the themes of the epistle to the Hebrews; the Lamb is the image in Revelation. On the other hand Paul interprets the death in terms of judicial language. All these themes can be developed doxologically in separate ways. David Power gives an example of a eucharistic prayer based around a theology of lament and confession.[29]

The relationship between Christ's action at the Last Supper, the death on the cross, and the Christian action in the Eucharist continues to be difficult for Anglicans to agree upon, and to articulate in the eucharistic prayer. There are certain expressions such as those in the Roman Catholic Eucharistic Prayer IV that would seem not only un-Anglican, but possibly even un-Thomistic and un-Tridentine.[30] Such phraseology would, we might expect, not be utilized in an Anglican eucharistic prayer. On the other hand the understanding of eucharistic oblation has been handled very differently in history, and there ought to be scope for a variety of articulation within as well as between Provinces.

Although in every age there are to found those who tend towards an Arian Christology, Anglican theology professes the Christology of Chalcedon, and an orthodox Trinitarian faith. This faith can be expressed in different ways in the eucharistic prayer. In clumsy fashion there are numerous ancient examples of eucharistic prayers where parts of the creed, or the Chalcedonian definition, are inserted to profess orthodoxy. But there are other ways in which orthodoxy can be expressed doxologically. The Economic Trinity immanent in history is well expressed in the 'Second Pan-Anglican' Document, and many recent Anglican eucharistic prayers. On the other hand, the anaphora of St James and the eucharistic prayer of Richard Baxter in 1661 show how by moving from address of Father to the Son and then the Holy Spirit the doctrine of the Trinity is not only confessed but also prayed. After the publication of a study by Jungmann, *The Place of Christ in Liturgical Prayer*, it was fashionable to believe that all orthodox prayer was originally addressed to the Father, and only later, through monophysite influence, to the Son. As the most recent edition of this work makes clear,[31] this is an exaggerated reading of the evidence, since there are many early examples of prayer addressed to the Son. Many hymns are addressed to the Son and to the Spirit; if hymns, why not also the eucharistic prayer?

The work of the Holy Spirit often features in the preface of many recent Anglican eucharistic prayers, as well as in various forms of epiklesis. On the other hand some Provinces seem shy of the Spirit in connection with the elements. A post-narrative epiklesis inspired by that of St James could actually be a powerful proclamation of belief in the Spirit.

God as Abba is an important image for the New Testament, and is likely to continue to be so in eucharistic prayers. But Abba is also the God of Abraham and Sarah, of Isaac and Rebecca, Jacob and Rachel, and 'He causes things to be'.[32] He is 'creator'. Praise of God as a compassionate Abba, as a shepherd who seeks the strays, as a woman who sweeps the house for the lost, and as a creator who cares for the lilies of the field and the sparrow, the God of justice and mercy, will also feature in eucharistic prayers, as well as an eschatological setting in which all our Eucharists take place.

Yet for all this, the eucharistic prayer, like all prayer, is the language of lovers — between the Bride and the Bridegroom. It will be more the language of the Song of Songs than of the Nicene Creed. Here is one of the problems with so many of the Anglican eucharistic prayers of the late 1960s and the 1970s. The language tried to reproduce fourth- and fifth-century terminology, with biblical phrases sometimes used without imagination, and some have felt that the end result has been 'Commission' and 'Synod' language.[33] This is not how Cranmer worked, nor the divines who improved his phraseology in 1661. The language of eucharistic prayers must be evocative, and it must be incarnational — expressing theological concepts in the culture of the Province. Inculturation — and therefore increased diversity — must be encouraged, even if mistakes are made. (Perhaps the ACC can act as an adviser, warning where it feels that inculturation has given way to syncretism.) Liturgical specialists do their best, but most know their limitations. They try to give the Church their best scholarship, theology and language. But for eucharistic prayers to be evocative, someone with an ear for the language of that country may in the end prove a better reviser than a Synod.

Finally, the Anglican Church has been a prime mover in ecumenical debate and co-operation. Already some Provinces have authorized for use eucharistic prayers which have been ecumenically compiled. We may assume that this will continue and be more common, and will itself be a sign of the Anglican commitment to the unity of the Church of God.

Notes

1 Godfrey Ashby, *Sacrifice: Its Nature and Purpose* (London: SCM, 1988), for a recent discussion of this.
2 George Herbert, *Prayer*.
3 George Steiner, *Real Presences* (London: Faber and Faber, 1989), p. 190.
4 'The meaning and unity of the Anglican Communion' in *The Lambeth Conference 1948* (London: SPCK, 1948), p. 85.
5 'Progress in the Anglican Communion — B. The Book of Common Prayer', 2.81 in *The Lambeth Conference 1958* (London: SPCK/ New York: Seabury, 1958).
6 Cited in C. O. Buchanan, *Further Anglican Liturgies 1968–1975* (Bramcote: Grove, 1975), p. 30.
7 C. O. Buchanan, *Lambeth and Liturgy 1988* (Grove Worship Series 106; Bramcote: Grove, 1988).
8 Apparently put forward by Professor Stephen Sykes (now Bishop of Ely): Buchanan, ibid., p. 4, note 3.
9 See S. Sykes and J. Booty (eds), *The Study of Anglicanism* (London: SPCK/Philadelphia: Fortress Press, 1988), where it is invoked by a number of contributors.
10 C. O. Buchanan, *What Did Cranmer Think He was Doing?* (Grove Liturgical Study 7; Bramcote: Grove, 1976).
11 E. C. Ratcliff, 'The English usage of eucharistic consecration 1548–1662', *Theology* 60 (1957), pp. 229–36; 273–80. R. Buxton, *Eucharist and Institution Narrative* (Alcuin Club Collection 58; Great Wakering: Alcuin/Mayhew-McCrimmon, 1976). Johnson was sent to prison, where he later died.
12 This view, still asserted by Marion J. Hatchett, *The Study of Anglicanism*, p. 124, has long been demolished by Brightman in 1927, and subsequently by Frere and Ratcliff. See Bryan D. Spinks, ' "And with thy holy spirite and worde": further thoughts on the source of Cranmer's petition for sanctification in the 1549 Communion Service' in Margot

Johnson (ed.), *Thomas Cranmer* (Durham: Turnstone Ventures, 1990),
pp. 94–102.

13 R.C.D. Jasper, *The Search for an Apostolic Liturgy* (Alcuin Club;
London: Mowbray, 1963).

14 See C.O. Buchanan, *The Development of the New Eucharistic Prayers of
the Church of England* (Grove Liturgical Study 20; Bramcote: Grove,
1979); *Anglican Eucharistic Liturgy 1975–1985* (Grove Liturgical Study
41; Bramcote: Grove, 1985).

15 H. Boone Porter, 'An American assembly of anaphoral prayers' in Bryan
D. Spinks (ed.), *The Sacrifice of Praise* (Bibliotheca Ephemerides
Liturgicae Subsidia 19; Rome: CLV, 1981), pp. 179–96.

16 See Buchanan, *Anglican Eucharistic Liturgy 1975–1985*.

17 D.R.G. Owen, 'Is there an Anglican theology?' in M. Darrell Bryant
(ed.), *The Future of Anglican Theology* (Toronto Studies in Theology 17;
New York and Toronto: The Edwin Mellen Press, 1984), pp. 3–13; J.E.
Booty, 'The judicious Mr Hooker and authority in the Elizabethan
Church' in S. Sykes (ed.), *Authority in the Anglican Communion*
(Toronto: Anglican Book Centre, 1987), pp. 94–115.

18 E.g. L. Ligier. 'The origins of the Eucharistic Prayer: from the Last Supper
to the Eucharist', *Studia Liturgica* 9 (1973), pp. 176–85; T.J. Talley,
'From *berakah* to *eucharistia*: a reopening question', *Worship* 50 (1976),
pp. 115–37; 'The Eucharistic Prayer: tradition and development' in K.W.
Stevenson (ed.), *Liturgy Reshaped* (London: SPCK, 1982), pp. 48–64;
H. Wegman, 'Généalogie hypothétique de la prière eucharistique',
Questions Liturgiques 61 (1980), pp. 263–78.

19 Paul F. Bradshaw, 'The search for the origins of Christian liturgy: some
methodological reflections', *Studia Liturgica* 17 (1987), pp. 26–34.

20 Bryan D. Spinks, 'Beware the liturgical horses! An English interjection
on anaphoral evolution', *Worship* 59 (1985), pp. 211–19.

21 J.H. Charlesworth, 'A prolegomenon to a new study of the Jewish
background to the hymns and prayers in the New Testament', *Journal of
Jewish Studies* 33 (1982), pp. 265–85.

22 G.J. Cuming, *He Gave Thanks: An Introduction to the Eucharistic
Prayer* (Grove Liturgical Study 28; Bramcote: Grove, 1981).

23 Bryan D. Spinks, *The Sanctus in the Eucharistic Prayer* (Cambridge:
Cambridge University Press, 1991).

24 Bryan D. Spinks and Kenneth W. Stevenson, *Patterns for Worship: Essays
on Eucharistic Prayers* (GS Misc 333; 1989).

25 David N. Power, 'The Eucharistic Prayer: another look' in F.C. Senn
(ed.), *New Eucharistic Prayers: An Ecumenical Study of Their
Development and Structure* (New York: Paulist Press, 1987), p. 243.

26 Bryan D. Spinks, 'The institution narrative, eucharistic prayers and the
Anglican liturgical tradition', *Record* (Church Service Society) 21 (1989),
pp. 3–10.

27 Buxton, op. cit.

28 William R. Crockett, *Eucharist: Symbol of Transformation* (New York:
Pueblo, 1989), pp. 18–19.

29 Power, op. cit.

30 'We offer you his body and blood'. Aidan Kavanagh, 'Thoughts on the

new eucharistic prayers' in R. Kevin Seasoltz (ed.), *Living Bread, Saving Cup* (Collegeville, MN: Liturgical Press, 1987), pp. 108–9.

31 London: Geoffrey Chapman, 1989, with an introduction by Balthasar Fischer.

32 E.g. Patrick D. Miller, *The Divine Warrior in Early Israel* (Harvard Semitic Monographs 5; Cambridge MA: Harvard University Press, 1973).

33 Richard K. Fenn, 'The secularization of the liturgy' in Bryant (ed.), *The Future of Anglican Theology*, pp. 103–15.

9

The pastoral offices

Kenneth W. Stevenson

The Pastoral Offices is a title normally given to the services that appear in the Book of Common Prayer for marriage, visitation of the sick, and burial. It appears to be a twentieth-century title, one of those convenient terms of liturgy that helps put things in their place, into the right category. It also has convenient, even happy, resonances with such studies of the nature and function of ordained ministry that Anthony Russell[1] (among others) has made. The very name, 'pastoral offices', implies the Church's exercise of special rites to meet certain intimate experiences in the human lifecycle.

If one compares this threefold list in 1662 with the provisions of the American Episcopal Book of Common Prayer (1979),[2] there is a complete contrast, for, in addition to marriage, sickness, and death, there also appear the following:

Confirmation
A Form of Commitment to Christian Service
Additional orders for Marriage [i.e. blessing, and a less formal rite]
Thanksgiving for the Birth or Adoption of a Child
Reconciliation of a Penitent [NB: taken out of the Visitation of the Sick]
Ministration at the Time of Death [expanded from Visitation of the Sick]
Additional Burial rites, including a less formal one.

The American Book of Common Prayer (1979) must not, of course, be taken as the norm of modern Anglican liturgy, but it is a well-established fact that the Scoto-American family of rites within Anglicanism has been vigorous since the seventeenth and eighteenth centuries, and both they, and many other Provinces, have found regular liturgical revision relatively easy, convenient, and a useful way of showing how the Church in a given area can adapt to new circumstances. On face value, the new American list (and others like it) would seem to illustrate a Church turning the Reformation clock back, to a time when there was a rite for everything. It will be the intention of this essay to show that such a judgement is a superficial one, and that, so far from being anachronistic, that list reflects a pastoral and theological rigour that would be even more admirable if it were to take account of some of the insights of anthropology. To that we must first turn.

Van Gennep and marriage

In 1909, the French scholar Arnold Van Gennep, now widely regarded as the father of social anthropology, published his *Les Rites de Passage*, subsequently translated into English as *Rites of Passage*.[3] His pioneering study brings out the way in which primitive societies cope with change in human experience. He discerns three stages that undergird any rite of initiation. First, there is a rite of *separation*, in which the person to be initiated is marked off from the community, with a view to eventually rejoining it. Secondly, there is a time of *liminality*, when the person is on the edge of the community, often deprived of privileges, even the object of some derision, and is actually preparing for new status. Finally, there is the rite of *incorporation*, in which the new initiate rejoins the community in the new status, and receives special privileges, honour, and even respect.

Van Gennep's threefold scheme has been the object of much further study. Rather like Gregory Dix's *The Shape of the Liturgy* (1945), it has been refined, and adjustments have been made; but its basic thesis stands firm. The interesting factor in our story is that it has not so far had much effect on liturgical revision. But it *has* thrown fresh light on the way in which the history of liturgical origins has been rewritten. It is impossible to understand the evolution of the early catechumenate and baptism sequence without having recourse to these three 'deep structures' of Christian Initiation.[4] It is, furthermore, abundantly plain that these 'deep structures' lie at the heart of many of the so-called pastoral offices, which are supposed to be the Church's means of responding to human need at important stages in human life. Marriage can be divided into three stages, consisting firstly of betrothal (the rite of *separation*), secondly of the period of engagement (the time of *liminality*), and thirdly of the rite of marriage itself (*incorporation*).

The ancient marriage rites, and those of the Eastern Churches today, and some of those of the early mediaeval West, all show signs of preserving these 'deep structures'. All that history seems to have done is to place them closer and closer together, by means of 'surface structures'. Thus betrothal becomes the rite of active consent in the marriage rite itself, and, in the mediaeval West, instead of phasing the marriage service through different stages of human experience, as had been known before, it was phased through using different parts of the church *building*. What Cranmer inherited from the mediaeval rites of England was a particularly rich example of the Latin services, hence the fact that the 1549 (and 1552) marriage rites are far more elaborate than those of Luther or Calvin (or, for that matter, those of the *Rituale Romanum* of 1614). Cranmer still uses the church building, but in an attenuated form, with the rite of consent at the head of the nave, and the solemn prayers at the altar, a preparation for the nuptial Eucharist he so strongly wanted but which in practice seldom (if ever) happened.

The Reformation inheritance, therefore, appears for what it is — a logical Protestantized version of the mediaeval. But there is no attention paid to the 'deep structures', because history had obscured them. Our own age, by contrast, sees an overwhelmingly greater knowledge of the past, which is, moreover, of benefit to an era in which the shape of historic Christendom is giving way to a secular form of society in which the old structures of religion are replaced by an atmosphere in which Christianity has to take its place side-by-side with other religions (and none). Thus, Van Gennep's insights into anthropology illuminate the way in which marriage is experienced, where many people are. It could be suggested that the sixteenth-century Reformation solution brings separation and incorporation together, and delays liminality until *after* the wedding. A renewed rite, even if optional, would provide a form of public betrothal, to be followed by a time of liminality, to be followed in turn by a rite of final celebration, the result of a process, not a marginalized packed twenty-five minutes in church on a Saturday afternoon.

Along with better and richer symbolism, such as anointing (as in the Coptic rite, an extension of baptism), or the use of the mediaeval canopy (connoting the presence of God) held over the couple, such a pattern of marriage rites would provide a suitable alternative in new service books to stand alongside the more recent post-mediaeval solution reached by Cranmer and his colleagues.[5] At a time when the very institution of marriage is under such pressure, it would be advantageous to the Churches to strengthen it by providing such a pastoral underpinning to its liturgical practice. Another symptom of the post-mediaeval is the proliferation of blessings in the traditional Anglican marriage rites, which, in the second half, could well be replaced by a long intercessory prayer for the couple, and a solemn blessing, with laying-on of hands.

Does Van Gennep go further?

The threefold scheme suggested here can be applied further than marriage. It can also throw light on the next set of 'phases' in the lifecycle. The 1662 Prayer Book in its Visitation of the Sick brought together a whole series of mediaeval offices which were usually celebrated together, including prayer with the sick, communion, absolution, and commendation of the dying.[6] (1549 had an anointing, a practice Martin Bucer did not like, which was therefore dropped in 1552 — unlike the nuptial Eucharist, which other Reformers disliked, but Bucer admired, so that remained, as an ideal only.[7])

It is not our task here to go into the complex interrelation of these rites in history. Suffice it to say that the 1979 American Prayer Book adopts a policy of separating them out again, in a recognizably Anglican form, laced with prayers based on the writings of that great pastor of Anglican pastors, Bishop Jeremy Taylor.[8] But once again, the question may legitimately be asked, have these rites gone far enough? Have they some sense of internal coherence? It is a well-known fact of liturgical and pastoral life that a rite is only of use if it fulfils a need and can be celebrated with integrity and appropriateness.

The answer to these questions is partly to be found in what belongs where. The Reconciliation of a Penitent has for long been the poor relation of the Pastoral Offices. Although long practised in Anglicanism (and Lutheranism), it has only appealed to a small minority. And the controversial nature of the 1662 form of absolution (the 'I absolve thee' formula) has rendered it something of a no-go area in liturgical discussions. Interestingly, the Canadian *Book of Alternative Services* (1985), avoids such a form of absolution, and both it and the American Prayer Book try to give the rite a more public ambience.[9]

And yet, it could be asserted, this may not be the right place to begin. In many parts of the Western world, and the Third World, the Churches have all had to rethink their attitudes to healing and wholeness, and at many a public service of healing, the private words exchanged between priest and faithful are more likely to be confessions than anything else. In such a context, the Reconciliation of a Penitent — so far from being detached from the whole pastoral scheme — belongs firmly where Cranmer put it, under the Visitation of the Sick, but, of course, with a slightly more modern-sounding title! Cranmer got it right, partially.

There is a sound Anglican principle, articulated by Richard Hooker, that there are those things which are necessary for salvation, and there are those things which are secondary, 'accessory', which are obviously subject to change, according to circumstances.[10] Here, it would seem, the message of God's healing forgiveness is what is 'necessary'; and what is 'accessory' is the exact context in which it is proclaimed and made known. Van Gennep's insights from anthropology bring out how the individual feels. Thus the person who is in need of 'reconciliation'/ 'healing' is, in a special and highly personalized way, on the edge of the community. It is not for the Church to provide in this case an elaborate set of rites of passage, but rather to show the level of its concern and understanding in the way these rites are shaped and expressed. It

would seem that the proper conclusion of the development of healing and wholeness is to place the Church's ministry of healing and
reconciliation together, and to put anointing as an option within that
framework. A possible norm would be provided by the Public Service
of Healing in the American *Book of Occasional Services* (1979),[11] but
with a better title. In that public norm would appropriately be fitted a
form of absolution, and it would be made clear that this public liturgy
(with its related private counterparts) is the fullest expression of the
Church's celebration of forgiveness, especially when the Eucharist is
celebrated. Those who come to these liturgies undergo in personal
microcosm the Van Gennep process of separation, liminality, and
incorporation.

Courageously, the American Prayer Book places Confirmation at
the head of its pastoral offices. Much has been made of the place of
confirmation in the twentieth-century Church.[12] And much of the
drift of historical research has served to undermine its position of
pre-eminence before Holy Communion. Patterns of initiation have
changed, and it is possible to see even in the 1662 provision for a service
of baptism for those of 'riper years' the Anglican Church adjusting to a
fresh situation that did not exist in 1549 or 1552. Similarly, most of the
new service books of worldwide Anglicanism today produce two main
patterns. First, there is the theoretical norm, of the liturgy of adult baptism, confirmation, and Eucharist, taken straight from the twentieth-
century Church's reading of its all too admired patristic past, with or
without the catechumenate. Secondly, there is the pattern of popular
religion, with infant baptism, followed by confirmation (before or after
first communion), and with a strong accent placed on the paschal character of that liturgy.

But there is a third pattern which is emerging, which matches well
with the renewed and 'wider' approach to confirmation that is to be
seen in both the American and Canadian books of recent years. This
third pattern accepts by implication that people become Christians
by one or other of the first two routes, but that they often come once
again to Christian faith in such a way that requires a further rite of
passage. There is the person brought up in another Church, albeit
with a similar ecclesiology. Then there is the person who lapses
altogether, or who undergoes an experience of personal renewal that
may place prior experience of Church life in that person's mind in
jeopardy.

Here, once again, we have the Van Gennep pattern operating. The
person who comes from another Church wants to join the Anglican
Church, and after leaving the previous Church (separation) stands on
the edge (liminality) of the new. The form of 'reception' provided in the
American and Canadian confirmation rites meets that need for a rite of
passage without negating what has gone before. Then, the person who

either has lapsed or, while still a churchgoer, undergoes a conversion experience of some kind, has the benefit of reaffirming the baptismal covenant and of receiving also the laying-on of hands of the bishop, in affirming the person's faith. The Van Gennep pattern works again, perhaps heightening the sense of separation and liminality and the drama of the incorporation. Moreover, Anglicanism, with its distinct emphasis on the office of the bishop, at last finds a useful role for episcopal confirmation, moving it away from being a barrier before communion (always a risky business, from an historical point of view) to becoming part of the bishop's pastoral liturgy.

The Prayer Book is remarkably lean on variety in its Pastoral Offices, and it is well known that one of the 1604 Canons allowed clergy who were so minded to adapt the Visitation of the Sick to suit circumstances.[13] This is exactly what the revisions of the present century have achieved, and it is a process that will doubtless go on for many centuries to come, in fact until the end of time, in one form or another.

Funerals

The Funeral rites are another area of considerable movement. As with the Visitation of the Sick, Cranmer's intention seems to be to bring together various offices which sat uneasily with each other. But it is clear, from the further restructuring in 1662, that the finished product was not entirely satisfactory; and the provision for a funeral Eucharist in 1549, which was abolished in 1552, is another feature of recent reforms.[14]

Van Gennep can help here, too, for it is in the rites for the dying, at the time of death, and afterwards, that another pattern of separation (death itself), liminality (rites immediately after) and incorporation (the funeral) expresses the movement of feelings and the adjustment at the personal level. It is for this reason that new funeral services need to be conceived, as in the 1979 American Prayer Book, as part of a series — not a one-off that somehow 'goes chink' in heaven and that is that. Cranmer's overreaction to mediaeval requiem Masses and their own peculiar subculture is understandable, but we are no longer living in the shadow of that foreign world.

There is, too, a theological aspect of this part of liturgy that Cranmer overlooked, deliberately, and it concerns prayer and the departed. That wonderful ending to the 1549 Communion rite's prayer of intercession ('that at the day of the general resurrection . . . Come ye, blessed of my father . . .') is taken from the Collect at the Mass of the Five Wounds of Christ.[15] It was a brave attempt to say something about commending the departed to God, in the hope of the end of the world, a theme underplayed by Cranmer elsewhere, but taken up by subsequent hymnwriting. Some modern prayers take up John Cosin's rendering of a mediaeval prayer, 'Acknowledge a sheep of your own fold, a lamb of your own flock, a sinner of your own redeeming'.[16] Such imagery is both realistic (funerals are mournful), and theological (funerals are also expressions of the Christian hope).

Other rites

Meanwhile there are other rites which are provided in official service books as well as in accompanying supplementary ones. In the nine-teenth century, the *Liturgy and Other Divine Offices of the Church* (1880)[17] of the Catholic Apostolic Church (sometimes called Irvingite) contained a very elaborate set of pastoral rites, by comparison with which the American Prayer Book's list quoted above looks paltry. It includes a set of prayers for use at the Eucharist 'on behalf of a young person about to engage in any occupation in life'. It is interesting that the American list should include a similar such form, for 'Commit-ment to Christian Service'. The Catholic Apostolics were keen, as a tiny Church, to exert strong pastoral bonds around their own. We in our own age seem to want to do just that, but in a way that asserts, too, our sense of Christian vocation in the world, what has sometimes been called 'secular obedience'.

It would be imprudent for new books to go overboard with rites for everything. Nonetheless, it is significant that Churches of the Anglican Communion, with their rich past tradition of euchology, official and unofficial, should produce forms of prayer to meet important human need, or rather, those human needs *it* deems important! For example, there is some debate about whether blessing same-sex relationships and providing a service for the termination of marriage should be the next step. As to the former, it is inappropriate for official public services to be authorized unless and until the Churches reach a common mind on a very controversial matter, although it is known that such services take place in private, where they are not subject to the same level of mis-understanding that they would otherwise provoke in public. As to the latter, it would seem to be more in line with Christian tradition if the individuals concerned sought the Church's rites of healing and recon-ciliation, and thus place the failure of what is past more completely under the loving power of God, rather than focus on that failure while the spotlight falls relentlessly on the little world of people that have been part of a crumbling family. Had we as a Church taken Cranmer's rite of Reconciliation out of the Visitation of the Sick much sooner and taught about it rather more, the demand for such services might not have arisen.

Other issues

But the world has changed further than the collapse of Christendom and the development of anthropology. The Church's own self-understanding has grown apace with its renewed liturgies, most significantly in the way the ministry functions. In all the rites under scrutiny here, be 'pastoral office' ever so widely or narrowly defined, there is an apparent sharing of ministry within the rites themselves and within the pastoral relationships to which they are applied. Whereas Cranmer's local ecclesiastical polity saw the priest operating within a pastoral context of himself as the professional minister, and the congregation, today's world could not be more different. Even though that 'professionalism' was heightened in the nineteenth century as a result of the founding all over the Anglican world of theological colleges, today's pastor is more likely to have a group of other ministers. They may be pastoral assistants, special ministers, readers, deacons, or called by other names.[18] They may even be rectors in all but name of outlying parishes where the ordained priest only visits occasionally.

The point is that with a delegation of ministry, whether because of a local substratum or because of an actual shortage of clergy, all these pastoral offices will be carried out in a very different way. The couple may be prepared for marriage by some of them; the lapsed may be helped towards recommitment; the sick may be visited or counselled; the dying may be prayed over; anointing and the laying-on of hands may even be performed by them. That places the presidential role of the priest under an implied pressure, such as is often to be found in the Sunday Eucharist. The priest has to be part of a whole network of relationships, which, moreover, may include some ministers who through professional training or personal expertise and inclination may carry out these roles better than in the old days — so often looked back to with a false nostalgia — when the priest did it all on his own, perhaps in a hurry.

There can be little doubt that the question of the shared ministry of the priest in the local community is going to continue, and it will increasingly set its stamp not only on the theoretical desiderata of reformed rites but also on how the next round of revisions are framed and set in order. The Church of England's *Ministry to the Sick* (1983) contains several important and strategic spin-echo resonances for the future.[19] Its vision of the priest is very much as the one who works in collaboration with others.

Another issue concerns the directions in which proliferation of such rites is likely to happen. We have already touched upon this, and it is important that it is not forgotten. The 1662 Prayer Book places the service of Churching between the Burial of the Dead and the Ash Wednesday Commination Service! There can be no clearer hint that such a rite was regarded as 'accessory', rather than 'necessary' for salvation (to use the terminology of Richard Hooker once more). It may well be that churching was taken to be a little suspect. Three centuries on in rural Lincolnshire, the writer encountered families where the churching service was no thanksgiving at all, but a rite for Mother to go through in order to be purified. (It is interesting to note the relationship between early churching rites, with their emphasis on presenting the child before God, and later ones, with their emphasis on purifying the mother, a similar development in the way the Festival of 2 February grew in the mediaeval West.)

The moral of the tale is that some people will 'hear' what they want to 'hear' in a rite that is close to experience and that is basic to human life, religious or not. And the next conclusion to draw is that when a new rite is being contemplated to match human need, the Gospel in all its fullness must be the principal criterion, not human therapy. We are living through an age that is consumer-orientated, and therapy-prone. It is right that Christian consumers should be heeded, otherwise liturgy would never develop. It is also right that pastoral offices should truly care for people, otherwise the liturgies under review here would never meet their purposes. But just as all heresies are logical, one-sided, neat and consistent (and therefore wrong), so an undue proliferation of rites and rituals runs the risk of being an end in itself, devised for those who are 'into' this sort of thing.[20] Cranmer was himself heir to many rites that seem to have lost their meaning, or else lacked their proper sense of direction. We may therefore understand why he took such a firm hand in setting them in order, even though he was by far the most conserving of the Reformers in the work that resulted.

Conclusion

In style, rather than substance, the Anglican rites of this century have altered almost beyond recognition from those of the sixteenth and seventeenth centuries. At times, these changes have resulted from better knowledge of the roots of Christianity than Cranmer could have had. At times, they have sprung from understandings of human science that both illuminate primaeval roots and throw into a fresh light the world we inhabit today, with its own peculiar blend of sophistication and barbarism. At times, too, we have to admit that there are basic theological insights that were part of Cranmer's world view; his notion of sickness as a judgement of God mixes strangely with all that is known of medical science today. At times, again, we have to admit that such a disparate group of Churches in communion with Canterbury as exists today has to produce multifarious rites, in face of the multifarious human needs that are deemed to be 'pastoral'.

According to the *Oxford English Dictionary*, the word 'pastoral' as an adjective is first used of a pastor in relation to the care of souls in 1526. The twentieth century has widened its scope, but tends to retain the nuance of spiritual care, even in the most secular of contexts. To speak, then, of 'pastoral offices' continues to be an appropriate assertion, even claim, for Anglicans today.

Meanwhile, the Churches of the Anglican Communion have to continue to adjust to living in a world that is far distant from the ideals of sixteenth-century English polity. And that may well bring to the surface a number of intrinsic and extrinsic issues.

First, given the kind of adaptation and renewal in pastoral liturgy that is under scrutiny here, and is likely to continue in the foreseeable future, there may well have to be a more flexible way of presenting these varying patterns of rites in a service book. If what we are arguing for is an extension and dispersal of those agglomerated rites that were brought together by Cranmer, then new service books simply have to cater for a both–and rather than an either–or public. In other words, we must expect baptism and marriage to be presented in such a way that both can be phased and both can be celebrated as one single rite. This is what is called legislating for flexibility, but it is only to be expected, given the fact that we are living through a time of considerable transition, and the fact that we are becoming an increasingly diverse Communion.

Secondly, when a sacrament or sacramental rite is phased, there needs to be clear agreement on where a special performative formula is required in order to ensure that the rites in question are in accordance with the mind of the Church as a whole. This does not mean a return to that obsession with 'magic words' which marked some eras of Western Christianity, and, indeed, is still with us today. But it does mean ensuring that when there is a rite for the catechumenate, there is a clear form 'admitting' the catechumen (a rite traditionally, as it happens, performed by the bishop). When there is a rite of betrothal, there is a clear form of future consent, which does not make superfluous the active vow to be expressed publicly at the marriage service itself. And when a penitent is forgiven, this should be a clear, ecclesial statement, not a vague wish.

Thirdly, Anglicans, wherever they are, may need to learn again what it is to celebrate pastoral rites which are *world-conscious*, not wrapped up in the tiny environment of the local religious ghetto, with everyone eagerly ministering to each other in a nice sort of way while the rest of society carries on regardless. The boldness and the strength of pastoral liturgies lie in their power to celebrate change in people's lives — their *whole* lives. This is an incarnational and an eschatological truth that is fundamental to the nature of our religion. Without it, we are simply playing at churches.

Fourthly, any renewed rites will have to stand the test of time, and that means facing up to the most difficult question of all. Are the Churches in general, and the Anglican ones in particular, sufficiently confident about their liturgical judgements to believe that a strong and vibrant liturgical culture will in fact be the result of all these new books and pamphlets? Will the dust settle, perhaps, at some happy day in the future, and an era of relative stability take over? History suggests, at least insofar as the pastoral offices are concerned, that the whole liturgical superstructure has been undergoing slow and organic change from 1549 — and before — and after, and undergoing such changes in response (usually indirect) to the pastoral infrastructure. It is true that people tend to be conservative and traditional in their liturgical expectations of pastoral offices. The *way* the changes come through — as the history of the rites demonstrate — is invariably when the people require or ask or need changes. A good test case is the *New Zealand Prayer Book* (1989),[21] with its rich collection of pastoral rites, that have burgeoned according to the way that particular Church has responded to a particular set of circumstances, while retaining a distinctively Anglican ethos.

One of the presuppositions of this study has been that the liturgy of the Church has more original righteousness to it than original sin: in other words, for all that mistakes have been made, are being made, and will doubtless continue to be made, the worship of God is part of the natural instincts implanted in us by the Creator, and that worship needs to take on a definite form, not least when it is avowedly 'pastoral' in its intent. Ultimately, therefore, the answers to these questions lie not in the work of Liturgical Commissions, or Synods, or even Bishops — all of whom can toil away, and discuss, and draft, and redraft, until the cows come home. The people about whom we are concerned are the ones who have always made the liturgy work, or put up with it, or adapted it — the priestly body, the baptized community. Anglicanism's history shows this story to be a mobile one from the beginning,[22] which is why it should not surprise the enquirer who lives in a very different world from Reformation England that these pastoral offices, with their nervous but judicious compendium of constants and variables, still manifest a powerful synthesis of word and prayer and symbolic action and praise for the community to identify as their way of expressing faith in a loving and redeeming God — who is with them in their need.[23]

Notes

1 A. Russell, *The Clerical Profession* (London: SPCK, 1980).
2 *The Book of Common Prayer* (New York: Church Hymnal Corporation/ Seabury Press, 1979), pp. 7–8. For the Prayer Book texts, and sources, see

F.E. Brightman, *The English Rite* II (London: Rivingtons, 1915), pp. 800–79. It is interesting to note that Confirmation immediately precedes Matrimony in the first English Prayer Books.

3   A. Van Gennep, *Les Rites de Passage* (Paris: Librairie Critique, Emile Mourry, 1909). See the full outworking of this thesis in Kenneth Stevenson, *To Join Together: The Rite of Marriage* (Studies in the Reformed Rites of the Catholic Church V; New York: Pueblo, 1987).

4   See, for example, Aidan Kavanagh, *The Shape of Baptism: The Rites of Christian Initiation* (Studies in the Reformed Rites of the Catholic Church I; New York: Pueblo, 1978).

5   The new South African book contains a service of 'Thanksgiving for a marriage': see *An Anglican Prayer Book 1989* (London: Collins, 1989), pp. 469ff. On symbolism, see Stevenson, *To Join Together*, pp. 194ff. See also Kenneth Stevenson, 'The marriage service' in Michael Perham (ed.), *Liturgy for a New Century* (London: SPCK, 1991), pp. 51–61.

6   For a discussion of these and the other Pastoral Offices, see G.J. Cuming, *A History of Anglican Liturgy*, 2nd edn (London: Macmillan, 1982), pp. 63–6 and *passim*.

7   E.C. Whitaker, *Martin Bucer and the Book of Common Prayer* (Alcuin Club Collections 55; Great Wakering: Mayhew-McCrimmon, 1974), pp. 124ff. (cf. pp. 120ff. on the marriage rite).

8   See Harry Boone Porter, *Jeremy Taylor — Liturgist* (Alcuin Club Collections 61; London: SPCK, 1979). See also Leonel L. Mitchell, *Praying Shapes Believing* (Minneapolis: Winston-Seabury, 1985), p. 231.

9   See *The Book of Alternative Services* (Toronto: Anglican Book Centre, 1985), pp. 166ff. In this book, Reconciliation follows Baptism, making another theological point. The prefatory note (p. 166) describes the 'I absolve you' formula as arising only in the thirteenth century and tending towards an individualization of sin and repentance.

10   See Paul Avis, *Anglicanism and the Christian Church* (Edinburgh: T. & T. Clark, 1989), p. 58.

11   See *Book of Occasional Services* (New York: Church Hymnal Corporation, 1979), pp. 147–54. This useful book also provides services for marriage anniversaries; the early sacramentaries sometimes made provision for this, as does the 1970 *Missal of Paul VI*.

12   See the recent study by Aidan Kavanagh, *Confirmation: Origins and Reform* (New York: Pueblo, 1988). Most of the reviews and articles provoked by Kavanagh's perceptive analysis have had to admit that this is an area that (to use the words of Robert Taft) can be described as 'problems such as Confirmation'.

13   See Cuming, *A History of Anglican Liturgy*, p. 105, but only by learned clergy!

14   See Geoffrey Rowell, *The Liturgy of Christian Burial* (Alcuin Club Collections 59; London: SPCK, 1977), pp. 84ff.

15   See F.E. Warren, *The Sarum Missal in English* Part II (Library of Liturgiology and Ecclesiology for English Readers IX; London: De La More Press, 1911), p. 66.

16   See also Kenneth Stevenson, ' "Ye shall pray for . . . .": the intercession' in Stevenson (ed.), *Liturgy Reshaped* (London: SPCK, 1982), pp. 46f.

17 *Liturgy and Other Divine Offices of the Church* (London; Pitman, 1880). The form in question is on p. 325.

18 See Russell, op. cit.

19 *Ministry to the Sick* (London; Privileged Presses, 1983), p. 3 (laypeople administering reserved sacrament to the sick), p. 27 (laypeople assisting in the laying-on of hands), p. 37 (prayer at the time of death).

20 See *A New Zealand Prayer Book* (Auckland: Collins, 1989), pp. 725ff.

21 See Aidan Kavanagh, *On Liturgical Theology* (New York: Pueblo, 1984).

22 See Kenneth Stevenson, 'Cranmer's Pastoral Offices: origins and development' in Margot Johnson (ed.), *Thomas Cranmer: Essays in Commemoration of the 500th Anniversary of his Birth* (Durham: Turnstone Ventures, 1990), pp. 82–93.

23 See Aidan Kavanagh, 'Liturgical inculturation: looking to the future', *Studia Liturgica* 20 (1990), pp. 95–105, for a perceptive, provocative, and prophetic analysis of this issue.

10

The Anglican Church and Holy Order

Bryan D. Spinks and Gianfranco Tellini

The Ordinal holds a crucial place in the Anglican Church, not because of any supposed liturgical merits, but because of its implications for Anglican ecclesiology. In the face of the earliest Roman Catholic accusations of nullity — whether on grounds of form, matter or intention — appeal was made to the Preface of the 1550 Ordinal which stated that the Church of England inherited and intended to continue the received and catholic threefold orders of bishop, priest and deacon.

It is certainly true, as E.C. Messenger demonstrated, and Paul Bradshaw reiterated, that Cranmer took as his model not the Sarum Pontifical, but Martin Bucer's ordination rite; but Cranmer also drew on the Pontifical to transform Bucer's single rite into three rites for the ordination of three separate ecclesial orders.[1] When changes were made to the services in the 1662 Ordinal, making clear which order was being conferred, Bishop Gilbert Burnet insisted that such alterations were not an admission of any previous defect, but simply making explicit in the services that which had always been implicit.[2] At the same time the 1662 revision removed what might have seemed the courtesy and ambiguity concerning the recognition of non-episcopal ministries. Paul Avis has sought to mitigate the change by describing it as an Anglican 'House Rule',[3] but the change in the Act of Uniformity and the Preface to the Ordinal had the effect of declaring non-episcopal ordinations invalid. Insistence on episcopacy was enshrined in the Chicago–Lambeth Quadrilateral, and wherever Anglicans have united with other Churches, they have insisted upon episcopacy and an Ordinal with the threefold ministry of bishop, presbyter and deacon. The Ordinal has thus come to represent a hallmark of Anglicanism, on the one hand in its belief in its fidelity to the tradition received and its own catholicity, and on the other hand allowing it to regard itself as a bridge Church between Roman Catholicism and Protestantism.

When Paul Bradshaw wrote his study *The Anglican Ordinal*, it was still possible to see that particular liturgical book (theoretically the Ordinal has always been separate from the Book of Common Prayer) as expressing the fundamental unifying rite in what was otherwise a Communion of considerable diversity. Indeed, although the 1958 Lambeth Conference report on the Prayer Book urged revision of the Ordinal, it also pleaded for conservatism, and no Province had made any radical change. However, Bradshaw, writing in 1971, suspected that the Church of South India and the English Anglican/Methodist Ordinals would together make changes to 'Cranmer's much-loved but liturgically unsatisfactory rite' inevitable.[4] Twenty years on, Bradshaw's suspicions have been confirmed and surpassed. Whatever may be the legal status of the 1662 Ordinal in England, in practice the rites normally used are those of the *Alternative Service Book 1980*, and other Provinces have produced new Ordinals which are far from the 1662 mould. The result is considerable pluriformity.

The stimuli for new Ordinals have been several. C. O. Buchanan lists the 1958 Lambeth Conference report in its more positive suggestions, the influence of 'unificals' — the rites of Ordination used in uniting Churches, particularly the creation of the English Anglican/Methodist Ordinal, and the new Roman Catholic ordination rites of 1968.[5] But equally important have been the studies on earlier ordination rites (some of the fruits, but by no means all, are to be seen in many of the new Ordinals), and greater ecumenical consensus on the ministry of the whole Church, and the ordained ministry within this greater ministry. The pluriformity of new Ordinals has not itself weakened Anglican identity (its return to sources has strengthened its claim to continue the received tradition) but it has shattered the method of those who have wished to place the locus of that identity in its common forms of worship and a reasonably common Ordinal.

When we look at the new Ordinals, two features strike us immediately. First, the *structure* of all the new Ordinals is practically identical, with the exception of the Scottish Episcopal Church Ordinal of 1984. Secondly, all the new Anglican ordination *prayers* derive largely from the English Anglican/Methodist Ordinal of 1968 — the main exceptions being again those of the Scottish Episcopal rite, and also the recent New Zealand rite.

There are two main ways to revise a liturgical service. One is to start from an existing formulary (new or old) that is considered to be fundamental in one's tradition and/or meets with the approval of the revisers in the light of recent research and discoveries. Such a method allows a Church to retain what it believes to be its roots, and at the same time — where new material is used — it allows new insights to be utilized. Experience shows, however, that this method is not always the most satisfactory, particularly where the inclusion of a new formulation is followed. The revisers will be trapped into using images and ways of expression which came naturally to the compilers, but do not necessarily come naturally to the revisers. It also results in 'tampering' with a text in order to show individual identity rather than creativity. Such an approach, while acknowledging that between the Ascension and the Parousia the Church is not a-historical, and its liturgy as such can never be a *creatio ex nihilo*, nevertheless runs risks. Liturgy has a habit of developing by gradual accretion and concretion, with the result that what is of secondary importance may come to be seen at a later date as being crucial, obscuring the original structure and theology. Alan Detscher has shown how this happened in the English ordination rites for priests between the tenth and fifteenth centuries.[6] An example is the *Veni Creator*, a late-comer into the rite, and now something of a *sine qua non* in Anglican rites!

This method has been the one largely adopted in the majority of recent Anglican Ordinals. The compilers seem to have had one eye on the 1662 rite, and the other upon the English Anglican/Methodist Ordinal.

The second method, though long and laborious, is to start all over again from first principles and without encumbrance of any one already-fixed formulary. In a Church which claims to continue the ancient received tradition of ministry, with regard to an Ordinal, this implies a willingness to sift the *whole* tradition of ordination rites to discover what is of primary importance; and in a Church committed to the authority of scripture, it means looking afresh at ministry as it unfolds in the biblical books. Our present 'story' of ministry (to use recent theological parlance) must coalesce with the 'story' of ministry in scripture, and in the early tradition, otherwise it will have little claim to be in any sense a continuation of the received tradition other than by the use of certain specific sources of the patristic or Reformation period.

This approach requires asking the question 'What is the service for?', and 'In the light of the purpose, what is and what is not negotiable in terms of its structure?' Having agreed on a basic, non-negotiable structure deriving from the nature of the service itself, one can then proceed to develop that structure in an organic way, and subsequently, to provide the full structure with suitable words and actions. The point in question is not: what is the structure of a document used as a source or model, but: what structure is demanded by the service itself? This actually involves asking searching questions about the nature of ministry vis à vis the Church, and the ministry of the Church vis à vis the world. It will involve at least the following considerations:

(1) What is the purpose of God's revelation? Is it to do with God's purpose in creation, with a new heaven and a new earth? Or is it about what items of doctrine ought to be preached and what specific words and actions to use in order to dispense God's grace? Classic Anglican Ordinals have tended to concentrate on the second rather than the first. It must be remembered that although ordination may be a churchly activity, it should point the gathered assembly outwards to the world.

(2) What is the relation of the task of the Church in ministry (the royal priesthood, established through baptism) to that of the ordained ministry? Recent ecumenical documents on ministry have stressed the Church's Christological basis and content. Through baptism all Christians share in the one (and only) priesthood of Christ. Although the ordained ministry does not exercise its office apart from the priesthood of the whole Body, neither is it derivative from the priesthood of the whole Body.[7] Yet at the same time the whole ministry of the Church is directed to the world. Thus T.F. Torrance could write:

> The real priesthood is that of the whole Body, but within that Body there takes place a membering of the corporate priesthood, for the edification of the whole Body, to serve the whole Body in order that the whole Body as Christ's own Body may fulfil His ministry of reconciliation by proclaiming the Gospel among the nations.[8]

(3) If all of us are to work together for the coming of God's Kingdom, the specific *function* of the ordained ministry within the overall ministry of the Church as a whole will have to be clearly identified, with notable consequences that may well cause a fundamental change in our generally accepted outlook on the subject.[9]

At least some of these questions were considered in the composition of the Scottish Episcopal Church's Ordinal (1984) — thanks to the inspiration of Geoffrey Cuming. Cuming was invited to address the Liturgical Committee of that Province, and led them in a brainstorming study day, urging them to start *de novo*: 'The great thing was not just to fiddle with one single existing rite, as we did.'[10] From the *liturgical* point of view, three elements were deemed to be essential to an ordination rite:

(a) The assent of the people.
(b) The prayer of the people.
(c) The laying-on of hands.

From the *theological* point of view, the context of prayer of the whole people of God is the most significant element, in that it acknowledges that it is God who ordains, and not human beings. God calls Christians to ministry through baptism; God calls an individual Christian from amongst the faithful to the ordained ministry (the call is from the Church, for the Church, even if as in the example of Ambrose, he was a catechumen and was baptized and ordained bishop in one go). Implicit in any ordination is God's call through the Church Universal. Thus in the 1984 Ordinal it was the *calling* of the candidate which was made the pivotal point, within the context of prayer, which *par excellence*, is the Eucharist.[11] The structure may be set out as follows:

In the context of the Eucharist
and in the context of Prayer

Presentation of the Candidate
Response of the Bishop
Declaration of the Candidate

Assent of the People

CALLING OF THE CANDIDATE

Prayer of the People:
Litany or Silent Prayer
Ordination Prayer with Laying-on of Hands
Porrectio Instrumentorum

Kiss of Peace from members of the Order in question

In this structure the 'story' of the Church, through scripture and tradition, and the 'story' of the candidate are carefully interwoven. Within such a structure, each ordination rite makes it clear that the call is from and to the Church of God, the Church Universal, of which the Anglican Communion claims to be a part. Thus specific reference to the 'Church of England', or in the Ordinal of 1979 to the 'Episcopal Church of the United States of America' seems to be an almost self-conscious hesitation as to whether or not this is ordination to the Universal Church. Attachment to what was sixteenth-century identity and defensiveness may now unintentionally hint at sectarianism.

How far the Scottish Ordinal is a fulfilment of Geoffrey Cuming's idea of what an Ordinal should be is difficult to say, but it represents once again his contribution to the future of Anglican worship.

In the making of an Ordinal, three further points need to be made as clear as possible:

(a) the relation of the ordained to the whole of the people of God.

(b) the relation of any one member of an order to the other members of the same order.

(c) the relation of any one order to the other two.

Not all of these can be made sufficiently clear by the structure alone; it is reinforced in the prayers, but above all by the praxis of the Church. We have already noted the agreement in many ecumenical documents that the ordained ministry cannot be divorced from the ministry of the people of God, the royal priesthood. At the same time the ordained ministry does not derive from it. In many new Ordinals (a) is expressed by the presentation of the candidates by clergy and laity. For example, in the Canadian Ordinal (1985), a bishop is presented by a priest, deacon and lay person, and priests and deacons by a priest and lay person (for the deacon, presentation by a deacon may be included in the rubric, 'additional presenters'). England is an unfortunate exception, where a bishop-elect is presented by two bishops, and the archdeacon or his representative presents priests and deacons.

With regard to (b), as the threefold ministry is widely understood, the 'college of bishops' represents the Church Universal, whereas the diocesan bishop presides over the 'college of presbyters'. This is symbolized most clearly by the fact that other bishops join in the laying-on of hands of a bishop—though the CSI rite allowed the presbyters to join in, which (as Bradshaw has suggested) may well have been the original usage in the *Apostolic Tradition*.[12] If the bishop is a sign of unity who presides over the college of presbyters, then immediately such an understanding of episcopacy is compromised by the excessive Anglican use of suffragan bishops. Ordained by the same rite as a diocesan, they lack the same ecclesial symbolism. As Peter Moore writes:

> The position of suffragan bishops is not one that should be further developed or maintained. They have not enabled episcopacy to shine with a primitive light. They have made possible the proliferation of committees and the feeling of remoteness which many priests and parishes feel from the bishop. The only solution is to restore episcopacy to its proper form.[13]

It is likely, however, that Anglican expediency will continue to take precedence over sound theology.

The collegiality of presbyters is expressed by the long tradition of them joining in the laying-on of hands on a new presbyter. What of deacons? In the Armenian rite deacons join in with the bishop, and Bradshaw suggests that this was probably true once for the Maronite and Syrian Orthodox rites.[14] It may be un-Western, but here Western tradition can usefully adopt an Eastern-rite practice, particularly in view of the revival of the diaconate in today's Church, and its actual way of functioning.

The most difficult to express is (c), partly because the relationship between bishop and presbyter is still far from settled. According to the recent study by Aidan Nichols (a Roman Catholic) the bishop may be understood as the result of an amalgamation of a once distinct two-tier ministry — that of the Apostles and apostolic delegates, who were 'universal'; and the local ministry centred upon the college of presbyters who elected a proto-presbyter who had *episkopē*. The apostolic delegate and the proto-presbyter combined to give the bishop who on one hand is a successor to the apostolic ministry in terms of representing the Universal Church, but is also head of the college of presbyters in so far as he also represents the local Church.[15] The duties of bishops and presbyters overlap, and where presidency of the Eucharist is seen as providing the setting and rationale of ministry,[16] little difference can be seen between the two orders.

The diaconate was in the direct service of the bishop, though in practice today the deacon is usually an assistant to a presbyter. Until recently both the Roman Catholic Church and the Church of England could be accused of paying only lip-service to the diaconate, for in each it was but a tiresome stepping-stone to the presbyterate. The admission of married men to a permanent diaconate in the Roman Catholic Church, and the ordination of women deacons in the Anglican Church has forced both Churches to reconsider this ministry, and give it some distinct status. It is to be hoped that as Anglican Provinces allow ordination of women to the presbyterate, this will not have the negative consequence of once more reducing the diaconate to insignificance. Churches without a threefold ministry can hardly be expected to take it seriously if episcopal churches themselves mutilate one or other of the orders which they profess to take so seriously.

The distinct nature of each order is underlined in the Presentation or the Declaration of Anglican Ordinals, as well as in the prayers. Yet having been slow in identifying the unchanging function of the ordained within the ministry of the People of God, most new Anglican Ordinals seem to limit their understanding of the function of bishops, priests and deacons to a factual description of a day in the life of a bishop, priest or deacon — the Church of England 'Declaration' in the ordaining of priests being a most glaring example.

The custom of the *porrectio* (e.g. handing over of chalice) has been restored at least as an option in many of the new Ordinals, and such secondary symbolism can serve a useful purpose, providing that it is remembered that it is but secondary.[17] However, given that ordination is to service, one wonders whether the staff, towel and bowl might be a better symbol for bishops rather than a mitre (a quaint piece of headgear suggesting that God has a sense of humour!) and ring. Episcopacy has been and is too often seen as bureaucratic authority and leadership rather than as the *kenōsis* model of the one true High Priest. In this connection it is interesting to note that the draft Scottish Episcopal rite prescribed that at the ordination of a new bishop, the Primus, accompanied by the two co-ordaining bishops, should come down to the candidate and kneel in front of him, and say: 'The Holy Spirit calls you to be the Bishop of N. What is your answer?' The Primus, however, was in no mood to kneel in front of anyone, and it was rejected!

Most new Anglican Ordinals seem to have been compiled in the mistaken belief that the identity of Anglican worship and its ministry can only exist in the dependence of their formulations on a single document deemed to be 'Anglican enough' — in this case usually the Ordinal of the ill-fated Anglican/Methodist reunion project. Strange customs still linger for scarcely apparent reasons, such as the insistence on having the *Veni Creator* for all three orders. Other customs seem to continue for more affective than effective reasons, such as in the giving of the Bible to the newly ordained. That each one of the three orders and its specific function is somehow intimately connected to the canonical books that contain God's revelation is perfectly obvious and beyond question. But why confuse the issue by giving the Bible in all three orders with the *same* formula — and why does the Church of England give only the New Testament to deacons, as though there was something Marcionite about this order?

Revision of the Ordinal should stem from a *total* reappraisal of our position on the subject. What we should not do is to allow ourselves to be trapped into accepting uncritically the hidden assumptions of any one already existing Ordinal. Furthermore, the Church cannot escape the judgement of God. Writing out an Ordinal for the Church *as it should be* will inevitably result in a serious indictment of the Church as it actually is.

Notes

1 E. C. Messenger, *The Lutheran Origin of the Anglican Ordinal* (London: Burns, Oates and Washbourne, 1934); Paul F. Bradshaw, *The Anglican Ordinal* (Alcuin Club Collections 53; London: SPCK, 1971).

2 Gilbert Burnet, *A Vindication of the Ordinations of the Church of England* (London: Chiswel, 1677), pp. 71–4.

3 Paul Avis, *Anglicanism and the Christian Church* (Edinburgh: T. & T. Clark, 1989).

4 Bradshaw, op. cit., p. 211.

5 C. O. Buchanan, *Modern Anglican Ordination Rites* (Alcuin/GROW Liturgical Study 3; Bramcote: Grove, 1987).

6 Alan Detscher, 'The ancient English ordination rites for presbyters', *Ecclesia Orans* 2 (1985), pp. 139–61, 241–64.

7 *God's Reign and Our Unity* (Anglican–Reformed Dialogue) (London: Church House, 1984), p. 79.

8 T. F. Torrance, *Royal Priesthood* (Scottish Journal of Theology Occasional Papers 3; London and Edinburgh: Oliver and Boyd, 1955), p. 81.

9 Aquinas argues that to be vested with a sacramental character is to be charged with an essentially instrumental function. There is no need to drive a wedge between ontological and functional. See *Summa Theologica* IIIa, q.63, a.3, corpus.

10 Letter from Geoffrey Cuming to Gianfranco Tellini (31 March 1981). The 'we' refers of course to the Church of England Liturgical Commission.

11 Torrance, op. cit., p. 74.

12 Paul F. Bradshaw, *Ordination Rites of the Ancient Churches of East and West* (New York: Pueblo, 1990), pp. 60–1.

13 Peter Moore (ed.), *Bishops But What Kind?* (London: SPCK, 1982), p. 172.

14 Bradshaw, *Ordination Rites*, p. 72.

15 Aidan Nichols, *Holy Order* (Dublin: Veritas, 1990).

16 Torrance, op. cit.

17 Bryan Spinks, 'Symbolism in the sacraments' in Kenneth W. Stevenson (ed.), *Symbolism and the Liturgy* II (Grove Liturgical Study 26; Bramcote: Grove, 1981), pp. 24–33.

11

Is there an 'Anglican' liturgical style?

David S. Stancliffe

'Now I know why the churches are true', said a four-year-old, watching a televised service from Exeter Cathedral; 'The people in them enjoy singing, and walk about in patterns.'[1]

This acute observation sums up the popular appeal of public worship for many people: the spontaneity of hearty congregational singing and the security of decent ceremonial. But beneath the surface of these apparently unlikely companions — spontaneity and order — lie deeper currents; and any attempt to describe or evaluate a distinctively Anglican style in worship needs to look beneath the surface of the patchwork quilt of Anglican liturgical practice in an attempt to discern the underlying patterns.

Our experience of worship

We begin with 'enjoying singing'. It is good to sing together: it draws people into a sense of fellowship and camaraderie; but just what you sing doesn't seem to matter much, provided that the tunes are the right ones. But while the Anglican Provinces (or most of them) have an immensely complex process of check and countercheck for authorizing the liturgical texts of service books, the texts of the hymns and songs we sing have never been authorized, nor have they been scrutinized by anybody other than the editorial team of the hymn or songbook that a particular Church happens to use.[2] We must indeed be thankful that the hymnbooks of the Anglican communion are so full of the hymns of, for example, the Wesleys, with their robust and Reformed yet Catholic theology, but what hymn singing does is essentially to generate religious warmth in a way which excludes some of the more excessive expressions of enthusiasm. Its countercheck is the decent order provided by the dignified and restrained ceremonial of formal processions: we 'walk about in patterns'. In spite of this attachment to 'decent order', there is often a residual suspicion of ritual — of the ceremonial expression of liturgical worship in movement, vesture and gesture. Yet exotic clothes and endless processions — provided that they have no doctrinal significance — are universally popular. Why?

There are several occasions which exhibit these characteristics and are reckoned to be popular enough to sustain a slot in the broadcasting networks each year without fail.

One act of worship in the Church's year is regularly broadcast at a fixed time and from the same place. It is transmitted the world over — my elder daughter heard it from a hotel room in Uruguay — and this year it was repeated twice on the network the day after. A televised version was also shown, and countless articles in newspapers and references in — for example — seasonal cookery programmes, indicate that it is an essential ingredient in many people's celebration of Christmas. It is the Festival of Nine Lessons and Carols broadcast on BBC Radio 4 at 3 p.m. on Christmas Eve from King's College Chapel, Cambridge, for more than half a century without a break.

The only occasions remotely comparable in popular consciousness are the Remembrance Sunday observance in Whitehall, and the distribution of the Royal Maundy on Maundy Thursday.[3] While they are acts of worship, both of these are 'royal' occasions in the sense that they show the British Sovereign — whether with a wreath of laurels or a purse of silver — stepping out alone to remember the humblest of her subjects, whether a fallen soldier or an elderly pensioner. In both cases the ceremonies are enacted — as were the rituals of the Davidic kingdom — by the Sovereign in person, and beneath them both we hear echoes of the new style of kingship to which the Canticle of Christ's Glory (Phil 2.5–11) bears witness.

At the heart of all these observances is the celebration of the divine humility; but it is a ceremonial remembrance rather than a sacramental celebration. It is the incarnation — the fact that God comes among us and shares our human life — which is central to the Festival of Nine Lessons and Carols, and it is this sense of coming among and identifying with her people, and so giving them a sense of worth and dignity, that is characteristic of the 'royal' occasions too.

The common factor here is that these rites are reflective and inclusive commemorations touching everyone, and not just the confessing Christians, rather than distinctive sacramental celebrations for church 'members' only. This is in contrast, for example, with the current stance of most of the worship of the contemporary Roman Catholic Church which is almost exclusively sacramental, and often therefore appears less woolly in its proclamation. But while there are strong currents in, for example, the Church of England which would like to make it more self-consciously the Church over against the nation, the post-Elizabethan sense of partnership between Church and State which exists for the common good and seeks to sustain our common life is much more deeply embedded historically in England than, for example, in Italy, where the Concordat between two separate sovereign states is uneasily maintained, let alone in post-Revolutionary and anti-clerical France. Nor is this an exclusively English phenomenon: the Anglican tradition of partnership rather than polarization is visible in varying degrees throughout the Anglican Communion.

Is there a demonstrable link between the doctrine of the incarnation and such a 'reflective and inclusive commemoration'? When the Roman Catholic Church held the Pastoral Congress in Liverpool in the early 1980s, they emerged with the slogan 'We are the Easter people, and our song is Alleluia'. In the Anglican Church, one would be tempted to respond 'We are the Christmas people, and our song is Once in Royal David's City'. Our focus seems to be located more comfortably in the incarnation than the resurrection — in the commemoration of a past and particular event, rather than in the celebration of a present and continuing reality. It is probably true that Anglicans have a strong sense of history as part of their corporate identity; it is certainly the case that we prefer the comparative safety of conserving the past, which provides an interesting story without necessarily committing us to vigorous action in consequence, to the adventure of exploring the present, with the attendant risks of being caught up in a pattern of response which demands commitment.

To polarize these attitudes is, of course, unfair both to the Roman Catholic sense of historical rootedness in the tradition and to the very real Anglican commitment to following the risen Saviour in our pilgrimage of Christian discipleship. Elements of both are found in both Churches. But there is, I believe, a very real difference which can be articulated in terms of both theological emphasis and temperamental preference.

Our experience of God

In theological terms, a contrast has traditionally been made between the different ways in which God's relationship to his creation is experienced and expressed. Which of these we warm to may depend on temperament, conviction or experience. Some people experience God primarily as the one who stands beyond the created order, and whose principal action is one of rescue. God is known in the voice which challenges the wickedness of our ways, and he calls us out beyond the limits of our own experience to a new life — 'out of darkness into his marvellous light' (1 Pet 2.9). The primary religious experience to be celebrated is this change, this conversion, from darkness to light, from sin to new life, from death to resurrection — which we call 'salvation'. This is the pattern which the Church celebrates liturgically each year in the paschal cycle, beginning with Ash Wednesday and concluding with Pentecost, with its peak at the Christian Passover, the *transitus* or 'crossing-over' from death to life celebrated dramatically in the Easter Vigil. A vivid contrast is made between Lent and Passiontide, culminating in the keeping of Holy Week, in which the call to conversion from the ways of sin is central, and Eastertide, when the risen life of Christ offers the baptized a taste of freedom, and affirms their place in the new creation.

By contrast, others experience God principally as the one who is discovered in their midst, who meets them in the homeless and stranger, and whose primary act is to share our life — his creation — in order that we may come to realize our divine potential. Instead of inviting us to turn our backs on a sinful world, God asks us to help bring about his new creation. We glimpse signs of that Kingdom in the Son of Man who came not to be saved but to save. The primary religious experience to be celebrated is the recognition of God's presence with us, and our consequent participation in seeking the establishment of his Kingdom. This is the pattern which the Church celebrates liturgically each year in the celebration of the incarnation, beginning with Advent, and ending Epiphanytide with Candlemas, the festival of the recognition of Christ as light of all the world. There is no one dramatic change, no point of sudden conversion to celebrate, but a gradual, progressive revelation of God-with-us, as the circle of recognition widens, and the first martyr Stephen is joined by the Saul who supervised his death.[4]

Two approaches to celebration

There are several consequences for the way in which we worship which derive from these two distinct but complementary ways of celebrating our encounter with God. First, there is the general style of the worship. The paschal celebration with its primary emphasis on change from death to life leads most naturally to sacramental celebrations in which the worshipper is offered a rehearsal of that change — 'Once you were no people but now you are God's people' (1 Pet 2.10). This is most obviously true in the sacraments of initiation and reconciliation, where a radical change of status is celebrated as an individual worshipper moves from death to life, but the same is true of the sacraments of Order, of Anointing and of Marriage, where change — from lay to ordained, dis-eased to whole, single to married — is being performatively celebrated. Above all, it is true of the Eucharist, where the scattered company of wayward individuals is yet again being made one in the Body of Christ.

The incarnational celebration, on the other hand, centres not so much on the change effected in us as on the recognition of the one who comes among us. Our task as worshippers is to learn to recognize the signs of God's presence, and then to tune ourselves to co-operate with his activity. The daily prayer of the people of God has as its focus the lectern and its Gospel Book, rather than the font or altar. At Morning and Evening Prayer the emphasis has come to be on the recitation of the psalter, reflective reading of the scriptures, and then, buoyed and expectant, to have our eyes opened to the signs of his kingly presence as we recite the gospel canticles of the incarnation. In a small but significant way the whole incarnational cycle is rehearsed daily in these Lukan gospel canticles: the Benedictus at Morning Prayer alerts us to expect his coming; the Angelic Salutation at mid-day celebrates the promise of his presence; the Magnificat at Evening Prayer recollects the astonishing upheaval of his Kingdom that we have witnessed — and even taken part in — during the day; and the Nunc Dimittis at Night Prayer reminds us, as we hand the day back to God, that the light of life is a gift we are called to share with all the world.

A Church which went overboard for one approach to the virtual exclusion of the other would end up with a seriously distorted Gospel, as well as an unbalanced liturgical life. Nevertheless, for reasons of tradition and temperament, as well as theological conviction, these distinctions are visible in the life of the different Churches.

An example: baptism

We can clarify our perceptions of these two models, and begin to gain a sense of the distinctive ecclesiologies they spawn, by looking at the way in which fashions in baptismal theology and practice have developed in the recent life of the Church. By the third century, Easter was *the* time for the celebration of baptism, and indeed Lent and Eastertide have been shaped liturgically largely in response to pre- and post-baptismal catechesis.[5] This was an emphasis which the architects of liturgical reform in the 1950s and 1960s sought to draw to the surface. To be baptized was to die and rise with Christ, and Romans 6.3–11 was the key reading for a celebration of baptism at the Easter Vigil, a reading which not only made clear the once and for all nature of baptism as the intelligent response of the believing adult to what God had done for him or her in Christ, but which also linked the moment of conversion, of becoming a Christian, with the celebration of Christ's dying and rising in the dramatic, once-for-all symbol of drowning. Such a view tends to view baptism as an anamnesis, a 'remembrance', of Christ's baptism.

But in addition to Eastertide, the Church has traditionally had another baptismal season, and a complementary baptismal model. Baptism also marks God's anointing of his chosen at the start of their discipleship, when the seeds of the new creation are sown. The out-pouring of the spirit on Jesus at his baptism in the Jordan (Mark 1), and the new birth by water and the Spirit (John 3) are key elements in the baptismal tradition, particularly of the Eastern Church, and such a tradition has its focus in the celebration of the Epiphany, the manifestation of Christ to the Gentiles. This pattern says more about God's act in his new creation, and hints at a theology of baptism which allows for gradual growth towards maturity rather than a sudden moment of conviction. It takes seriously Jesus' own baptismal anointing as marking the moment when a new and different quality of relationship with the Father emerged — a relationship that was not sealed till the moment of final surrender on the cross. Such a view tends to see baptism as an epiclesis, an 'invocation', of God's promises in the future.

Anglicanism has always believed in the rightness of infant baptism as a sign of God's prevenient grace, freely bestowed; infants are not baptized solely on the ticket of their believing parents and sponsors by extension with the household baptisms of the first few centuries. For in baptism a work of grace begins to be articulated, which it is the Church's task to nurture and make visible. However, in the Roman Catholic Church the reform of the Holy Week rites in the 1950s stripped from the prayer for the blessing of the water at the restored Easter Vigil all references to the acts of God in creation and the new creation.[6] Similarily, in the Church of England, the baptismal theology of the 1960s which found its way into the Initiation Rites of the *Alternative Service Book 1980* leans almost exclusively on the paschal model. Little wonder, then, that the 1980 Initiation Rites have been interpreted as a tool for dividing 'true believers' — as they seem to the eyes of the incumbent or local church — from the rest, and that we have witnessed movements not only for the reform, but also for the abolition of infant baptism.

Theologies of the Church

A further consequence follows: different theologies of initiation sharpen the question of church membership, and here is the point at which different ecclesiological presuppositions surface most clearly. Is the Church *ecclesia contra mundum*, a body called out of the world to witness to a distinct and separate life? Is it the ark, outside which is no salvation, floating on the stormy seas of the wicked world, rescuing people by hauling them aboard? Is the model for the Church's life a monastic/desert model of withdrawal from the social and political realities of current confusions in order to point to a more excellent way, and prepare for a Kingdom not of this world? Part of the tradition says 'Yes' to this, and the Church of the elect, the self-consciously saved, knows what the rules for membership are, where the boundaries are, and can celebrate the moment when these boundaries are overstepped with great clarity. Whether consciously or not, the favourite ecclesial image of the *Alternative Service Book* — 'We are the body of Christ' — emphasizes the gathered club membership of the Church in a way that has undoubtedly confirmed and strengthened the regular eucharistic community, but has not made it particularly easy for those who are feeling their way towards faith, who might be helped by the less self-confident sounding model of 'fellow-disciples on the way together' which is where the emphasis would fall in a parish adopting a more catechetical style.[7]

Reading the church building

And ecclesiology, whether consciously articulated or not, is expressed not only in the way the liturgy is celebrated but also — though this frequently contradicts the liturgy itself — in the way in which the church building is ordered for worship. Many of our parish churches exhibit a whole range of architectural styles; and the accumulation of furnishings, fittings and monuments over the centuries gives, for example, an English church interior what can best be described as a layered feel, a strong witness to a continuing tradition. In churches like these an implicitly twentieth-century ecclesiology is often uncon-sciously expressed in the presentation of the liturgy and in preaching only to be robustly contradicted by an essentially Tractarian — and therefore linear and hieratic — arrangement of the building. The resulting muddle is satisfying to no one. But is the attempt to turn a thoroughly ordered Tractarian church into a bijou drawing-room, com-plete with fitted carpet and potted plants, any better? And what do these matey church interiors seek to achieve, unless it is to substitute a superficial togetherness for the terrifying and awesome encounter between the believer and the Maker, which the death of the Lord alone has made possible?[8]

But is modern building any better? As an example of that central focus, that gathered concentration on the broken bread and poured-out wine on the Lord's Table at the heart of the community, the Metro-politan Cathedral of Christ the King in Liverpool could hardly be bettered. Yet the community gathered for worship there is looking inwards, and although the focus of its concentration is the transfigured signs of the new creation, the bread of life and the cup of salvation, there is a sense in which the building leads nowhere. How do we balance that incarnational sense of gathering around a focus with the need we all feel to be taken out of ourselves, and led further in our pilgrimage? Here is an area where those who design churches, and especially those who reorder the older buildings, need not only to be sensitive to the grain of the building and the expressed functional needs of the congregation, but also to have a fine sense of both the liturgical and ecclesiological expression of the church community for whom they are working. The Anglican tradition has a strong incarnational theology, and encourages an inclusive sense of community in worship. But at the same time, the Anglican tradition is sensitive to the beyond. We expect to meet a God who reveals himself gradually, in response to the probe of intellect. The Church's liturgy will provide a patterned and ordered backcloth against which our fragments of experience will begin to make sense. Our liturgies present an ordered drama, and seek to enfold our experience in the story of what God has done for his people in such a way as to give value, meaning and direction to our lives. We are changed gradually, step by step; not yet in a moment, in the twinkling of an eye.

The liturgy as drama

The need for a dramatic presentation of the liturgy was understood by that eccentric Cornish parish priest in the nineteenth century, Parson Hawker of Morwenstow. When he had baptized a child, he would then hold it above his head as he strode to the chancel step, 'thundering forth with his rich, powerful voice, the words: ''we receive this child into the congregation of Christ's flock . . .'''.[9] Hawker had grasped the teaching power of underlining liturgical texts by suitable visual expression. It is to him too that we owe the creation of Harvest Festivals, at any rate in their modern form.[10] He perceived, like Pope Gregory who, when he sent Augustine to England, exhorted him to 'baptize' the pagan shrines and the pagan festivals, that the instincts and rhythms of agricultural life were the seedbeds of religious awareness. He knew that the natural sense of thankfulness experienced after the relief of a successful harvest could be directed towards God, rather than be absorbed in self-congratulation. Behind this perception lies an instinctive understanding that the focus of worship is God, not ourselves, and that that heart of worship is giving, not getting, the selfless offering of praise and thanksgiving, rather than the manipulation of the deity to achieve what we want. This essentially Judaeo-Christian insight was picked up and given a very Anglican expression by Parson Hawker in a way which underlines the essentially Catholic nature of Anglican worship. Something of the robustness of this dramatic sense is an important ingredient: a few drops of water sprinkled from a bird-bath font may be a valid administration of the sacrament of baptism, but they hardly serve to express the powerful imagery of drowning and being raised to new life which is there in the liturgical texts.

This sense of the dramatic possibilities of the liturgy has, of course, a long tradition. Pre-Reformation England had more than its fair share of drama in the liturgy, whether one thinks of rites like the burying of the Host on Good Friday, or the *Quem quaeritis?* of Easter, and similar quasi-liturgical dramas.[11] The Christian year was patterned with fasts and festivals, and processions — the religious 'demonstrations' of their time — occupied a prominent and popular place, as did the more arduous pilgrimages.

At the Reformation, Cranmer's native sense of the dramatic did not desert him; and although it is fashionable to decry his eucharistic liturgies, if they were celebrated according to his intentions, with the communicants coming to stand around a free-standing table in the otherwise empty chancel as he envisaged, the integration of liturgical text and significant movement in his novel and rememorative rite could be admired for its forceful incorporation of the people within the drama, even if its theological emphases were not obviously ours.

Instead, it is Cranmer's liturgical texts as emended and improved a century later in the 1662 Book, not his liturgies as he originally drafted them, which have been held up for admiration. And this means that his admirers have grasped only part of his significance. For it is not only the Order for Holy Communion which makes dramatic use of movement as the worshippers leave the nave, the place of the ministry of the Word, for the chancel, the place of the celebration of the sacrament. The Solemnization of Matrimony provides for the solemn exchange of vows to take place before 'their friends and neighbours' in 'the body of the church'. After that, they move to the chancel for the prayers, and for the celebration of the Holy Communion which the Prayer Book assumes will conclude the rite.

At a funeral too, the movement throughout the rite expresses the sense of a continuing journey better than any words. The body is met at the gate, and sentences and the penitential psalms accompany the procession into church. Psalms and a substantial lesson take place in church, after which the burial takes place, followed by the Prayers. While the Order for the Burial of the Dead is no more than a shadow of what the whole series of rites in the pre-Reformation Church had provided, the sense of accompanying the body on its last journey is still present.

Do these ingredients add up to anything that can clearly be labelled 'Anglican'?

First, there is an integrated feel about Anglican liturgy which has its origins in the union of heart and mind, of word and sacrament, of text and ceremonial. Our worship is earthed in a theology which is incarnational, and a sacramentality which is organic and affirmative. We belong in a tradition which retains strong echos of the Benedictine pattern, with its emphasis on ordered worship, serious study and common life. While the English cathedrals, for example, consciously reflect this inheritance, it is true also of the parochial ministry, where the parsonage house has traditionally been a place not only of prayer, but of study and hospitality. Our liturgy is ordered, not regimented, and it is related to how we think and how we live.

Second, and closely related, we are people of the book or rather, of a family of books. In spite of cultural differences, the revised books for worship produced by the Churches in the family of the Anglican Communion still show a remarkable family likeness. That is also true of ceremonial. The movements we make — to describe ceremonial in its plainest terms — are, in terms of Frere's distinctions, always functional, frequently symbolic, but never simply allegorical.[12] In terms of the relationship between word and action, the Prayer Book of 1662 is neither prescriptive, like the late mediaeval books or the *Missale Romanum* of 1570, nor suggestive, like the Roman Missal of 1970. We have a minimalistic approach of our own sort at this level, which has perhaps allowed the Anglican tradition to take root and flower unselfconsciously in very different contexts. Our tradition does not exist in the abstract: it needs to find its own climate and memory in order to embody its dignity.[13]

And third, there is an elusive but very distinctive Anglican style, which has a lot to do with the acceptance and integration of a number of different layers, which create a sense of unity by inclusion, rather than of uniformity by exclusion. Liturgies may draw on both the Eastern and the Western tradition; for example the Kyries in Greek, hymnody of the eighteenth century and the prayers of priest and people from *An Australian Prayer Book 1978* with the Mass in Four Parts by William Byrd will provide an integrated and harmonious whole. It is this inclusive quality, with its unspoken capacity for growth, which has the potential to lead us and point us beyond where we might have travelled on our own. Like the parish churches of sixteenth-century England, which Cranmer understood to be a series of liturgical spaces, each with a proper focus of its own, yet each pointing up the steps or through the screen to the one that lay beyond, Anglican liturgy is more than the sum of its parts, and always holds within itself the possibility of pointing God's people beyond where they could ever imagine themselves on their own, to the very throne of God himself.

Notes

1 Quoted in *Patterns for Worship: A Report by the Liturgical Commission of the General Synod of the Church of England* (London: Church House Publishing, 1989), p. 5.

2 See the dilemma that faced Charles Gore as Bishop of Birmingham on the publication of *The English Hymnal* in 1906: G. L. Prestige, *The Life of Charles Gore* (London: Heinemann, 1935), pp. 300ff.

3 On the footwashing and its royal associations (not just in England), see J. W. Tyrer, *Historical Survey of Holy Week, Its Services and Ceremonial* (Alcuin Club Collections 29; London: Milford, 1932), pp. 109ff.

4 See *The Promise of His Glory: Services and Prayers for the Season from All Saints to Candlemas: A Report by the Liturgical Commission of the General Synod of the Church of England* (London: Church House Publishing, 1990); also *The Promise of His Glory: Services and Prayers for the Season from All Saints to Candlemas* (London: Church House Publishing/Mowbray and Collegeville, MN: Liturgical Press, 1991).

5 See, for example, Maxwell Johnson, 'From three days to forty: baptismal preparation and the origins of Lent', *Studia Liturgica* 20 (1990), pp. 185–200.

6 See Dominic E. Serra, 'The blessing of baptismal water at the Paschal Vigil', *Worship* 64.1 (1990), pp. 142–56.

7 See, for example, Peter Ball, *Journey into Faith* (London: SPCK, 1984), pp. 32–42.

8 Much of this religious subculture receives a deserved corrective in Aidan Kavanagh, *Elements of Rite: A Handbook of Liturgical Style* (New York: Pueblo, 1982).

9 S. Baring-Gould, *The Vicar of Morwenstow* (London: Methuen, 1899), p. 84.

10 See S. Baring-Gould, op. cit., p. 190.

11 On the history of this fascinating area, see O. B. Hardison, Jr, *Christian Rite and Christian Drama in the Middle Ages: Essays in the Origin and Early History of Modern Drama* (Baltimore: Johns Hopkins University Press, 1965).

12 See W. H. Frere, *The Principles of Religious Ceremonial* (The Oxford Library of Practical Theology; London: Longmans, 1906).

13 For parallel thinking, see Mark Santer, 'The praises of God' in Michael Perham (ed.), *Liturgy for a New Century* (London: SPCK, 1991), pp. 1–8.

12

Liturgy and society

Donald C. Gray

It is all too easy to idealize any historic connection between Anglican liturgy and society. In England, although claims can be made, and often are, for the integral place of the Book of Common Prayer in the life, consciousness and culture of the nation, on careful examination they can be seen to be, to a certain extent, elitist claims made by and for a section of society in which there was both the time and the opportunity for worship. There were huge areas of England in the eighteenth, nineteenth and the early part of this century, involving thousands of people, where the writ of the Prayer Book did not run, and where ignorance of its contents and provisions were widespread. And this despite the heroic efforts of those who were engaged in the Church of England's huge stake in the growing educational provisions, to say nothing of the devoted labours of hundreds of Sunday School teachers in the parishes of the nation.[1]

Cosmo Gordon Lang (Archbishop of Canterbury 1928–42) described the period 1890 to 1914 as 'The Golden Age of parochial work in the towns of England',[2] yet in the middle of the War, in 1916, a survey revealed that 80 per cent of soldiers from the Midlands had never heard of the sacraments. 'Repentance, grace, forgiveness, baptism, confirmation is hardly known by the great mass of them', it was stated.[3] In the middle of the Second World War, in 1943, at the request of the Church Assembly the Archbishops of Canterbury and York set up a Commission which was asked to survey:

The whole problem of modern evangelism with special reference to the spiritual needs and prevailing intellectual outlook of the non-worshipping members of the community, and to report on the organisation and methods by which such needs can most effectively be met.[4]

The result of this survey, published under the title *Towards the Conversion of England*, concluded, among other things, that 'it is difficult to find any contacts between the liturgical worship of the Church and the minds of a generation to whom all forms of worship, however simple, are unfamiliar'.[5]

Forty-five years later the situation seemed to be unchanged; indeed the report *Faith in the City*, in 1985, confirmed this:

> A Church which has only a single highly intellectual style of doctrinal formulation and which orders even its most contemporary forms of worship by reference to a closely printed book of over a thousand pages can never hope to bridge the gulf which separates it from ordinary people.[6]

The Church in the Urban Priority Areas recognized not merely the Book of Common Prayer, but also the liturgical provisions of *The Alternative Service Book 1980*, as blunt instruments in their hands as a means of effective worship for the people in the society in which they were set.

Although the Church has continued to play an integral part on the rural scene (its presence, it is said, 'is woven into the very fabric of rural community life'),[7] no easy assumptions about the way in which liturgy is perceived by that section of society should be made, as the report of the Archbishops' Commission on Rural Areas (ACORA) made quite clear in 1990. There is in the countryside the opportunity for what might be termed 'natural religious experience'. In parenthesis: perhaps this is only true because so few have made the attempt to harness industrial and urban concepts for the purposes of proclaiming or revealing God's wonders; Richard Jones's 'God of concrete, God of steel' has had pitifully few imitators.[8] Nonetheless, many have found that nature in its rural setting can be specially evocative of God's glory. Bishop Jeremy Taylor described it over three hundred years ago:

> God is glorified in the sun and moon, in the rare fabric of the honeycomb, in the discipline of bees, in the economy of pismires, in the little houses of birds, in the curiosity of an eye, God being pleased to delight in those little images and reflexes of himself from those pretty mirrors, which like a crevice in a wall through a narrow perspective transmit the species of a vast excellency.[9]

There is, therefore, an expectancy that there might be implicit religious fervour within countryside matters and the ACORA report hopes that in the future the Church will promote this expectation. At the same time the report would not want anyone to be misled, and says:

> We believe that Christian worship should not stifle implicit religion. On the contrary Christians are challenged to articulate and make explicit in public worship what many people feel implicitly outside the setting of formal worship. Thus the Church should respond to the hunger for spiritual expression, which is at times outside the limited range of its authorised liturgical offering.[10]

Thus in both town and country alike there would appear to be a yawning gap between the Church's liturgy and men and women, whether they be in city streets or village lanes.

Where have we gone wrong? Is it that we tried to make the connection with tools that are unable to finish the job? The Church of England's liturgical bequest to the Anglican Communion was the Book of Common Prayer. For many years, up to and including the 1978 Lambeth Conference, this common heritage was assumed to be a boon and an asset. But since then, one by one, the Churches of the Anglican Communion have chosen to go their own way, having realized that along with Gothic buildings and *Hymns Ancient and Modern*, the Book of Common Prayer did not 'speak' to their people or, if it did, it spoke as an uncomfortable reminder of the colonial past. The 1988 Lambeth Conference said:

> The presuppositions of the 1662 Book itself were of a static 'Christendom' England, so that little awareness of mission touches its pages; its requirements of the laity were of largely passive participation; and, for all its ancient beauties, its liturgical structuring has been called heavily into question in Province after Province by scholars, pastors, and worshippers alike. There is inevitable pain for those who for perhaps half a century have found the approach to God through a well-loved pattern of language, and who then find it removed from them almost literally within a single night. But once a general direction of change is set, the transition, however painful, is better undertaken than evaded.[11]

The societies in which these Churches have now long been set are far removed from the seventeenth-century paternalistic, stratified, hierarchical régimes which the Prayer Book took for granted. Only at a few points is that Prayer Book still able to provide items for inclusion in a liturgical vocabulary that is able to sustain the devotions of members of the Anglican Communion outside the British Isles. The need to reflect the society in which a Church is set is well stated in the Introduction to the Canadian *Book of Alternative Services*:

> The gospel is truly perennial: unchanging but ever new in its confrontation and transfiguration of the world. Liturgy is the means by which the Church is constantly invested in that gospel, in the reading of the scriptures, in proclamation, in praise, in prayer of deep concern, and in those sign-acts which wordlessly incorporate the believer in the Word. Liturgy is not the gospel but it is a principal process by which the Church and the gospel are brought together for the sake of the life of the world. It is consequently vital that its form wear the idiom, the cadence, the world-view, the imagery of the people who are engaged in that process in every generation.[12]

If this is true of Canada, Australia, the United States and so on, it is also demonstrably true for England, as both the Urban and Rural Church Reports have now revealed. The Book of Common Prayer is by no means the devotional *lingua franca* of the nation and any attempt to make it so would be futile and silly. To say that is not for one minute to deny to those churchpeople who wish to continue to use it their right to do so, or to call into question the spiritual benefits which they derive from its use.

The lack of a practical liturgical vocabulary is most clearly revealed when arranging the details surrounding pastoral offices. Then it becomes obvious that there is pitifully little knowledge of any liturgical material with the exception of a very narrow selection of hymns. This selection is thought to be equally applicable for all church occasions, without any discrimination.

Further evidence of this sort of liturgical ignorance is currently available in the choices made for suggested inclusion in one particular liturgical growth area in Britain — the memorial service. Although such services do occasionally occur in other parts of the world, it is mainly a British phenomenon.[13] In Britain it is increasingly requested that the funeral service should be a private affair for the family only and 'A memorial service at a date to be announced' is promised. For these services there is no officially devised order of service in England.

At first, such services seemed to be the preserve of 'the great and the good' and were only held in certain 'prestigious' churches, but the court pages of the newspapers now daily contain a batch of announcements of memorial services which are to be held in a whole variety of churches across the land.

It must be admitted that such services would not be a feature of life in an Urban Priority Area parish, but rather do they reflect the aspirations of those who have 'something of this world's goods'.

This latter fact might be thought by some therefore to presuppose the possession of something of that liturgical vocabulary which we have said is not always the stock-in-trade of some parts of society. Unfortunately this is not the case. The request is made for the inclusion of those same hymns that might serve for a wedding or a baptism; and it also becomes obvious that the knowledge of scripture does not go far beyond 'Let us now praise famous men' or 'If I speak with the voice of men or of angels', although 'a reading from the works of Canon Scott Holland', as the newspapers describe it, is almost always preferred to either. This passage, which is passed on from service to service, and has been described by a slightly irreverent American as 'I'm not dead, I'm just on hold', is torn from its context.[14] It started life as a sermon by a Canon of St Paul's who held firm Christian Socialist views, a fact which would shock many of those being memorialized — if they are, indeed, 'on hold'.

From time to time the Church of England has made attempts to interpret liturgically events which were not contained within its own Church calendar. A number of them had political overtones, the Gunpowder Plot for instance, while others were connected with the Royal

Family (e.g. the Royal Accession and the Restoration of the Monarchy). These were intended to forge links between Church and State and also, presumably, the general populace. They fell out of use in 1859.[15] Other parts of the Anglican Communion have not generally attempted to initiate services, although the Church in Australia did issue *A Book of Occasional Services* in 1944, published under the authority of its General Synod, which included *inter alia* services to commemorate the formation of the Commonwealth, Anzac Day and a form for services 'for centenaries of religious and national history and the remembrance of great personalities'. These services were not continued in *An Australian Prayer Book* of 1978.

An exception to this rule might be said to be Independence Day and Thanksgiving Day in the United States. For these day propers are provided, but not a form of service.[16]

If the provision of liturgies for secular occasions is not to be the way to associate the liturgy with the lives of the generality of the population, perhaps the pastoral offices can do this. All Anglican liturgical revisions of the past twenty years have attempted to make the pastoral offices accessible to those who participate in them without sacrificing their fidelity to Christian truth or the traditions of the Church. By language, sign and symbol they have attempted to give a Christian dimension to the occasions of human happiness and sadness. In many parts of the Anglican Communion there has also been a discernable attempt to domesticize some liturgical actions. One such ceremony is strictly domestic by definition — the Blessing of a Home. *A New Zealand Prayer Book* prefaces its service by saying:

> It is in the home that the first experience of love occurs; it is there that love is nurtured and grows to maturity. The Christian home is also the ground for much of people's spiritual growth.

> The ministry of Jesus occurs in many different homes. Therefore to hallow the home as an environment for nurture and renewal, is a deeply felt need by many Christian households.

> The blessing of a home encourages Christians to dedicate their life at home to God and to others.[17]

The Book of Alternative Services of the Anglican Church of Canada contains a section of over a dozen pages entitled 'Home Prayers'. The introduction admits that it is impossible to offer just one form of prayer which will meet all needs, 'indeed it is not desirable to do so, for each community is shaped by God in a unique way'. The basic form is that of the Divine Office, but it is capable of much adaptation. There are also a number of useful suggestions for ways in which the Church's seasons can be marked at Home Prayers; by an Advent wreath, for instance, or by the table being decorated with the symbols of the saint being commemorated on a particular day. The focal point for these Home Prayers is a lighted candle and the content of a Preparation (which may be used as a separate devotion) contains elements of the *Lucernarium* which is also a feature of the Evening Prayer contained in the same Canadian book.[18] Thus a link is made between church and home and the liturgical vocabulary used within the church building is shown to have a wider application.

A New Zealand Prayer Book, in the service for the Blessing of a Home already noted, has a section entitled 'The Family Liturgy' which can be used apart from the Home Blessing. Once again candles are a feature, but the form is not this time that of an office. A very simple 'office' form is to be found among the Liturgies of the Word in that book entitled 'Family Prayer'. This does not however contain the *Lucernarium*.

These must be viewed as ideal situations where there is regular prayer in the home. However undoubtably right and proper it is to provide such material in any revised book of services, it will not be in this way that the liturgical vocabulary of large numbers of people will be added to. We are still very much within the Church family. In fact, there is probably no guaranteed method of doing this, apart from a slow process of taking the opportunity, whenever possible, of putting suitable material on public show.

Although it may now be one of that pitifully short list of well-known hymns that has already been criticized, the paraphrase on Psalm 23 known as 'Crimond' is an interesting textbook example of how something which was previously only known by a group of churchgoers has found a place among everyone's best-known hymns. It was chosen by HM The Queen for her wedding in Westminster Abbey in 1947, but it was not suggested by the Abbey authorities. It arose out of the fact that the Queen had been taught it by her lady-in-waiting, Lady Margaret Egerton, who in turn had been taught it by the minister of her local Kirk in Scotland.[19] By this complicated process this Scottish paraphrase came into prominence.[20]

This example highlights the responsibility that rests upon all those who plan national and other liturgical occasions which attract media attention. Equally, those responsible for diocesan or local occasions must see to it that what is 'on offer' is carefully chosen in order to demonstrate what is the best and the most appropriate. The wise householder brings out the old and well-tried but there is an equally important place for the new and the unfamiliar. Modern society has not a natural aptitude for Christian liturgy. It needs to be provided with one by a sympathetic and sensitive Church. The problem is that what the Church most easily produces is material which is primarily for its own 'internal' purposes. *The Alternative Service Book 1980*, and its equivalents throughout the Anglican Communion, are by definition 'Church' books, they have been designed to fulfil the needs of already worshipping Christians. George Guiver CR has pleaded for a determination to produce a 'kit of activities, understandings and rigmaroles in which our profoundest selves can be brought to birth'. But it all sounds like a 'kit' which will only stimulate the already committed. It seems to start from where churchpeople already are:

> Part of the task is not to create a new vocabulary of activities, but to make more of all that we already have, by taking more seriously the liturgy of the Church, and its outward paraphernalia and customs and traditions. All we need to do is treat things more carefully, rediscover the traditional ways in which they have been understood, and generally accord to what we already do in liturgy and prayer a greater importance. Prayer can be informal and still transcendent. Worship can be relaxed and have a family atmosphere and still be mysterious and have a profound sense of history. In a sense we need to stay with what we have, but discover its hinterland.[21]

The only set of liturgical texts which has taken seriously the needs of those outside the Church, and the subsequent need to provide them with, in Guiver's phrase, a liturgical 'kit', a liturgical vocabulary, has been the report of the (English) General Synod's Liturgical Commission which is entitled *Patterns for Worship*. Originally commissioned in response to the criticisms made in *Faith in the City* about the inadequate provisions made for Urban Priority Areas in that 'closely printed book of over a thousand pages', it has taken seriously the width of the gap of worship experience which exists between those *within* the Church and those who are *outside*. This has long been obvious and the Family Service was introduced in many places to help solve some of the problems that the success of the Parish Communion movement created. *Faith in the Countryside* quotes the result of the Rural Church Project which discovered that Communion services formed well over half of the total services held in the rural benefices surveyed:

> This is not surprising for it is precisely suited to the small band of the faithful needing to affirm the validity of their call to be God's people in that place. By comparison all other services have come to seem second class to many. The disadvantage is that the so-called 'parish communion' is the exact opposite: it excludes half the parish. And this exclusion is often deeply felt by adults who are not confirmed (and even by unconfirmed children).[22]

If this is true in the countryside, it is certainly equally true in an urban context.

It is this problem that Family Services have been attempting to solve. *Patterns for Worship* believed that the phrase 'Family Service' creates further problems:

> We do not think the title 'Family Service' should be adopted formally by the Church of England, and we look for a more

satisfactory alternative to emerge. The 'pilgrim church' model provides some exciting educational (and processional') possibilities, but we doubt whether 'Pilgrim Service' would convey the required image.[23]

Faith in the Countryside recommends what it believes is a less exclusive title, 'Parish Worship'. Whatever name you give to these services, they are an attempt to produce a more widely available and acceptable liturgical context for the worshipping participation of a larger cross-section of society.

Liturgy, at least Christian liturgy, rather than the rituals of modern society, has to win its place in that society, without ever cheapening and distorting its message or debasing the coinage. The Church must seek to design liturgical material which could be a means of enunciating the aspirations and hopes of the average person, but which is within a recognizably Christian context and is in clear continuity with the history and traditions of the Church. This is no easy task and is not one to which liturgical revision has as yet put its mind. We have been preoccupied with getting our own 'internal' liturgies right and have not too often looked outside the confines of our Churches. It may be that we have much to learn from the world outside. For that world is also God's.

Notes

1 *The Army and Religion, An Enquiry and its Bearing upon the Religious Life of the Nation* (London: Macmillan, 1919), pp. 121–2.
2 J. G. Lockhart, *Cosmo Gordon Lang* (London: Hodder and Stoughton, 1949), p. 155.
3 Report of a private enquiry made from Chaplains in connection with the National Mission, *The Army and Religion*, op. cit., p. 448.
4 *Towards the Conversion of England* (London: Press and Publications Board of the Church Assembly, 1945), p. vi.
5 Ibid., para. 319, pp. 140–1.
6 *Faith in the City. A Call to Action by Church and Nation. Report of the Archbishop of Canterbury's Commission on Urban Priority Areas* (London: Church House Publishing, 1985), 3.39, pp. 66–7.
7 *Faith in the Countryside. A Report of the Archbishops' Commission on Rural Areas (ACORA)* (Worthing, West Sussex: Churchman Publishing, 1990), p. 128.
8 Richard G. Jones in *Hymns Ancient and Modern New Standard* (Norwich: Hymns Ancient and Modern, 1983), no. 366.
9 Jeremy Taylor (1613–67), *Twenty-eight Sermons*, quoted in Richard van de Weyer and Pat Saunders (eds), *The Creator Spirit* (London: Darton, Longman and Todd, 1990), p. 194.
10 ACORA, op. cit., p. 182.
11 *The Truth Shall Make You Free, The Lambeth Conference 1988. The*

Reports, Resolutions and Pastoral Letters from the Bishops (London: Church House Publishing), para. 185, p. 68.

12 *The Book of Alternative Services of the Anglican Church of Canada* (Toronto: Anglican Book Centre, 1983), p. 10.

13 *A New Zealand Prayer Book. He Karakia Mihinare o Aotearoa* (Auckland: Collins, 1989), p. 869. *An Anglican Prayer Book 1989* (London: Collins, 1989), pp. 553–7, contains material for a memorial service.

14 Henry Scott Holland, 'The King of Terrors' in Christopher Cheshire (ed.), *Facts of the Faith* (London: Longmans, Green, 1919), pp. 125ff.

15 Frank Streatfeild, *The State Prayers and Other Variations in the Book of Common Prayer* (London: A.R. Mowbray, 1950), p. 34.

16 *New Zealand Prayer Book*, op. cit., lists national days of remembrance (p. 13) but has also included mention of the possibility of diocesan, tribal, local or other commemorations (p. 11). Liturgical material is not provided for any of these days.

17 Ibid., p. 762.

18 *Lucernarium* is also a feature of *The Book of Common Prayer According to the use of the Episcopal Church (USA)* (New York: Church Hymnal Corporation, 1977), pp. 108ff. See also Marian J. Hatchett, *Commentary on the American Prayer Book* (New York: The Seabury Press, 1980), pp. 134–5.

19 John Colville, *The Fringes of Power. Downing Street Diaries 1939–1955* (London: Hodder and Stoughton, 1985), pp. 619–20.

20 Another example, this time of organ music, is the popularity of the Toccata in F from C.-M. Widor's 5th Symphony, which was generally unknown except within the circle of organ aficionados until the wedding of HRH Princess Alexandra of Kent and the Hon. Angus Ogilvy in 1963.

21 George Guiver CR, *Faith in Momentum* (London: SPCK, 1990), p. 25.

22 ACORA, op. cit., para. 9.26, p. 189.

23 *Patterns for Worship. A Report by the Liturgical Commission of the General Synod of the Church of England* (GS 898; London: Church House Publishing, 1989), p. 4.

13

Whose culture and why?

George Mathew

The aim of this essay is to investigate the worship of the Churches which are part of the Anglican Communion, and to examine how far this is suitable for the life and mission of the Churches in their respective contexts. This observation is limited to the Church of North India (CNI), the Church of South India (CSI) and the Church of Sri Lanka. The need for inculturation of liturgy and worship is also discussed. A survey of the inculturation experiments taking place within these Churches is undertaken, and some practical guidelines for inculturation are suggested towards the end of this discussion. These are mainly based on my experiences and observation of these Churches, as a priest of the Mar Thoma Syrian Church, which is in communion with them and at the same time not part of the Anglican Communion.

A brief history of the Anglican Church in India

With the establishment of trading stations in India, the East India Company appointed resident chaplains there. Later in the eighteenth century the SPCK employed Lutheran missionaries in South India. But it was the East India Act of 1813 which led to the establishment of the Anglican see of Calcutta, and, later on, the sees of Madras, Bombay, and Colombo. The Act of 1813 opened India to missionary societies.[1]

The Church Missionary Society (CMS) began its work in 1814, and SPG took over the SPCK mission in 1825. The Church of England Zenana Missionary Society began its work in several parts of India. More people were converted to Christianity, especially from the lower-caste people known as untouchables. The Book of Common Prayer was the unifying factor of these new Churches as Anglican.

In 1947 India became independent from the colonial rule of Britain. The younger Churches were left with the Book of Common Prayer as their only liturgy. During the same year four Protestant Churches in South India, including the Anglican, united as the Church of South India. But again the liturgy of the new Church was predominantly Western or Anglican rather than indigenous. Similarly, different Protestant Churches and the Anglican Church united and formed the Church of North India in 1970. Their liturgy was also mainly Western or very similar to the Anglican liturgy. So the post-colonial Western Churches in India inherited the liturgy and ethos of worship of their colonial fathers. Here we have to answer the question whether it is a suitable pattern or model in the Indian context. Is there any need for indigenization and local adaptation of worship at all?

In the introduction to 'the inculturation statement' of the Third International Anglican Liturgical Consultation (1989) held in York, it is stated that 'liturgy to serve the contemporary church should be truly inculturated'.[2] The Consultation further reaffirmed two of the Lambeth Resolutions (1988), i.e. 22, 'Christ and culture', and 47, 'Liturgical freedom':[3]

> This Conference (a) recognises that culture is the context in which people find their identity; (b) affirms that ... the gospel judges every culture ... challenging some aspect of the culture while endorsing others for the benefit of the church and society; (c) urges the church everywhere to work at expressing the unchanging gospel of Christ in words, actions, names, customs, liturgies which communicate relevantly in each society.

> This Conference resolves that each Province should be free subject to essential Anglican norms of worship, and a valuing of traditional materials, to seek that expression of worship which is appropriate to Christian people in their cultural context.

The Prayer Book tradition which determined the norm of the Anglican Communion is largely shaped by British and European ideas and culture. In following this culture, the Churches in non-European countries had to live in two cultures; first the culture of their religion and second that of their own society.[4] In the early stages of missionary expansion the success of the missionary task depended upon how far they were Westernized.[5]

The areas where inculturation is necessary

The York Consultation pointed out areas in general where inculturation is needed. Some of these are relevant in the Indian context. So let us examine these areas.

The language and idioms of worship should be vernacular. It need not be mere translation of the English liturgy, but indigenous thinking and style of expression should be used.

Vestments of both clergy and choir need not be copied from the West. In Indian worship, vestments which are simple and more suitable to the hot climate can be used. This will create closeness to Indian culture.

Regarding church music, is it necessary to follow the four-part singing of the Western Church? Or is it suitable for the Indian Church? India itself has a rich variety of musical heritage, and so more indigenous music needs to be adapted. Even in the time of missionaries there were very good Christian hymn writers like N. V. Tilak, Justus Joseph, K. V. Simon and Mosavalsalom. Their hymns are written in Indian style, very similar to the Hindu *bhajans* (praises). This kind of Christian music will be appreciated by the local people. Now there is a rediscovery of such hymns in the Indian Churches through radio and the circulation of cassette recordings.

In India there are a variety of musical instruments which are traditional and used by all religions. For example, tabala, hand cymbals, harmonium and different types of local drums can be used for worship in church and on other occasions. Now the trend in church is to use more Western musical instruments rather than the local ones.

Using oil lamps was considered as pagan practice by some missionaries. Indian religions have several festivals of lamps. In the Hindu temple different types of lamps are used for worship. Some ancient Churches in South India use oil lamps in church. In some Roman Catholic churches, along with candles they use oil lamps for worship which symbolize 'Jesus Christ the light of the world'. Inculturation in this area makes the worship more meaningful to the local people.

The architecture of the church need not necessarily be Gothic in structure with steeples or towers. It can be constructed by simple local methods. The trend today is for simple constructions rather than Western architecture. Before the arrival of the Portuguese and thereby the Roman Catholics in South India, the structure of the Syrian churches was identical to that of the Hindu temple, with gates and compound walls. For example, the Old Syrian church in Chengannoor, Kerala, was built like a Hindu temple.[6]

The lay-out and the fittings of Indian churches are replicas of Western churches. Before the coming of the missionaries , the ancient churches, like the Hindu temples, had no furniture or pews inside them. The Syrian churches in South India do not provide any furniture even today. (However, the Mar Thoma Church provides pews for the worshippers in almost all its churches, probably due to the influence of Western churches.) People sit on coir mats, plain floor or carpet. Most of the time they stand or prostrate themselves. Sitting during the worship is unusual in the Eastern Churches.

Worshippers began to use footwear inside church only after the advent of missionaries. In the Hindu temple, the mosque and the Syrian churches of India, footwear is kept outside. In the West it is a must because of the cold climate. The practice of entering the church bare-footed is disappearing due to Western influence. Local cultural adaptation is to be continued, otherwise Christianity will be considered as a foreign religion by the majority of the Hindus.

Hindu festivals like Deevali (the festival of light which commemorates the victory of good over evil), the Kerala festival of Onam (this is a harvest festival which symbolizes prosperity, equality and justice) can be reinterpreted to convey Christian messages like 'Jesus Christ, light of the world' and Christ as 'the king who reigns with righteousness and justice', which are the values of the kingdom of God.

Local arts, symbols and paintings can be used as a medium to communicate Christian themes, especially where people cannot read and write. It is also helpful for the Christian education of children. Bishop Azariah of Dornakal, the first native Anglican bishop, for example, used some local symbols like banana buds (which symbolize new life) as a symbol of resurrection in his design for the cathedral.[7] The lotus, which is very popular in the Hindu religion, typifying beauty out of filth, seems a natural metaphor of Christian redemption and is coming into increasing use within the Church.

More participation by the congregation is necessary in the Indian Churches. In some of the Western liturgies the priest does everything and the members sit like spectators. If the congregation have a Hindu background, more involvement of the worshippers is inevitable because they want something different from their Hindu way of worship.

So far we were trying to discover the areas of worship where inculturation is needed. Now let us examine a few specific experiments in inculturation that have taken place recently in the liturgies of CSI, CNI and the Church of Sri Lanka. The experimental liturgies in CSI and CNI are given in an article by Virginia Kennerley in *Studia Liturgica*.[8]

Liturgical experiments

In the Indian Churches the search for a more authentic way of worship goes back to the nineteenth century. But in the Roman Catholic Church, the process of inculturation has gathered momentum since the Second Vatican Council (1962–65). The Catholic Bishops' Conference of India (CBCI) appointed Fr D. S. Amalorpavadass as the head of the National Biblical Catechetical and Liturgical Centre (NBCLC). The Conference accepted 'twelve points' on Indian-style ritual action in liturgy and published a *New Order of the Mass for India* (1974).[9]

The Church of South India

The need 'to be a more Indian Church' has been felt ever since the formation of the CSI in 1947. Even before that, some native Anglican theologians like Bishop Appaswamy and P. Chenchiah attempted to produce an Indian way of worship and theology. After the independence of India, the need for a more indigenous way of expressing Christian faith was felt even more strongly. Yet very little was attempted towards this goal in both CSI and CNI until 1980. Virginia Kennerley writes as follows:

> So the Protestant work in this area is only beginning to emerge. The CSI and CNI experimenters have avoided what they see as the elitism of the NBCLC and adopted only generally accepted Hindu and indigenous imagery and ritual, along with expressions of the folk culture of the villages and of other locally prominent traditions.[10]

Under the chairmanship of Dr Eric Lott, an Englishman on the faculty of the United Theological College, Bangalore, with his colleagues like Dr Christopher Duraisingh and R.S. Prabhakar, a eucharistic liturgy has been published and accepted officially by the CSI Synod for occasional use.

The CSI Indian Liturgy for celebrating the Eucharist was published in 1986 along with seven other experimental liturgies, and accepted with certain modifications as an alternative by the CSI Synod. The rite is divided into five parts: Entrance into the presence of God; Awakening to the Word of God; Recalling and Offering (including prayers of the Church, offertory and institution narrative); Sharing; and Commissioning. In this liturgy specific Indian motifs include: the chant of *Saranam* (song of refuge sought in God under various attributes) both at the lamp-lighting preceding the confession and as an alternative to the Sanctus: the use of the *Asato* (a prayer from the *Brihadaranyak Upanishad* which begins 'Asato ma sat gamaya', meaning 'Lead me from the unreal to the real') in the Awakening litany preceding the readings; provision for a reading from an Indian scripture on special occasions; the idea of God as 'greater than all names and forms, our inmost self' in the newly drafted affirmation of faith at the close of the liturgy of the Word: the *Namajapa* (the recital of all the names of Christ in an Indian language) while the table is prepared before the institution narrative; the prayer for *Darshana* (awareness of Christ's presence), before the sharing of the bread and wine.

Except for the *Asato* and *Saranam*, there are no references to Vedic tradition and no Sanskrit words. The themes of liberation from oppression and the Church's responsibility for social action are more emphasized. The themes run through the bread prayer which follows the institution narrative and continue in the closing prayer before blessing.

The CNI's proposed Indian Contextual Liturgy

The CNI's proposed Indian Contextual Liturgy follows the CSI Liturgy with variations at certain points. The draft was drawn up in 1986 by Rev James Massey, Secretary of the CNI Liturgical Commission. This has been used experimentally in 'schools of worship' for various areas of the CNI. So far no decision has been made on this experimental liturgy.

This liturgy uses the same affirmation of faith and also offers the Apostles' Creed as alternative. It omits the offertory responsory but continues with an almost identical offertory prayer, *Saranam*, and the simple *Namajapa* of 'Jesu Om': a chant which in classic Indian style fades away into silence as the name is interiorized by the worshipper. For the closing prayer, the triumphal words of the seventh-century Hindu poet from South India, the Savite Appar, are introduced. The text ends with the grace pronounced by the presbyter and no further blessing or commission.

Though the CSI and CNI experimental liturgies consider the 'twelve points' of the NBCLC text, they deviate from the Sanskritic tradition of Vedas to the more spontaneous *bhakti* (devotion) stream of Indian spirituality with an emphasis on the local folk-culture. Some current issues, like the oppressed, the sick and the unemployed, are also included in the liturgy.

The Holy Eucharist or Lord's Supper — A Liturgy for Sri Lanka (1988)

In 1988, an experimental liturgy for Sri Lanka was authorized and published by the two bishops of Colombo and Kurunegala to use along with the BCP of 1662 and the Ceylon Liturgy (1938).[11]

In the Liturgy of Sri Lanka, various adaptations and more flexibility have been introduced. Some Buddhist ideas and terms are used in the liturgy (Sri Lanka is a country where the majority of the people are Buddhists). A brief analysis of this liturgy will show the inculturation process that has taken place.

During the Preparation, after the psalm/hymn in the rubric it is given:

1. All may stand at the beginning of the service, and the clergy and people may exchange greetings in a suitable manner such as the traditional *ayubovan/namoskaran* with palms together and/or a salutation.[12]

In the invocation the posture of hands and the words are adapted from the local religion and culture. The rubric is as follows:

3. The following invocation or other suitable chant or prayer such as the Prayer for Purity may be used. Repeat line by line by priest or leader with palms joined together:

    We worship you Creator, We worship you Liberator, We worship you Sanctifier, We worship you O Trinity, . . . Now taking refuge in Him completely . . .[13]

The invocation 'Now taking refuge in Him completely' is identical to the 'threefold refuge' chant (I take refuge in the name of Buddha, I take refuge in thy law of good, I take refuge in thy order: *Buddham saranam, Dharmam saranam, Sangom saranam*) in Buddhism. Probably this is an adaptation from the local religion.

The intercession is known as the Prayer for the People. Some new and more relevant prayers are included in the intercession.

14. For the peace that is from above and liberation of all people everywhere let us pray to the Lord.
For all industry and agriculture, that we may be spared from scarcity, famine and disaster, and we may use the fruit of the earth and of labour to your glory and for the good of all mankind, let us . . .
For the poor, the exploited, the oppressed, the hungry, orphans and widows and them that suffer persecution, let us . . .[14]

During the offertory there is an optional song. The rubric says 'Offering of the bread and wine. Alms and other offering may be presented.'

Before the Communion, the rubric is given which says: 'Prostrate or kneel.'

After the Communion and the thanksgiving prayer, before the dismissal, the following canticle is said/sung by all:

I take my refuge in you the Father accepting you as God
I take my refuge in you Son accepting you as Lord
I take my refuge in you blest Spirit accepting you as Lord
I take my refuge in you Three acknowledging you one God

I look for refuge in your holy Church
I look for refuge in your own precepts and laws
I look for refuge in your noble word
I look for refuge in this your brotherhood.[15]

Here also one can see the parallelism with the Buddhist chanting of the 'threefold refuge' or *saranam* and the eight-times refuge symbolizing 'the eightfold paths' (*Ashtanga Marga*) of Buddhism.

The Church of Sri Lanka is trying to do more experiments in liturgy and worship and thereby make them more indigenous and relevant to that particular society. For example, on International Labour Day they conducted an ecumenical service bringing all the labourers together. The vestments of the bishops and clergy bore the trade union symbols of hammer and sickle. There was also a service of dedication of tools and implements. Hindus have a similar practice during a festival. Through these practices the Church tries to identify with working-class people and inculturate its worship.

Some suggestions for inculturation of liturgy and worship

A liturgy to be relevant or contextual to a particular society and culture needs to reflect the spiritual and social issues of that society. Each society varies from others in the problems and challenges it is facing. Here I would like to point out some areas, untouched by the liturgists, which need our attention in the process of inculturation.

In India large sections of the population are still under oppression and exploitation by the dominant caste or class. In certain areas a feudal system is still in existence. The liturgy of the Church should reflect the pain and suffering of its people. More prayers with the theme of liberation and justice should be introduced. Some progress has been made in this area recently in the liturgies of CSI, CNI and the Church of Sri Lanka. The liturgy should further emphasize God's bias to the poor, liberation and justice for both the oppressed and the oppressor.

Another area to which Indian liturgy should give attention is the fight against fatalism, the belief that one's present state of life is the result of deeds in a past life; therefore one cannot get rid of one's present state, which is believed to be one's fate. This idea is derived from Hindu philosophy, and can lead a person to apathy and passivity in life. Poverty is often seen as a hallowed state. This view of human life is very strong in Indian society, even among Christians. The Christian message of hope and life-giving power of resurrection must be stressed as against this belief.

Western values such as individualism, consumerism etc. should not dominate in the Indian liturgy. More importance is to be given to ideas of simple and community life. The dignity of human beings as created in the 'image of God' and co-workers with God is to be emphasized. This emphasis is lacking in the present Indian liturgies.

Unlike in the West, the value and merit of the joint family system need to be given due importance. For example marriage is not merely a contract between the man and wife, but it is a bond of relation between two families, taking place in the context of the Church, the body of believers. Now the Western influence on the family is too high in India, especially in the cities. But cultural adaptation of wedding songs, dress, tying of *mangalsoothra* or *thali*, garlanding etc. is already included in the rites of matrimony: this will make the Church Indian rather than Western in its outlook.

Through the liturgy the believers need to be challenged to take this life seriously. Faith and worship should be a reality of life in this world and in the immediate context. Salvation is not something to be experienced only in life after death, as seems taught by some branches of the Western Church. Of course the consummation of it is only at the *parousia* (coming) of Christ.

The Hindu concept of *nishkama karma* (the deed without expecting any reward) can be reinterpreted and linked to the Christian understanding of *agapē* or the self-giving love. This will help to reveal the depth of Christian love in a more meaningful way to Indian Christians and Hindus alike.

Worship should not be confined to the time and space of the church. Informal and spontaneous gatherings should be arranged for singing, music and different ways of expression of faith. For Hindus there are rites and ceremonies from birth to death. They are very much involved in religion. When they become Christians, they should not be allowed to be passive or inactive. More meaningful ways of expressing faith should be provided.

The classical Indian idea of *bhakti* (devotion) should be encouraged in worship, which will make the faith personal as well as spontaneous.

Inculturation is necessary in ministerial training too. At present the training programme is a mere copy of the West. Most of such training is irrelevant to the challenges of India. Theological books are mainly Western and as a result, theological thinking and interpretation reflect Western influence. Ministers are more attracted to the Western way of life. In such situations inculturation is rather difficult. More and more theologians and liturgists should come forward from within the Indian Church for the adaptation of relevant liturgy.

The theology and doctrines of the Eastern Churches are not codified like the Thirty-nine Articles or the Westminster Confession, but they are inherent in the liturgy of the Church. Similarly the doctrines of the Indian Church should be reflected in its liturgy. The liturgy should also be used as a vehicle of Christian education of believers.

The search for more indigenous liturgy should be made in the ancient liturgies of the East. The Eastern liturgies have already influenced the Churches in the Anglican Communion in India. For example the Trisagion, and the kiss of peace by holding the palms against one another etc. are adapted from the Syrian rite. In Korea the kiss of peace is in their traditional manner: each person bows to whoever stands near him.[16] Practices like this which are suitable to Indian culture need to be experimented with.

A detachment from the religious culture of the colonial past and a move to an inculturated church life is inevitable for the Indian Church. Indian spirituality always challenges us towards a simple way of life. A highly Westernized Church will alienate Christians from the mainstream of Indian society. Even after four decades of independence from the colonial régime, Christianity is still considered as a foreign religion in India, except in the south. Such an image will affect the life and witness of the Church. The ashram movement (people living as a community with vows of poverty, chastity and obedience and sharing everything in common) founded by certain pioneers in the early part of this century, paved the way for integration as well as evangelization in various parts of India. Eastern monasteries were the centres of liturgical treasures and theological treatises in the early centuries. In the same way ashrams can contribute towards the noble life through a simple life-style and without compromising with the pressures of modern society.

This suggestion for inculturation can be summarized in the words of J. W. Grant. In his article 'Indian ways of worship', he writes:

> A worship that remains set in the European pattern is evidence of a faith that has not yet quite come to grips with its Indian task. On the other hand, worship conforming to the pattern of Hinduism would

betray a religion that had lost its hold on the distinctive faith of the Church. A worship at once Christian and Indian, would be evidence that the gospel had become firmly rooted without losing its integrity and its universality.[17]

Precautions

The use of indigenous sacred literature and theological concepts in the liturgy of the Church should be approached with proper caution. The inculturation process must be judged by its motives: does the use of the scriptures and theological concepts of other religions help the mission of the Church? Indiscriminate borrowing of Hindu practices and concepts leads to syncretism and risking the unique position of Christian faith. The majority of the exponents of inculturation say that the aim behind it is not conversion of people to Christianity but to keep 'good relations and real communication with fellow-Indians'.[18] If that is the purpose, such Christian worship will remain only a duplication of Hindu worship. The task of Indian liturgists is not to provide a variety of worship patterns for Hindus but to challenge them to accept Christ. The Hindus would not find it difficult to accept Christ as one among many *avatars* (incarnations) or as *ishtadevan* (personal deity). Here the Christian message is at risk. So if inculturation leads to syncretism, such attempts should be discouraged. Today the trend is that some of the Hindu concepts and practices are adapted into the liturgy without proper reinterpretation. This will lead to confusion and chaos not only for Hindus but also for Christians.

Another sociological factor which needs our attention is that the use of Hindu scriptures and practices is a challenge to the Christians who have converted from a low-caste Hindu background. By embracing Christian faith, they gained social mobility from their low position on the social ladder. Through such inculturation they may be asked to accept the practices they once abandoned. There is a psychological barrier for them against accepting such practices.

Many of the theologians and liturgists who introduced the experimental liturgy are either Westerners or Western-trained. They do not necessarily know all the needs of the Indian Church. Of course there are quite a few local liturgists who propagate inculturation. Most of these experiments are taking place in ashrams, seminaries and such small communities, and not in a real parish setting. So they do not always reflect the genuine religious experience and feelings of the people. Through inculturation some theologians accept the view that Christianity is the answer to and continuation of the expectation of the Hindu scriptures. That this is acceptable to the Church Universal is doubtful and needs further study.

Conclusion

The inculturation process should not alienate Christian worshippers by becoming too extreme. Christian theology must always be made clear. Even the same terminology can mean a different thing in each religious context. For example, the Hindu concept of *moksha* (salvation) is different from the Christian doctrine. Salvation according to Hinduism is the liberation of the individual soul from the cycle of birth and death and merging with the supreme soul *Brahma*, whereas in Christianity salvation is redemption from sin, achieved through the death and resurrection of Christ, and experiencing eternal life with him. But in both religions the same term is used in India.

All inculturation attempts must be measured by certain criteria such as the Lambeth Quadrilateral (1888), the Lambeth Conference Resolutions, etc. They should provide the basic framework for inculturation. Based on these principles, there can be a plurality of rites within the Anglican Communion. There is no need to think of a single liturgy like BCP or ASB as the only authentic expression of unity of the worldwide Anglican Communion. In India, for example, the Roman Catholic Church has three rites (the Syro-Malabar, the Syro-Malankara, the Latin rite) which vary considerably and yet are in communion with Rome. Such kinds of liturgical flexibility and diversity should be allowed in the Anglican Communion.

In short we can say that the liturgy of the worldwide Anglican Communion need not be the Western or European model. It can be adapted, amended and revised whenever and wherever necessary. There is no single liturgical model.

Any attempt at inculturation must come from within the Church and not outside. If it evolves from the grass-roots level, that will be more genuine and acceptable. To achieve this purpose, further learning and research is essential. Inculturation should be ethno-centric and mission-oriented. It should challenge people to accept Christ and bring them closer to God.

With an extract from the Inculturation Statement of the Third International Anglican Liturgical Consultation, this discussion on inculturation can be concluded:

> Inculturation must therefore affect the whole ethos of corporate worship . . . True inculturation implies a willingness in worship to listen to culture, to incorporate what is good and to challenge what is alien to the truth of God. It has to make contact with the deep feelings of people. It can only be achieved through an openness to innovation and experimentation, an encouragement of local creativity, and a readiness to reflect critically at each stage of the process — a process in principle never ending. The liturgy rightly constructed, forms the people of God, enabling and equipping them for their mission of evangelism and social justice in their culture and society.[19]

Notes

1 Colin Buchanan (ed.), *Modern Anglican Liturgies 1958–1968* (Oxford: Oxford University Press, 1968), p. 261.
2 David Holeton (ed.), *Findings of the Third International Anglican Liturgical Consultation* (Bramcote: Grove, 1989), p. 3.
3 Ibid.
4 Elisha Mbonigaba, 'Indigenisation of liturgy' in T. J. Talley (ed.), *A Kingdom of Priests: Liturgical Formation of the People of God* (Alcuin/GROW Liturgical Study 5; Bramcote: Grove, 1988), p. 4.
5 Ibid.
6 L. W. Brown, *The Indian Christians of St Thomas* (Cambridge: Cambridge University Press, 1982), pp. 213–14.
7 John W. Grant, *God's People in India* (London: 1959), p. 58.
8 K. Virginia Kennerley, 'The use of indigenous sacred literature and theological concepts in Christian eucharistic liturgy in India', *Studia Liturgica* 19 (1989), pp. 143–61.
9 *New Orders of Mass for India* (Bangalore: NBCLC, 1974). For a critique from an Anglican theologian and liturgist, see Bryan D. Spinks, 'The anaphora for India: some theological objections to an attempt at inculturation', *Ephemerides Liturgicae* 95 (1981), pp. 531–49.
10 Kennerley, art. cit., p. 147.
11 *The Holy Eucharist or Lord's Supper — A Liturgy for Sri Lanka* (1988), p. 1.
12 Ibid.
13 Ibid., pp. 2–3.
14 Ibid., pp. 7–8.
15 Ibid., pp. 14–15.
16 Colin Buchanan (ed.), *Further Anglican Liturgies 1968–1975* (Bramcote: Grove, 1975), p. 307.
17 John W. Grant, op. cit., pp. 56–7.
18 Kennerley, art. cit., p. 157.
19 David Holeton, op. cit., p. 4.

14

An African perspective

Dinis Sengulane

Preamble

Africa is a vast continent with a wealth of cultures and values. Anglicanism is also very vast, and growing fast. At the present time, there are no fewer than ten Anglican Provinces, and some of these countries are joined to another Province outside Africa; for example, Egypt, Ethiopia and others take part in the life of the Jerusalem and Middle East Jurisdiction. For these and other reasons, any generalization when talking about a so-called 'African perspective' would fall short of the truth. What we are going to try and do here is to give one person's experience and perception of the Anglican presence in Africa, both in terms of what goes on now and also in terms of what could develop in the future.

Worship creates an opportunity for teaching the Christian faith, for evangelism, pastoral care, healing, stewardship and deepening of the fellowship; indeed, the communal aspect of worship is usually extended afterwards in the context of a meal. One could say that the liturgy is an occasion for the building-up of the Body of Christ, and many of these occasions are unplanned-for.

Further, colour and movement carry a strong message in many aspects of African tradition. To celebrate or mark a special occasion, the use of colour and movement adds something which words cannot adequately convey. For this reason, liturgical colours which are used in so many parts of the Anglican Communion find a welcome home in some African societies.

From time to time, we hear a word of caution coming from some quarters of the continent, warning us that some of the loudest advocates of simplification of the liturgy are not in fact from the continent itself, and these voices even point to the fact that some of the 'specialists' in African language are not African, but have very little actual experience of Africa. Indeed, some of the 'African liturgical dances' being experienced in some Christian communities seem too organized, too unnatural to be called truly African. This is a complaint aired by some people, which needs to be heard.

Liturgical year and seasons

One of the most common answers to the question 'Why do people choose to become Anglican?', where such a choice exists, is 'the liturgy', especially because of its variety and the way that it takes into consideration the situations people find themselves in. Such interest is growing more and more. To give one example, children ask for prayers before their exams and then come to thank God for the (good) results! Sometimes, the Eucharist is even celebrated in a parish at the request of the students or their parents, or at the initiative of the parish priest, in connection with exams.

Looking further into African traditions, it is possible to see that Traditional African Religions have special prayers for certain seasons and occasions. These include initiation rites, seasons relating to agriculture, when there is an epidemic, in connection with rain (drought or flood), when there is infertility of crops, when naming a child. All these — and many other — occasions are brought before the gods. They can also be brought before the One True God Christians worship. When Anglicanism comes with its liturgical richness, which takes into consideration the agricultural year, commerce, and industry in the Rogation season, this makes good sense to Africans. To have always the same style of worship and to be rigid in approach produces a liturgy that is remote from people's daily experience, and is little more than meaningless. The liturgical year makes sense to an African mind.

An engaged spirituality

At the end of the Partners in Mission consultation of the Church of the Province of Southern Africa in 1987, there was a strong call for a deeper spirituality which should also be an engaged one. For a Church that was wrestling with the pain of apartheid, our spirituality should not neglect the spiritual dimensions of the sin of apartheid, nor should we allow our spiritual pilgrimage to be an excuse for ignoring the practical, physical realities which affect the lives of so many with whom we have day-to-day dealings.

How, then, do we find such an 'engaged spirituality'?

First, an engaged spirituality means to many Africans that the *ministry of healing* needs to be taken up seriously in our presentation of the liturgy. For many tribes, when people greet one another, they are automatically thrown into considerations of a person's health and the health of those around him. Not to deal with health in worship is to neglect a vital aspect of the lives of so many of our people. Perhaps it is in this context that we see in the liturgical revisions and practices a strong message concerning the ministry of healing. Ministering to the sick in the context of the liturgy has become a normal practice among some African Anglicans, or, at least, the beginning of a process for such a ministry. In a certain African country where Christian worship was severely restricted for a number of years, a certain priest found an excuse for celebrating the Eucharist for the whole village, by ministering to a sick person. A private service of this sort was permitted, so one person volunteered to be considered sick in order that the priest could come into the village and celebrate in his home, and he then invited his neighbours to be with him while the priest carried out the visit. The priest, needless to say, ended up celebrating the Eucharist for about sixty people under the umbrella of such a ministration! During this Eucharist, there was baptism of infants and teaching of the Christian faith, as it was the norm for that particular priest to use the eucharistic celebration as an opportunity for teaching and for deepening Christian understanding and nurture.

There is a lot of work to be done in creating a proper 'natural' understanding of the place of healing in worship, but a lot has been achieved in some areas, so that there is hope for a firm place for this type of ministry in the life of the whole Church. The reading out of the names of those in need of healing does not come naturally to everyone, but personal requests on the spur of the moment by both children and adults are a normal feature of worship in some places. The enriched rites that have come to us in liturgical revisions, the efforts towards restoring a proper understanding of the place of the sacrament of anointing in the life of the Church, and the growing interest in reading the scriptures are all a real blessing in this field of healing. To many of us, such healing ministry includes the need and practice of exorcism. This has to be handled with care, like many other aspects of our faith, but handled it still must be, as always, by pointing to the power and victory of Jesus, as we engage ourselves in the experience of the person who is, or who believes himself to be, demon-possessed.

Secondly, while considering exorcism, it is opportune to highlight the importance of the blessing of homes, and similar places of permanent use or concern to human beings. If the Church does not make a public expression through a visible sign that the Spirit of God is being invited to take over a certain place, some people will ask the witch-doctor to come and ask another kind of spirit to take over. As far as Africans are concerned, Anglicanism got it right when it allowed and encouraged the blessing of houses, boats, schools, fields, factories.

Thirdly, fasting is a religious observance which Africans can and do follow without much difficulty. But how engaged are we when we fast? There are two approaches. One is to say that, like the people of Nineveh (Jonah 3.6ff.), we fast together for one common cause, for example, observance of Lent, or interceding for peace. Another is to maintain that fasting is not about postponing a meal until a later time, but is actually about cancelling it, and using the resources for the glory of God. The time that should be spent eating is used for a devotional purpose, and the money that should have paid for the meal given up is used for the purpose of the fast, or some other cause which a person may choose for the glory of God.

In such ways as these, we engage ourselves in the spiritual observance of fasting.

Children

When one considers children and their participation in the life of the Church, it has to be said that gestures like the Anglican Consultative Council Meeting in Wales (1990) and its 'Letter to our children' serve to demonstrate the pre-eminence that they have in the life of the Church by virtue of what God did for them. The blessing of children is a vivid example of a sacramental gesture which can have such a strong impact that inherited practices and disciplines are called into question, if not reconsidered afresh.

Many children are becoming regular worshippers because their friends told them about Jesus or about the Church, or even about how the priest lays his hands on the heads of young children. What is clear to us is that they become regular worshippers. They may be as young as three to six years of age. Their friends may be baptized because their parents are Christians, but they either have to wait until they are old enough to answer the questions for themselves, or have to find Christian parents. Godparents also have to be much older than the kind of children we have 'doing mission' in our midst. Under these exciting circumstances, are we to maintain the discipline of only receiving children whose 'natural' relatives can ensure that the children will grow up having their faith nurtured? Are we to maintain an age restriction on godparents? Or does our engaged spirituality demand another dimension of engagement by the children themselves in the spirituality of baptism?

If we are to continue to have our little ones engaged spiritually in our Churches, neither the separation of the public liturgy into one part for adults and another part for children, or the division of preaching into one style for adult intellectuals and another for children can remain unchallenged. Africans believe strongly in family life. Anglicans believe that Anglicanism is a family, and that the Church is a family. The worship of the family should be an activity in which all members of that family participate, whether or not there are special parts of the worship in which only some members may participate fully. Anglicans got it right when the divine service of the Church was defined as 'common prayer', for the whole family. But they got it wrong when preaching is regarded as catering only for one group, to the exclusion of the little ones.

Litanies

Litanies are forms of prayer which provide the opportunity for the participation of members of the worshipping community. The litany is thoroughly Anglican, and it is also biblical in its underlying ethos, with its focus on request and response. But it is also very African. Prayers for rain, and concerns for fields and animals, often find expression in litany-type prayers in the Traditional African Religions. These fall badly short of the biblical, Christian ideal, for a number of reasons, including the fact that such prayers can be no more than a series of curses, whereas the Christian litany is addressed to God, and makes its whole body of prayer focus on the divine will, through Christ, and in the power of the Spirit. The 'spirit' of the litany (if one may coin such a phrase) is indubitably strong among Africans, and it is a welcome and easy way of building up an engaged spirituality, through its simplicity and rhythmic directness, where people can participate either by responding to the requests or by adding their own, or both.

Anglicans in Africa got it right when they encouraged new litanies, but they got it wrong when there has been a stiff attitude to this kind of participation, or to other yet more vivid forms of sharing in public forms of intercessions with their short, pungent responses.

Remembering the dead — 'I believe in the communion of saints'

The clearest and most vivid manifestation of belief in the communion of saints which I have come across in my life is to be found in Africa. Revolutionaries, religious and anti-religious people seem to meet from time to time in an act of remembering their departed ones. Whether the Church allows it or not, our people follow these practices, and take them seriously. The methods and styles vary a great deal. There are, understandably, things about these observances which are unacceptable to Christians, just as there are other things which fall into other categories, and can be described as neutral or commendable. My conviction is that belief in a larger family than just the living, a belief in a continued, active existence of the departed, and a belief in man's need of salvation or security or happiness through the shedding of blood, among others, are the pillars which sustain the continuous practices of remembering or commemorating the dead. It is not within the scope of these remarks to explain or explore what is done, but only to raise the issue as one which should be looked at from a liturgical point of view, over and above the doctrinal and pastoral issues which it raises. One may note in passing how prayer for the departed has found varied forms of expression in Anglican prayers in different parts of the world, and an African variation in this regard would seem to be a legitimate and thoroughly Anglican development.

Anglicans got it wrong where they bluntly forbade their members to commemorate departed loved ones, and where they turned a blind eye to those very practices as they persisted. Anglicans declare daily 'I believe in the communion of saints' — aren't these 'saints' the highly-respected members of the family of the faith whose lives have influenced ours in our pilgrimage? Aren't the people Africans commemorate highly-respected members of their family whose lives have influenced theirs? The question needs to be opened, positively.

Anglicans got it right where they have engaged in a dialogue, or at least a study of this matter, and have tried to 'baptize' some of the good and godly things that exist in African commemorations. Anglicans got it right when they faced the reality and told their members where they were erring, and tried to seize these opportunities to proclaim the message of eternal salvation, to teach the faith, and to enrich the liturgical life of the Church.

Conclusion

When liturgy takes into account children, the young, adults, the old, the departed, spiritual beings (whether regarded as angels or demons), rain and environment, national leaders, heaven and hell, houses and fields, colour and movement, gestures and symbols, then it is dealing with what concerns African peoples, as it builds up the worship of God, Father, Son, and Holy Spirit. In this worship, Anglican openness allows room for the realities of people's convictions to gain shape and to be properly expressed, thus enriching our universal way of worshipping God.

From an African perspective, this is what we have in liturgy today. A great deal more exists both to be explored and to be exposed, for liturgy is in the heart of the mission of the church.

15

An outsider's view

John F. Baldovin SJ

In the preface to the first edition of his *History of Anglican Worship* Geoffrey Cuming made the wise observation that reading about liturgies cannot serve as a substitute for reading the liturgies themselves.[1] One needs to add that reading the texts of liturgies is an inadequate substitute for a fuller 'reading' of the liturgies which includes not only the texts but also the action of the liturgy as a whole, including the church environment, the social setting, music, the nature of the worshipping assembly, etc. Reading only texts and rubrics tends to give a one-sided understanding of worship, biased to its purely rational components. What I intend to do in this essay is to give the fuller 'reading' to the extent that my experience of and familiarity with Anglican liturgy allows.

I will begin, then, by describing the extent of my experience with Anglican worship, most especially the limits of that experience. I was introduced to Anglican worship, at age seventeen — just before the reforms of Vatican II were implemented, at Evensong on the Fourth Sunday of Advent at St Thomas Episcopal church in New York City. The physical setting, music and prayers were all of such beauty that I knew this was a place where I could feel at home in pouring out praise to God. Since then I have sought out participation in Anglican services of worship on a fairly frequent basis. There are, however, definite limits to my experience. I have worshipped mainly at what could be called 'High' churches, mainly in urban settings, in the United States, England and in (of all places) Italy. In addition, with the exception of a few weddings, my experience of Anglican worship has been confined to celebrations of the Eucharist and of Morning and Evening Prayer.

I had the good fortune to receive the greater part of my seminary training at a Roman Catholic school which was closely allied both in terms of spirit and facilities (we shared the chapel) with the Episcopal Divinity School in Cambridge, Massachusetts. In fact I was ordained a deacon in the EDS chapel. In Cambridge I also became familiar with the Cowley Fathers (Society of St John the Evangelist), who have a monastery on the Charles River. I once made my annual retreat there and found the setting quite congenial, not least because of the presence of a stained glass window of Ignatius Loyola in Ralph Adams Cram's lovely chapel.

In the course of my graduate studies I encountered two Anglicans who were to influence me considerably: Professor (now Bishop) Jeffery Rowthorn of Yale and Professor Thomas Talley of General Theological Seminary. A significant portion of my studies were given over to Anglican sacramental theology in the nineteenth century, with particular emphasis on the Oxford Movement and the ritualist controversy of the latter part of the century.

Since it is my conviction that worship must be studied in context,[2] I trust that I have established two things here: that I am not unfamiliar with Anglican worship in practice, and that my experience, though rich, is severely limited both geographically and in terms of the style of worship. My task, of course, is to write as an outsider, but it should be understood that I write as a *sympathetic* outsider who has profited considerably from worship with Anglicans both here and abroad. As an outsider I propose to do the following. First, I will discuss liturgy as an action (as opposed to a text). Then I will reflect on the aesthetic aspects of Anglican worship. Finally, and very much consciously from the point of view of a Roman Catholic, I will comment on a selected issue: calendar and lectionary.

I. Liturgy as activity

In an extremely perceptive essay published in 1980, R. T. Scott showed that the most pertinent questions relating to the revision of the Book of Common Prayer in the American Episcopal Church do not relate so much to text as to the need to appreciate liturgy as an activity.[3] Liturgists, as well as theologians in general, tend to focus on what they know best: discourse. But logical and rational discourse has an effect on people only within a setting in which they can commune. That this is not an overly cynical estimate of the limits of human reasoning must be admitted by anyone who has engaged in argument, convinced of the correct reasoning of his or her position and yet unable to reach an interlocutor. No, the conditions for genuine communication in worship — both in terms of God and one another — strike at roots far deeper than rational discourse.

This is not to argue that words are unimportant in worship, for they inevitably conjure up images that shape not only the way we think but also the way we live. Part of the difficulty faced by a change in language, whether from Latin to modern English, as in my own Communion, or from a more traditional Elizabethan English to contemporary idiom, as in many revisions of the Book of Common Prayer, is that a new language implies adoption of a new worldview, which at the same time may be more biblical in its thrust.[4] But even renewed language is bound to be ineffective in a context which contradicts it. As someone once said, there

is considerable lack of consistency in Pope Paul VI attacking trium-
phalism from a throne under the Bernini baldachino in the lavishly
Baroque St Peter's Basilica. The activity, which includes the physical
setting, must match the language if liturgy is to be effective.

At the heart of the question, then, is liturgy as activity — and not only
activity in general, but corporate activity. This is the genius of Scott's
treatment of liturgical revision — the recognition that what is most
essential to Christian worship, namely corporate activity, is that which is
most problematic at least in contemporary 'First World' post-industrial
societies. This is, of course, the theme which undergirds Gregory Dix's
classic book, *The Shape of the Liturgy*.[5] Aidan Kavanagh employs Erving
Goffman's analysis of social relationships to show that worship is an
activity where the many relate to the many (as opposed to one-to-one or
one-to-many relationships). These occasions require a certainly formality and ritual repetition to enable a congregation to cohere as an assembly
rather than a gathering of individuals.[6] But even prior to these ritual
determinants of effective liturgy is a question about the faith that brings
these people together to celebrate. The best way to put this question is:
'What is at stake?' If a liturgical assembly has nothing *in common* at stake
when they come together to worship, I doubt that the liturgy can
effectively form them into the Body of Christ, which I take to be the goal of
worship. My present task is not so much to comment on faith and culture
as it is to shed some light on Anglican liturgy from the outside. It seems,
however, that anyone considering worship as an activity rather than
merely as a text must take the social milieu of the worshipping congregation into consideration. At least on the face of it, I assume that an assembly
of South Africans in Cape Town has much more at stake when it meets to
worship than, for example, one in suburban San Francisco. This does not
mean that there is no hope for liturgy in affluent or urbanized cultures, but
rather that those responsible for worship will probably have a more difficult time establishing what is at stake for assemblies in those cultures. In
short I would be willing to bet that liturgies which occur in societies
experiencing oppression or common need are far more powerful than
those which take place in societies where it does not seem to matter
terribly whether one goes to church or not. The rôle of liturgy in particular
here is to create an atmosphere in which worship conveys a sense of common importance for the assembly. Such atmosphere is created by reverence as well as by powerful preaching and the linking of worship activity
to the needs of the extra-liturgical world.

II. Anglican worship as aesthetic experience

Given the necessarily corporate nature of worship, it is important to look
at what is usually thought most characteristic of Anglican worship (at

least by outsiders), namely its aesthetic quality. I have argued above that liturgy must be understood as a corporate experience that involves whole persons. As the sagacious observer of the liturgical scene, Robert Hovda, once wrote, specifically with regard to liturgical vesture:

> Like so many experiences which rationalist types dismiss as trivial, liturgical vesture has a considerable impact on the feelings of the assembly as a whole as well as on those exercising a particular role of leadership. Anyone who contrary to the most elementary human experience, persists in the stubborn conviction that ideas, points, arguments are the stuff that move human beings, is natively unfit for liturgical leadership, if not for liturgical life.[7]

This is not to dismiss rational thought as a vital aspect of human experience, but rather to emphasize the non-verbal or aesthetic elements that go to make up worship as a powerful experience. Even when it comes to liturgical language, the poetic quality or aesthetic beauty of the words is at least as important as the concepts that are being communicated. Thus, much of the criticism levelled at contemporary revisions of Anglican worship has dealt with aesthetic issues rather than theological ideas. Of course the challenge to proclaim scripture and to pray in language that is both understandable and beautiful is a considerable one. It seems to me (very much from the point of view of an envious outsider) that current revisions of texts for Anglican worship have met that challenge rather well — or at least better than many English-language revisions of Roman Catholic texts have done. I will give only one example — from Eucharistic Prayer C in Rite II of the American *Book of Common Prayer*:

> Deliver us from the presumption of coming to this Table for solace only, and not for strength; for pardon only and not for renewal. Let the grace of this Holy Communion makes us one body, one spirit in Christ, that we may worthily serve the world in his name.

Here language and concepts come together so well that I would not be surprised if after a number of years of use, people who hear this prayer could repeat it from memory. No one would argue that it doesn't take great genius to write memorable English that is at the same time clear and contemporary, but to charge that this cannot be done today (or has not been done with some success in current Anglican revisions), as some have, tends to make Cranmer into rather more an idol than a fine exemplar of liturgical revision.[8]

Attempts to render Christian prayer in a contemporary idiom will also inevitably have to deal with the question of inclusive language. Here the *Alternative Service Book 1980* (for example, in the Collect for Pentecost 8 and the Collect for the Last Sunday after Pentecost) has not attempted to change from generic uses of 'mankind' and 'man' to more inclusive language. I am told that consciousness of the need for inclusive language is not high in Great Britain, but it is difficult to imagine that future revision of the Prayer Book will not have to face this issue, as has been the case in the American Prayer Book of 1979.[9]

Obviously language is not the only concern of liturgical aesthetics. Architectural space, music, decoration, and choreography are all important here. These all go into making up what one might call the typical 'style' of Anglican worship. I will admit that most of my experience of liturgy in Anglican churches has been in the milieu of a Gothic, or better, neo-Gothic style. I do not, however, think that this particular style is inherent to Anglican worship. If that were the case it would be impossible to inculturate Anglican worship in Asia, Africa or Latin America. At the same time there is a certain formality which I think is indispensable for worship of an Anglican cast, and which runs in many contemporary cultural situations directly counter to the current fashion. By formality I mean attention to detail, careful choreography, and a certain lack of 'folksiness'. On this side of the Atlantic most people (innocent of the history of such things) would call this 'High Church'. I am convinced that this formality is a necessary antidote to the desire for informality and intimacy which cannot be successful in the arena of common worship.[10] On the other hand, what I am loosely calling 'High Church' worship cannot be successful if it remains stiff and distant. 'Formal' and 'stiff' are not equivalents. The best example I have known of a very formal liturgy which at the same time was warm and unpretentious took place regularly at Christ Church, the Anglo-Catholic parish in New Haven, Connecticut. The combination of a formal style with engaging preaching and a lack of pretence in ceremonial is the best course for Christian worship bent on acknowledging both the transcendence and nearness of God. It is what I call 'High-Church-with-a-heart' and currently is one of the best gifts of the Anglican Communion to the Church as a whole.

What is at stake here is not so much the preservation of a cultural heritage, let's say sixteenth- or seventeenth-century church music, as attention to quality. That such attentiveness can render worship successful in a very contemporary idiom is evidenced by an Episcopalian parish with which I have some acquaintance — St Gregory Nyssen, San Francisco. There a curious blend of the Prayer Book, chants and troparia in the Eastern Christian mode, and congregational participation go to make up a liturgy that is at once traditional and contemporary. The secret of this particular liturgy's coherence seems to be the success in having the entire congregation participate in stylized movement, which some would call dance. I realize that this combination of liturgical activities must seem rather bizarre as I have described it, but it works. And it works because while very creative (even in terms of the 1979 Prayer Book) there is no attempt to think up something new each week. While the congregation is engaged, it is not pandered to by a misplaced desire to be relevant or up-to-date.

It is the kind of adaptation or inculturation that I have just described that remains true to the Anglican heritage of worship while for going any attempt to import a foreign cultural style into contemporary worship. This is not a style which will 'sell' everywhere, nor should it, for the aesthetic challenge to worship today is to attend to tradition in such a way that it comes alive here and now.

One final comment: the firm impression I have been given by most of the Anglican liturgies I have attended is that we have assembled to worship something (someone) greater than ourselves. This may seem rather obvious if one is to talk of worship at all. My experience of other worshipping assemblies, however, including even at times Roman Catholic congregations, is that we have been so concerned with relevance and the nearness of God that the overall impression is one of a religion (and liturgy) that *we* are constantly making up. Tradition is the vehicle by which social groups are brought into contact with something greater than themselves. It seems to me that those concerned with Anglican worship will neglect a sense of reverence and obedience to the tradition to the peril of the people's faith — and faithfulness. By 'reverence' and 'obedience' I do not mean anything slavish, but rather an attempt to respect the traditional nature of Christian worship while at the same time attending to the assembly's needs here and now. Of course, this is far more easily said than done.

III. A selected issue: calendar and lectionary

Along with the artistic and architectural environment for worship no element is as influential on liturgy as the articulation of time. A calendar provides a whole system of orientation to life. Needless to say this is an extraordinarily important issue for the Churches today and I cannot pretend to deal with it in any depth. The liturgical calendar conflicts and will continue to conflict with all sorts of other articulations of time: national, civic, academic, economic, etc. The church calendar therefore provides a certain counter-cultural understanding of reality. Within this broader framework we will limit ourselves to the specifically liturgical aspects of the calendar.

The calendars of the various Churches within the Anglican Communion respect the fundamental genius of the Christian liturgical year — the observance of Sunday as the Lord's day. The calendars of both the *Alternative Service Book 1980* and the American Prayer Book of 1979 also point to the importance of Easter, Pentecost and Christmas in the articulation of liturgical time. They also make provision for the celebration of lesser saints and festivals, which of course has been a major battle with sabbatarian churches since the late sixteenth century. Both of these calendars exhibit a certain largeness of heart by including holy men and women of other churches, e.g., Francis Xavier, Francis de Sales

(ASB), the Martyrs of Japan and the Martyrs of Uganda (BCP 1979).

On the whole the American Prayer Book follows much more upon the revised Roman calendar of 1969 with its four Sundays of Advent and the omission of the pre-Lenten 'Septuagesima' period of three Sundays. The ASB on the other hand provides nine Sundays before Christmas, although for five of these Sundays the colour green is employed rather than the Advent colour of violet. Here the ASB opted for more consistency with regard to the lectionary with its pre-Christmas eschatological themes as opposed to the more traditional season of four Sundays in preparation for the feast of the Nativity. Using the colour violet for all nine of these Sundays would be more consistent. One should not underestimate the non-verbal impact of colour and decoration in the liturgical environment. I suspect that it speaks louder than the title for any given Sunday.

Somewhat more puzzling is the ASB's provision of nine Sundays before Easter, thus perpetuating the old Septuagesima season in fact if not in name. Once again the colour scheme does not change and green is used for the first three Sundays. The colour changes to violet (or Lenten array) only on Ash Wednesday. It is true that there has been a tendency to extend the Lenten penitential season before Ash Wednesday (or the official beginning of Lent) in both East and West, but there seems no need to do this today.

With regard to the lectionary for the Sunday and feast day Eucharist two different principles are at work in the American Prayer Book and the ASB. The BCP 1979 follows the three-year pattern adopted by the Roman Church in 1969. In content it varies only in a few places from the Roman readings. The virtue of this lectionary arrangement is, of course, the proclamation of a great deal of Scripture over the three years and the ability to preach strategically on one central gospel for each year (Year A: Matthew, B: Mark, C: Luke) with Johannine readings provided for Lent (especially in Year A), Easter and during the post-Pentecost season in Year B (called Sundays of the Year or Ordinary Time in the Roman calendar) when John 6 is read to 'fill in' for the brevity of the Markan Gospel. The weakness of the American calendar, which has been adopted by a large number of churches, is the second reading taken from the non-evangelical New Testament writings, which at least during the post-Epiphany and post-Pentecost seasons follows a method of continuous reading rather than correspondence to the other readings.

The ASB, on the other hand, has opted for a two-year cycle of readings that renders a rather thematic approach.[11] The problem of a second reading, not in accord with the other selections from scripture, is avoided in this lectionary. Only two readings must be used and the preferred reading is marked by an asterisk. There are no doubt benefits to the ASB lectionary system, but one wonders if these advantages are outweighed by being out of step with the majority of Christian Churches which follow a lectionary.

Conclusion

This view from the 'outside' obviously has its advantages and disadvantages. The great disadvantage is the author's lack of breadth and depth in the actual experience of Anglicans at worship. A possible advantage is the opportunity to take a look at Anglican worship from a different and perhaps less heated perspective than is sometimes done, especially in recent debates over Prayer Book reform. I hope that it has been clear that my perspective is one of a sympathetic observer — one whose faith has been deepened by worshipping with fellow Christians in the Anglican Communion and whose understanding of liturgy itself has been greatly advanced by Anglicans who are colleagues, not the least of them the late Dr Cuming, and whom I have had the privilege of calling friends.

Notes

1 Geoffrey J. Cuming, *A History of Anglican Liturgy*, 2nd edn (London: Macmillan, 1982), p. xi.
2 On the question of method and the necessity for studying liturgy in context, see Kevin Irwin, 'Method in liturgical theology: context is text', *Eglise et théologie* 20 (1989), pp. 407–24.
3 R. T. Scott, 'The likelihood of liturgy: reflections upon Prayer Book revision and its liturgical implications', *Anglican Theological Review* 62 (1980), pp. 103–20.
4 See, for example, David R. Holeton, 'The formative character of liturgy' in Thomas J. Talley (ed.), *A Kingdom of Priests: Liturgical Formation of the People of God* (Alcuin/GROW Liturgical Study 5; Bramcote: Grove, 1988), pp. 9–12.
5 In addition to Dix, see M. Francis Mannion, 'Liturgy and the present crisis of culture', *Worship* 62 (1988), pp. 98–123.
6 Aidan Kavanagh, *On Liturgical Theology* (New York: Pueblo, 1984), pp. 136–8.
7 Robert Hovda, 'The vesting of liturgical ministers', *Worship* 54 (1980), p. 104.
8 See, for example, the numerous criticisms of language revisions in David Martin and Peter Mullen (eds), *No Alternative: The Prayer Book Controversy* (Oxford: Blackwell, 1981), esp. pp. 57–72, 96–124, 149–61.
9 On this subject, see the fine essay by Vivienne Faull and Jane Sinclair, *Count Us In — Inclusive Language in Liturgy* (Grove Liturgical Study 46; Bramcote: Grove, 1986).
10 On this issue see M. Francis Mannion, op. cit., esp. pp. 107–13.
11 As one can see from the thematic table, ASB, pp. 1092–3.

16

A future for Anglican spirituality:
a Methodist view

Gordon S. Wakefield

Historical background[1]

Thoughtful observers who are not especially learned in spiritual writings or conversant with modern developments would probably find it easy to describe the Anglican ethos. The pervasive presence of the institution in English life has left indelible impressions.

Such people might speak of reverence in worship and decorous behaviour in church, of a mistrust of enthusiasm and heartiness, 'sweet singing in the choir' rather than swelling lungs in the congregation; and of the end of religion as being 'a godly, righteous and sober life' in conformity to the State. Anglican Christianity is not revolutionary. It is good citizenship and 'the conservation of socially recognized values'. It is concerned with the moral consequences and practical outworkings of Christian belief, though more in personal lives than by radical social change since society is protected and made just by the hierarchical order of the establishment. A good conscience and a sense of duty and obligation are paramount. And the whole is sustained by a uniform, legally binding liturgy from which there should be no unauthorized departures.

This is no caricature. It describes what has been the shop front of the Church of England for many generations. It may still represent the religion of some members of the Conservative Party and it is displayed to the nation on State occasions. It encapsulates both the strength and the weakness of Anglicanism: the strength, a prevailing moderation in spite of some bitter conflicts, the persistence of nominal Christianity in English life, the stubborn belief, at least until recently, that this is a Christian country and that although many are lukewarm, few are hostile and even among the ignorant and the deprived there remain many who would turn to the Church in times of need, of sorrow and of joy; the weakness, that Anglicanism is the religion of the governors, of the old aristocracy and the socially privileged, that it has been protected by law and immune from persecution since the Restoration. Complacency and 'effortless superiority' have sometimes taken it far from the Christ of the Gospels and what A. N. Whitehead called 'the Galilean vision of humility'.

There have always been tensions, as is inevitable in a system which rejoices in the middle way, the 'golden mediocrity' of seventeenth-century claims. In 1690, Tillotson complained in a sermon that 'those odious and unhappy names of difference' which the need for unity against James II seemed to have buried were risen from the dead.[2] And there have always been those who could not be content with the Church as it was.

The Non-Jurors detached themselves not only because they could not forswear their oaths to the Stuarts; they sought a richer, more Orthodox liturgy and a faith more firmly founded on the historic creeds than the moralists and the latitudinarians emphasized. Yet the latter represent an Anglican strain which has been there from the seventeenth century. What has come to be called 'liberalism' in the English Church did not begin with media-conscious clerics of our own time. On the other hand there has always been a High Church tradition, 'high and dry' till the Oxford Movement fertilized it with a more intense and awesome spirituality, leading to the colour and ceremonial of the Anglo-Catholics, which removed that dreariness from Church of England worship which the Roman Catholic Newman bemoaned. Some attempt to revive Caroline spirituality was accompanied by methods of devotion derived from continental Catholics.

And Calvin has had his Anglican disciples, who burgeoned in the Evangelical Revival and made their witness, sometimes with their lives, in the mission fields and the philanthropy of the nineteenth century. Their piety, though morally strict, was fervent and tender and centred on Christ. The mission hymn 'Safe in the arms of Jesus' was played at Lord Shaftesbury's funeral in 1885 by the band of the Costermongers Temperance Association.

It has been said that the English Christianity of this century is the creation of the last. And it was the nineteenth century which saw those changes of which we are the heirs, not least in our devaluation of their legacy in our time. Then, the English Church spread into the world of Empire and other races came under its influence and slowly, very slowly, began to reciprocate. Then, modern ecumenism began with the need for international consultation, the scandal of rival Gospels on the mission field and the discovery of many new means of communication. The Christian social conscience, never entirely asleep or indifferent to the poor, was awakened under the impact of the Industrial Revolution, and some saw the necessity of political action supported by organized Christians, so that by the 1980s the Church of England ceased to be seen as 'the Tory Party at prayer'. Then, Darwinism and the 'Essays and Reviews debates' demanded some re-presentation of Christian theology. The authority of the scriptures, so central to the Book of Common

Prayer, had to be reinterpreted, while Anglican Catholics and liturgio-logists alike became discontented with the work of Cranmer and of 1662. Its vestigial Catholicism, which the Anglican Newman had believed the Tractarians could rehabilitate, seemed inadequate beside the Roman use, or, for the better-informed, the liturgies of the early Church, some of which were being rediscovered.

To picture Anglican spirituality at what I would claim is its most authentic, we may consider two divines, one Victorian, one who died in 1988, both of whom, in differing degrees, represented it as they tried to come to terms with the world in which they lived.

1. Dean Church

Richard William Church (1815–90) was called 'the greatest of the Deans of St Paul's' by an eminent Methodist,[3] while the subtitle of his biography is 'the Anglican response to Newman'.[4] It was Newman at Oriel College, Oxford, who imparted a sense of 'the awfulness of things unseen' and drew out his capacity for the spiritual and unearthly side of religion, which, for instance, Dean Stanley of Westminster lacked. There was in Richard Church a longing for God in sacramental worship, which was seen at the altar both in his village cure of nineteen years at Whatley in Somerset and at St Paul's. There is a sentence from his sermon on Pascal which perfectly describes his own spirituality: 'On our knees we need to remember the deep abysses of judgment and mercy in which the foundations of our prayers are laid.' Yet he knew that devotion could degenerate either into formalism, 'sleepy routine', or sentimental fussiness and affectation. He knew that Gospel did not mean the abolition of Law. A fine expositor of Bishop Butler, he warned against the deceits of antinomianism. 'Let us not think that because we frequent sacraments and delight in divine service and feel devotion and uplifting of heart in prayer, we need not fear the temptations which are "common to man"; that we can afford to indulge our dislike of trouble, or relax our care and vigilance, or neglect plain duties, or can be bold in things more dangerous still.'[5]

Church's teaching is palpably influenced by Newman, as when he quotes the famous words from the St Mary's sermons: 'Revelation was not given to satisfy our doubts, but to make us better men, and it is as we become better men that it becomes light and peace to our souls, even though to the end we shall find difficulties in it and in the world around us.'[6] He showed to Newman personally an unfailing loyalty and love; but he could not follow him to Rome. He remained a witness to that historic Anglicanism, biblical, reasoned, reverential, sacramental, which refused to seek refuge in a supposedly infallible institution. The human spirit must not be intellectually castrated. The truth of the Gospel must stand in its own strength. (This, remember, was at the time of the restoration of the Roman Catholic English hierarchy, of Pio Nono and, ultimately, Vatican I.)

Church, though an amateur by modern academic standards, was a born historian and, dare it be said, a better and safer one than Newman, for whom the past was so often a mirror in which he saw his own times. Church did not judge people of the past as though they lived in any time other than their own, though in the conclusion of his book on Anselm, there is a comparison between the account of Anselm's death-bed and that of Richard Hooker. For him the truth of Christianity rested on history and on the historic incarnation from which there is no escape. As for Ignatius Loyola, for Wesley, Bonhoeffer and Hammarskjöld, 'The Imitation of Christ' has a special place in his spirituality and the Christian character is simply one in which the love of God in Christ is seen.

Not only so, it was history which gave the English Church its rationale. Church was in the succession of Lancelot Andrewes, not only as the author of *Preces Privatae*, but as one who vindicated on behalf of the reformed Church of England the rights of Christian history: 'Andrewes claimed for the English Church its full interest and membership in the Church Universal, from which Puritan and Romanist alike would cut off the island Church by a gulf as deep as the sea.' History freed the English Church from the Reformed tendency to abstract and metaphysical argument and narrow biblicism, while it enlarged its ideas of the Church Universal, so that Rome was seen as Latin rather than wholly Catholic Christianity. So Andrewes prayed, 'for the Catholic Church, its establishment and increase: for the Eastern, its deliverance and union; for the Western, its adjustment and peace; for the British, the supply of what is wanting in it, the strengthening of that which remains in it'.[7]

Church was blind neither to the tragedy of life nor to the reality of sin. He wrestled both with the advent of modern science and with the poetry of Browning, to whom he gave much attention as 'a poet who handled the moral destiny of man as a live issue within the context of a world which is not simply Vanity Fair'.[8] He jibbed somewhat at *Lux Mundi*, published in the year before his death. And he knew that what his friends thought of him was not what his heart told him of himself or the verdict of Divine judgement. His only hope lay in the grace of Christ's Passion. On his tombstone at Whatley in Latin is the *Dies Irae*:

> Faint and weary thou hast sought me
> On the Cross of suffering bought me,
> Shall such grace be vainly brought me?

2. Archbishop Ramsey

Arthur Michael Ramsey (1904–88), Archbishop of Canterbury (1961–74), lived in more turbulent times and through the amazing changes of the twentieth century, when Anglican spirituality could no longer be rooted in country livings of a few hundred souls, and dignitaries lost their gaiters and some of their glamour. Unlike Church, he was not a cradle Anglican. It was spirituality in his undergraduate youth which turned him from Congregationalism to Anglo-Catholicism. At the parish church of St Giles in Cambridge, he found, says Owen Chadwick, quoting him, 'something of ... "the sense of mystery and awe, and of another world at once far and near ... a sense that we were vividly in the presence of the passion of Jesus and also vividly near to heaven, to which the passion mysteriously belonged, so as to be brought from the past to the present". His nonconformist origins made him find it strange, if not reprehensible, that at the main service of the day no one but the priest took the sacrament. Soon he came to value this practice very much. It left his mind free for "pondering, adoring".'9

As priest, theologian and bishop, Ramsey taught contemplation, but not mysticism, as the 'perennial philosophy' of Aldous Huxley's misnomer. It was contemplation of the glory of God in the face of Jesus Christ. That 'glory' was everything. 'The effect of contemplation is often not to cause the person to long for experiences so much as to love and serve God under the sovereignty revealed in Jesus. Indeed the validity of contemplation is often tested by the pursuit of the life of faith.' Such contemplation was not contrary to the Pauline doctrines of 'by faith alone' and 'by grace alone'.10 Like von Hügel, Rowan Williams and others, Ramsey saw affinities between the religion of Luther (and the Protestant Reformation) and the spirituality of St John of the Cross. In the latter's words, 'Pure contemplation consists in receiving'.

In the radical 1960s, Ramsey wondered if it had not been a mistake in the West 'to regard meditation as the norm for all Christians and contemplative prayer as reserved only for advanced souls'. 'Whereas mental meditation is something in which not every Christian will persevere because the powers of the human mind in concentration and imagination vary so greatly, the contemplation of God with the ground of the soul is ... accessible to any man, woman or child who is ready to try to be obedient and humble and to want God very much.'11

Ramsey never forgot the world in his teaching of prayer. 'The prayer with beautiful buildings and lovely music must be a prayer which also speaks from the places where men and women work, or lack work, and are sad and hungry and suffer and die. To be near to the love of God is to be near, as Jesus showed, to the darkness of the world. That is "the place of prayer".'12 St John was the evangelist who inspired him most, St John for whom the incarnate life is described 'as being all the way a journey to the Father ... But the journey to the Father was at every moment a journey deeper and deeper into humanity with its sin, its sorrow and its death. And nowhere was Jesus more utterly in the Father's glory than when in bearing the world's darkness and dereliction on Calvary he cried out that he was bereft of God. Towards heaven, towards the world's darkness: these were two facets of one journey and one Christ.'[13]

Like Church, Ramsey had the Anglican sense of history and deplored the tendency of some theologians to deny history to make room for faith. We may not know as much of the historical Jesus as we would wish or possibly as teachers like Church assumed, but we have enough certainties for faith, and Ramsey reaffirmed in his retirement study, *Jesus and the Living Past*, that there is a logical progression from the 'knowable person' of Jesus to the proclamation of the divinity of his life and work, and so to the cosmic Christ and the Church as the community of his death and resurrection.

Ramsey believed in the Church and in Catholicity as an essential mark. His awareness of Eastern Orthodoxy, his attraction to its theology of the Divine glory made him an ecumenist from the start. He wished for visible unity in the British Isles, and was heartbroken when the Anglican–Methodist Scheme failed in Convocations and Synod of the Church of England. Yet he never wavered in his insistence that the unity to be sought must be in truth and holiness. But though the Church is of God, the Gospel precedes it. The Church is utterly dependent upon Jesus and is judged by him.[14]

The future

What is the future of the spirituality thus illustrated from two renowned exponents? The question is difficult and fraught with dangers. One can but project from present trends, while being aware that prophecy may reveal more of one's own hopes and fears than of eventuality.

1. Liturgical change and flexibility

First we must notice the effect of liturgical change. The Book of Common Prayer no longer dominates worship in the English Church and soon its cadences will pass from English life. It had an influence almost greater than the Authorized Version of the Bible and Hardy's rustics were familiar with its phrases. *The Alternative Service Book 1980* is not so poor a thing in comparison as its detractors would say and it has both theological and liturgical advantages. Its great achievement has been to heal divisions between Anglican Catholics and Evangelicals and bring a unity and to some extent a discipline long belied. It has reconciled extremes, together with the success of the Parish Communion movement, which has ensured that the Eucharist is now the principal service of the Lord's Day in most churches. In consequence, there must now be a greater proportion of worshippers communicating frequently than at any time in the history of English Christianity. The Venerable Bede commented many centuries ago that the English were reluctant communicants and in the eighteenth and for much of the nineteenth century there was no weekly celebration of the Eucharist and the hallmark of Anglican worship became Morning Prayer with or without Ante-Communion!

This development is not regarded as spiritually efficacious by all. There is a feeling that it results in a famine of the Word. The older Evangelicals believed that Holy Communion should separate the nominal and conventional from the truly converted and committed. Bishop E. A. Knox in the 1930s looked back with regret to the days when that was so and communicants were 'marked out by the fact of remaining (after Morning Prayer) and were to some extent objects of criticism for not following the outgoing throng'. Then was felt the force of the words of the Independent Philip Doddridge's communion hymn which may well have been sung:

> Why are its dainties all in vain,
> Before unwilling hearts displayed?
> Was not for them the victim slain,
> Are they forbid the children's bread?[15]

Michael Ramsey was critical of the Parish Communion. In *Durham Essays and Addresses* (1956), he tilted at those who 'trip along to their communion' and regretted the passing of the quiet early celebration for which the devout prepared themselves carefully overnight. There is little doubt that he then hankered after Communion at 8 a.m. and contemplative non-communicating attendance at High Mass, which had first won him to the Anglican Church. It may well be that though the Parish Communion with its restoration of 'the kiss of peace' gives 'place' to worshippers, the passing of the old rites denies them 'space', to borrow a distinction of W. H. Vanstone's.

There is much more variety in Anglican worship than was traditionally permitted. There are para-liturgies and family services, with the possibility of enrichment provided by such proposals as those contained in the recent Liturgical Commission Reports, *Patterns for Worship* (1989) and *The Promise of His Glory* (1990). There are guitars and overhead projectors, choruses, uplifted hands, charismatic hugs and 'happy clapping'. Sometimes it is very noisy. The revival of evangelicalism and the charismatic movement have brought crowds to some churches. The Eucharist is sometimes obscured by enthusiasm, the pentecostalist manifestations of the Holy Spirit and the testimonies of the 'born again'. 'Reserve' has gone, along with uniformity. How the Tractarians would have shuddered! Yet Cathedral worship survives and witnesses to the beauty of holiness and opens for many the gate of heaven.

2. The contemplative way

At the same time, the teaching and practice of contemplation have increased. Retreats are well subscribed and there is some demand for these at Christmas as a silent protest against the commercial profanities of the season. Julian of Norwich and the English Mystics have now greater vogue than at any time in history. The Ignatian Exercises, though meditative rather than contemplative, in spite of their terminology, have transformed lives and fixed vocations. Anglicans have written on the Benedictine life. They have certainly ventured beyond the historic bounds of their own Communion, though from Pusey onwards Roman Catholic works of devotion have been available for Anglicans. Many use the Orthodox 'Jesus Prayer'; and the writings of Anthony Bloom and Kallistos Ware have great distribution among Anglicans.

There is increasing demand for spiritual direction and a union of ascetical theology with psychology and an awareness of the psychosomatic. This last has always been characteristic of the Judaeo-Christian tradition, sometimes crudely expressed. It is the basis of the counselling of so skilled a practitioner as Dr Martin Israel, who guides those whom he directs along the traditional ways of Christian mysticism, combining its deep understanding of the human and religious psyche with modern insights and pathology.

In short, Anglican spirituality on all sides is becoming increasingly ecumenical and this is bound to continue. Constitutional and sacramental unity may be denied us, but in spirituality the barriers are often down. The last to fall will be those around the altar, though Anglicans now accord eucharistic hospitality to other Christians of good standing even if they will not all — or officially — feel able to receive communion from the non-episcopally ordained.

Ecumenism seems, however, to look more in Catholic, Orthodox and charismatic directions than to a revival of the classic Anglican tradition of the Carolines and the Moralists as with Dean Church. Interest in Lancelot Andrewes, Jeremy Taylor and Joseph Butler has not revived, though scholars and cognoscenti find much food for thought there. And in spite of attempts such as those of Hodges and Allchin in *A Rapture of Praise* (1968) and Timothy Dudley-Smith in *A Flame of Love* (1988), the spirituality of the Wesley hymns has not captured Anglican devotion, and one suspects that in Methodism it is in danger of being supplanted by choruses.

3. The encounter with other faiths

To what extent must ecumenism embrace other faiths? They can neither be ignored nor written off, as by some Christian exclusivists, as heathen delusions. John 14.6 is a stumbling block which fundamentalists invoke and some liberals dismiss as of John not Jesus: 'I am the way, the truth and the life; no one comes to the Father except by me.' Recent commentators point out that in its context it is more a polemic against a Christianity solely of the Spirit than a denial of other faiths. Christianity is not a religion of the Spirit apart from the incarnate and crucified Jesus, who alone, by his glorification through the cross, releases that other Paraclete. And the one who speaks to his disciples is the Divine Logos, who is the *fons et origo* of all truth, 'the true light which gives light to everyone'.

Those Christians who do not feel threatened by other faiths have learned much by seeking 'dialogue' with them in penitence, humility and openness. Their own faith has been enriched, their Christian convictions strengthened. They must learn to live with paradoxes. The differences between the world's religions are great and must not be blurred by an indolent pretence that they are all one. I doubt if holism in this sense is compatible with intellectual honesty. Reconciliation will come through an understanding of differences and a mutual respect for beliefs based on clear commitment to one way, not by what used to be called syncretism; even though sometimes a Hindu prayer may express Christian beliefs, as in the use of a petition from the Upanishads in the 1975 Methodist rite of baptism: 'From darkness lead *him* to light, from death lead *him* to eternal life.' The Christian does not pray that as a Hindu would; 'eternal life' replaces 'immortality' and it is offered 'through Jesus Christ our Lord', yet by the use of this prayer there is a bond between them, a desire for understanding and for light in our darkness, which for the Christian is Christ, yet the cosmic Christ who transcends the narrow limits of our perceptions.

A small book about Muslim–Christian meetings in Birmingham has been written by Andrew Wingate, an Anglican priest, now Principal of the College of the Ascension.[16] There is no suggestion that all was easy or that there were not frustrations. There are some moving accounts of prayer offered in the forms of the different faiths for each other's needs, in sickness and in social deprivation and disorder. The spirit of the whole encounter is very much what Christians like to think is the spirit of Christ. Sharing each other's worship is valuable, without the folly of attempting to devise a form acceptable to all, which is impossible and a betrayal of what each separate faith believes to be the true way to God. Pluralism is profoundly unsatisfying and essentially shallow. But there is, arguably, scope for an inclusivism in the sense for Christians of a Logos Christology, of a God who loves the world and a Christ who died for all.

Wingate describes from his Indian experience as a prison chaplain how Hindu prisoners who desired to come were admitted to the Eucharist because there is proclaimed the forgiveness which was their greatest need. The word of absolution was not sufficient; they must receive the body and blood of Christ.[17]

4. The inner city and the prayer of faith

In the introduction to *Encounter in the Spirit* the leading Muslim participant writes, 'I believe deeply in the need for the involvement of all communities, regardless of creed, sex and nationality, in building up good will and the desire to live together, whilst letting each one be true to one's own faith. Love and mutual service should be at the heart of this sense of togetherness.' He has in mind the riots of Handsworth in 1985 and the problems of the inner city, those 'urban priority areas' with which the report *Faith in the City* (1985) was concerned. To live and work there has a profound effect on spirituality, though, for Christians, this means to reaffirm rather than revise the Gospel of the incarnation and the Passion of Christ. There the 'imitation of Christ' takes on new meaning. Christians feel that they are treading in the footsteps of his incarnate life. Some have felt that the *Alternative Service Book 1980* is 'too triumphalistic with too much use of resurrection imagery and "power" words'. Without denying for one moment the resurrection hope, they want something that reflects 'a little more realistically the pain of the cross. Part of the reality of the cross means speaking to God about vulnerability, about dying, about the complexity of life and of moral choices . . .'[18]

Some Anglicans have found it a new and moving experience to hear inner-city Christians, particularly of Afro-Caribbean origins, pray. They pour out their hearts to God without set forms, but as children talking to their Father. There may in the future be a revival of what Friedrich Heiler, in a not undisputed dichotomy, called 'prophetic' or 'faith' prayer.[19] For many years, what he classified as 'mystical' prayer has been in the ascendant and the prayer of petition and of words has been regarded as of a lower level, if indeed it has not been scorned.[20] And this in spite of scripture and of the teaching of Jesus. The June 1990 issue of *Concilium* powerfully redresses the balance with articles on 'Asking and Thanking', and though the contributors are Roman Catholic in the main and none of them is English, this may be a harbinger, along with the broadening of Anglican experience outside the old controversies with Nonconformists and Evangelicals, of a rehabilitation of the prayer which is conversation with God and not simply wordless contemplation; though in the end, as Hooker said, 'our safest eloquence concerning him is our silence' and our petitions and thanksgivings may lead to a state in which we are 'lost in wonder, love and praise'. What Michael Ramsey and others have said and so many have proved about contemplation will not be disowned, but it will not be regarded as the 'honours school' of prayer while the insistence of Jesus that we 'Ask! Seek! Knock!' is brushed aside. The difficulties of unanswered prayer in the light of the insistence of Jesus that requests will be granted are indeed acute and may lead to self-torture and a certain spiritual tyranny; but we cannot escape the fact that for Jesus prayer is 'an inter-personal "conversation" with God in which love is experienced and given and relationships of intimacy are founded'. And Jesus is urging us to ask not for 'casual favours' but for the Kingdom of God, while the intimacy leads to the absolute trust which, when our own human desires are not granted, says 'Your will be done'.[21] The prayer of Gethsemane is at once prophetic and mystical. All prayer leads to union with God, but for the Christian this is the union of love between persons, not mystical absorption, nor the monism in which the world, the self and God are all one.

The inner city finds book-liturgy and book-prayers alien, and demands a freedom of language as well as a moral tolerance for bingo halls, and pursuits often anathema to middle-class culture, and an awareness that Church organization as well as classic devotion may be daunting and meaningless. But the Christian story can be told and the Passion re-enacted through the tokens of bread and wine.

5. Feminism

Finally, there is the influence of feminism on spirituality. The increased role of women in the leadership of all institutions is a simple fact of human life in the Western culture of our time, which the Churches cannot forever resist, though reactionaries may hinder it. It may lead to a slow revolution, for women are different from men, and opponents of women priests are right in their feeling that the ordination of women will change the character of priesthood. It may result not so much in female storming of a hitherto male bastion as in a rediscovery of the priesthood of the whole people of God and a eucharistic and absolving ministry less 'set apart' from the rest of the people of God.

While women are denied ordination in those Churches which claim to be Catholic, there has developed a spirituality of protest, in some cases with its own liturgies or liturgical revisions. The life of prayer seems to be dominated not by the narrower issue of women priests, but by identification with all the oppressed. And all the traditional forms of spirituality have been questioned as covert instruments of subjugation.

The protestors are not more than a minority and a vote in a General Synod could bring them in from the wilderness to which some have felt themselves driven. But if this issue disappears, there will still be found need for protest against injustice and the cruelties and oppressions of conformists. The witness of the sectarians and dissenters in English Church history will have its successors, but need they form separate denominations? Their heirs are now found more among those who would still call themselves Anglicans than in the weakened ranks of historic dissent. Will not the Church of the foreseeable future have to live with the tension, or the dialectic, of those who uphold the tradition and seek where possible to live in co-operation with the powers that be and those who cannot forget that Church and society alike are always in need of reformation?[22]

There is spiritual danger when one particular temporal issue so dominates prayer that the mind becomes obsessed and direct awareness of God seems lost. He may be blotted out by the protest. This often happens quite apart from some great social question. A person may find prayer almost impossible because of a broken love affair, or business worries or 'envy, hatred, malice and all uncharitableness'. This is where one must remember that the one obsession of Jesus was the Kingdom of God, and all must be seen in the perspective of that prayer, which has its social and political implications, but which is made supremely in that sacrament in which we remember both the laying down of his life for it and the eternal rule of God. All Christian prayer is offered in union with Christ on the cross and from the heaven of his all-conquering love.

Feminists raise more than any other group the problem of language. This is agonizing, and not for them alone, because the language of the gospels themselves may be condemned by some as sexist, or at least patriarchal, and one cannot revise it radically without being in some sense 'post-Christian'. To refuse to say 'Jesus is Lord' assails the earliest Christian creed and contravenes the teaching of the New Testament. Yet there has to be a distinction between final truth and its cultural expressions.

The issue of the motherhood of God is not simple. There are a few similes in scripture which might justify it, though no metaphors. Some fear that any introduction of a 'goddess' element into theology and prayer might lead to Gnosticism. (Others would retort that these heresies, about which there is uncertainty and dispute, were condemned by men anyhow.) Helen Oppenheimer has argued that metaphors of fatherhood are more appropriate for our relation to God since the umbilical cord has to be severed and dependence on our mothers outgrown. Yet clearly God who is without sex has those qualities of undying mother love which are so elemental and powerful a part of human experience. We might, helped by the precedent of Anselm, use in our private prayers meditation on God who 'as with a mother's tender hand, leads his own, his chosen band'. (A recension of an Anselmic prayer has been provided by a member of the present Church of England Liturgical Commission.)

Conclusion: the necessity of history

The Anglican sense of history must not be lost. It is sad that the study has not its former place in the curricula of seminaries and theological colleges, for many students are 'new Christians' who happen to have been converted in Anglican (often Evangelical) congregations, and are ignorant of the tradition. History is an affirmation of our belief in the communion of saints, and although it is not hagiography and must not, *pace* Newman's strictures against Milman, be taught as a sacred subject without secular realism, it is necessary for our prayers, as much in its lessons of human frailty as in its evidences of 'the historic Christ in his fulfilment'. It unites us with the past, with those 'who wrestled hard as we do now, with sins and doubts and fears' and who won their victory through the incarnate God. The tradition saves us from the excesses of modern heresies, like Creation spirituality and the New Age, which, though rightly summoning us to revere nature and co-operate with her, ending the ravaging exploitation which is so great a crime, revive some of those dangerous and occult beliefs which *inter alia* make us ignore the gravity of sin. The tradition confronts us with the fact that our salvation depends on things which really happened in this world of time and space; that we have more than an inner light to guide us, rather a datable Jesus who lived and suffered and died and rose again to change the balance of spiritual forces in the universe and bring our humanity with the whole creation to God.

There is no need to despair. The tradition will not be lost, nor history forgotten, as long as the Anglican Church has scholars who combine deep learning and reverence for the past with an ability to read the signs of our times. And spirituality will move in the twofold direction which Michael Ramsey discerned in the Fourth Gospel — 'down to the earth' to which our Saviour came, while never losing the vision and the promise of the heavenly glory.

Notes

1 For more detailed studies, see C.J. Stranks, *Anglican Devotion* (London: SCM, 1961); S.H. Evans in Gordon S. Wakefield (ed.), *A Dictionary of Spirituality* (London: SCM, 1983); relevant sections in C. Jones, G. Wainwright and E.J. Yarnold (eds), *The Study of Spirituality* (London: SPCK, 1986); A.M. Allchin in Stephen Sykes and John Booty (eds), *The Study of Anglicanism* (London: SPCK, 1988); and Gordon S. Wakefield in Louis Dupré and Don E. Saliers (eds), *Christian Spirituality* III (New York: Crossroads 1989/London: SCM, 1990), pp. 257–94.

2 J. Tillotson, *The Way to Prevent the Ruin of a Sinful People*, Jer V. 18. A

Fast Sermon Preached before the Lord Mayor etc., *Wednesday 18 June*, *1690*.

3 W.F. Howard, *Christianity According to St John* (London: Duckworth, 1943), p. 60.

4 B.A. Smith, *Dean Church* (Oxford: Oxford University Press, 1958).

5 R.W. Church, *The Discipline of the Christian Character* (London: Macmillan, 1900), p. 49.

6 'Pascal and Other Sermons 122'. See J.H. Newman, *Parochial and Plain Sermons* I (Oxford: Oxford University Press, 1868), p. 229.

7 R.W. Church, ibid., pp. 90f.

8 B.A. Smith, op. cit., p. 224.

9 Owen Chadwick, *Michael Ramsey: A Life* (Oxford: Oxford University Press, 1990), p. 22.

10 Michael Ramsey, *Be Still and Know* (London: Fount, 1982), pp. 90, 91.

11 Michael Ramsey, *Sacred and Secular* (London: Longmans, 1965), p. 45.

12 Michael Ramsey, *Be Still and Know*, pp. 13–14.

13 Michael Ramsey, *Sacred and Secular*, p. 7.

14 Michael Ramsey, *Jesus and the Living Past* (Oxford: Oxford University Press, 1980), pp. 32–3.

15 E.A. Knox, *Reminiscences of an Octogenarian* (London: Hutchinson, 1935), p. 60.

16 Andrew Wingate, *Encounter in the Spirit* (Geneva: WCC, 1988).

17 Ibid., p. 73.

18 Trevor Lloyd, 'Inner City England' in David R. Holeton (ed.), *Liturgical Inculturation in the Anglican Communion* (Alcuin/GROW Liturgical Study 15; Bramcote: Grove, 1990), p. 43.

19 F. Heiler, *Prayer: A Study in the History and Psychology of Religion* (English translation; Oxford: Oxford University Press, 1932).

20 Cf. D.Z. Phillips, *The Concept of Prayer* (London: Routledge, 1965), and his essay in Basil Mitchell (ed.), *The Philosophy of Religion* (Oxford: Oxford University Press, 1971).

21 George M. Soares-Prabhu, 'Speaking to Abba', *Concilium* (1990/3; *Asking and Thanking*) (London: SCM, June 1990), pp. 33, 37ff.

22 On Anglican feminist spirituality, see Ursula King, *Women and Spirituality* (London: Macmillan, 1989); Bridget Rees, 'Wandering in the wilderness: a feminist reflects on education in spirituality' in Jill Robson and David Lonsdale (eds), *Can Spirituality be Taught?* (London: Way Publications, 1988). A fine historical and devotional study by Gordon Mursell, *Out of the Deep: Prayer as Protest* (London: Darton, Longman and Todd, 1989).

17

Anglican identity: a chapter of accidents

Kenneth W. Stevenson

It is always tempting in a concluding chapter to try to resolve every single loose end and ambiguity in sight. But this is more often than not a futile exercise, artificial and self-conscious. In doing some lateral thinking for Anglicanism's soul, these essays have tried to probe behind what is apparently happening worldwide, in the search for what is going on under the surface. It is already clear that many of these movements have been going on virtually since the beginning of Anglicanism's life. There has always been a tension about whether or not the Prayer Book should be revised, how that should be done, and how far a local manifestation of the Church, whether national or regional, should go its own way — following in Cranmer's footsteps in a judicious blending of new material with adaptations of older elements, as these are uncovered. It all seems to have happened by accident. Perhaps four of these stand out as pre-eminent in our story.

The accident of Canterbury

When speculation began early in 1989 about who would be chosen as the next Archbishop of Canterbury, most observers outside England (by which is meant England — not the United Kingdom!) took as their measuring-stick Robert Runcie's indefatigable commitment to travelling around the Anglican Communion, visiting individual countries, and both listening to and encouraging their Churches in what they were doing. Moreover, the focal point of the Archbishop's ministry in this regard was, by many accounts, the Lambeth Conference in 1988.

In peeling off the various layers of the Archbishop's job, one begins to see how accidental the development has been: Bishop of a diocese, Metropolitan of a Province, Primate of All England, and in effect presiding Bishop of the Anglican Communion. It was by accident, pure and simple, that Augustine set his episcopal seat at the capital of the East Saxons in 597. It was by accident that Canterbury, not London, became the archiepiscopal centre for the Southern Province, long after the East Saxons ceased to count for much. And it was this historic precedence that placed Canterbury over York, a see that had known many vicissitudes in the early years.[1]

At the Reformation, Canterbury and York ceased communion with Rome, and the Prayer Book became the rule of faith and worship for this new national Church. There was never any thought of exporting it to foreign soil, for even when the Scots were to use a Prayer Book, it was to be their own; and by one of those many ironies, the Scottish Prayer Book of 1637 was as ill-fated as it was an eloquent expression of classical seventeenth-century Anglican theology.[2] It was in the (later) Non-Juror tradition of the Scottish Episcopal Church that this theological drive became even more apparent. As every American Episcopalian knows well, the fact that their first native, independent, elected bishop, Samuel Seabury, was consecrated in Aberdeen in 1784 by three Scottish bishops gave a powerful steer towards a type of Anglicanism that was very Anglican, and decidedly un-English. Historians, commentators, and journalists repeatedly underestimate this side of the equation, especially if they are native English writers.

However small and insignificant Anglicanism outside the mother-country in the eighteenth century was, it showed its ability to adapt and grow on new terrain, with great theological riches, so that by the time of the first Lambeth Conference in 1867, the accident of Canterbury proved itself to be not only fortuitous, but widely accepted by an increasingly diverse Communion. We shall return later to some practical suggestions as to how Churches in communion with Canterbury could respond to the present liturgical growth industry. Meanwhile, it needs noting that from the very outset, Anglican identity is about *worship*, expressed in a family of liturgies that are related, but not identical, whether that is 1662, Scottish 1764 or the 1789 American book. That simple fact, and the primordial variety within the Communion, is inescapable.

The accident of the liturgical story

In the later Middle Ages, Canterbury may have been the metropolitan see, but it was the Sarum Use that held increasing sway in England. The ironies persist even further after the Reformation, for even though with each monarch, up to and including Charles II, there was a fresh Prayer Book, the actual way in which the book was used in parishes varied considerably. When investigations were made at the start of the reign of William and Mary in 1689 into the state of play in local churches, many anomalies and variations were uncovered, some of them of considerable soundness, for example in the adoption of a concluding collect to round off Cranmer's marriage service, which was originally intended to lead straight into a Eucharist but seldom (if ever) did.[3]

This tale also includes liturgical projects that were considered, or just appeared, but were not authorized, for example, in that much-loved quarry of Anglican spirituality, the collects. Whereas in 1662, the somewhat prolix collect for Advent 3 (probably written by John Cosin) replaced Cranmer's rather bald translation of the corresponding Latin prayer in the Sarum Missal, Simon Patrick's equally long suggested further replacements which appear in the 1689 'Book of Comprehension' were never authorized; but they are part of the same liturgical family, even if we may secretly give thanks that Cranmer's originals survived.

But whatever central authority decides in the face of new material that surfaces in connection with *public* worship, there is still the question of *personal* devotion, which has long nourished Anglican hearts. Simon Patrick, in the 1684 edition of his *Mensa Mystica* (Discourse on the Lord's Supper), produced a stream of intercalated devotional prayers, in a very rich and pictorial style, illustrating the doctrines propounded, and feeding the piety of the worshipper.[4] It may well be that this is what is badly needed today, as Churches (not just Anglican ones) search for ways of conveying a more 'holistic' theology that is (like Patrick's work in question) lay-oriented.

Another ironical accident can be perceived in the two seemingly contradictory directions taken by Prayer Book revision this century. They are apparent not just in the current ferment; they are equally obvious in the work done earlier in the century. One tendency is the desire for *flexibility*, so that the liturgy can be adapted to suit local circumstances, aiming at (among other things) a degree of discretion over what is mandatory and what is not. In the 1920s, this was particularly manifested in the revision of the Daily Offices, whereas today it is particularly true with the Eucharist, and those many other rites and sacraments that can be combined within it.

The other tendency is the desire for *enrichment*. Earlier on, it was expressed in alternative canticles and additional collects and prayers at the Offices; now, it is expressed in the variegated Eucharistic Prayers and forms of intercession that are common coin in the new books. The explosion of new material has been the greater, perhaps, because of the very different and pluralistic world in which we now live. It is also, I suspect, explained by the fact that we seem to have moved in our collective instincts to a looser view of liturgical norms, as embodying *tradition*, rather than *law*. The pitfalls of this growth are becoming obvious, but even the most conservative worshipper must be comforted that Anglicanism already experienced in 1662 the tensions of how far to allow new material in (like the Prayer for All Sorts and Conditions of Men, and the General Thanksgiving) and how far to exclude it (like the reunification of the Eucharistic Prayer along 1549 lines).

Perhaps another reason can be suggested for this dual pull towards flexibility and enrichment, and it has to do with the growth of liturgical studies as a science in its own right. Towards the end of his (much neglected) book on the Eucharist, Charles Gore makes some observations which, perhaps unintentionally, aptly state what many of us have been trying to do:

> ... there is a special vocation for scholars, and this vocation lies in great part in purging the current tradition, or enlarging it, by perpetual recurrence to the divine originals.[5]

Following in a great train of Prayer Book commentators, liturgical scholars have been trying to do just that — purge the current tradition, or enlarge it, by looking afresh at 'divine originals', some of which we know better than the Reformers, because the material is now available. Knowing a lot about the past, of course, is not always an advantage. It can be overwhelming, even stultifying, and it can induce a kind of paralysis in thinking that engenders fixed attitudes. But, with few exceptions, liturgists this century have tried to use ancient models in a creative manner, not slavishly aping Hippolytus (who appears to have had more influence on the twentieth century than on the third and fourth!), but looking for the deep structures and narrative character of prayer, and basking in some of the patristic theological sunshine of a Basil of Caesarea.

But there is another side to this, and it concerns the way in which Anglicanism, along with the other major Western Churches of the Reformation, has tried to converse with its roots. There has been a spate of studies of Cranmer and the Reformation. Here, opportunities for multidisciplinary approaches have not always been taken. While liturgists can be criticized for living in their own world, the same is sadly true of other branches of theological study. For example, the quincentenary of the birth of Thomas Cranmer produced laudatory lectures, but academe still shows signs of ignoring one important insight which liturgists have themselves brought to the fore this century, namely that Cranmer was Zwinglian in his sacramental theology,[6] and that the moves and shifts in Anglicanism after him, and discernible both in 1637 and in the changes made to the English Prayer Book at the Restoration in 1662, all show that the rank and file of churchmen and theologians were not happy, for example, with a prayer of consecration which was not called such. This factor has been one of the consequences in making liturgists, when they draft new prayers, conscious of the gulf of theological interpretation between 1662 as touched up and edited by the Restoration divines, and 1552 as drafted by Cranmer in the light of comments on 1549 by his Reformed advisers. The twentieth-century scholar, therefore, should be deeply, and naturally, suspicious of the folklore equation, 'Cranmer = 1662'.[7] Cranmer's narrow theological vision of the Church in 1552 had to be nuanced considerably in the next century to accommodate a much wider Church. The Anglican tradition is more complex, and this adds to our chapter of accidents.

The accident of revision and its critique

We have already drawn attention to the different kinds of debate about liturgical revision that have been going on ever since the sixteenth century. It is now time to look more reflectively at what is going on in our own times. Revision has continued apace under a head of steam already built up by the love of antiquity that has been there from the start, but was given fresh impetus by the Tractarian Movement. What has divided revision earlier this century from our own era is the twin developments of the change from 'thou' to 'you' language[8] and the growth of liturgical studies in their own right in the intervening years. To put it at the level of texts, the 1928-style Eucharistic Prayer still espoused the fourth-century Greek–Syrian texts, but in Cranmerian prose, whereas the post-1970-style Eucharistic Prayer is often modelled on Hippolytus' *Apostolic Tradition*, and is expressed in the new-style English language that is still undergoing evolution.

Roughly speaking, there have been five distinct strands of criticism of the newer liturgies. For the sake of convenience, the examples that I shall give are taken from the debate in the Church of England. By this, I intend no chauvinism, for although I happen to be a presbyter of the Church of England, I was born and bred a Scots Episcopalian, who through a Danish mother is descended from generations of Lutheran pastors.

The first concerns *language*, and the neglect of social roots. David Martin is the name most closely associated with this arena, though there are many others who voice it with considerably greater force.[9] The power and the passion of the Prayer Book as a social, motivating force is contrasted with the flat, banal, limp prose of, for example, the *Alternative Service Book 1980*. The Church is accused of withdrawing from the world where many people supposedly are, in order to become a tightly-knit ghetto on the fringes, full of self-discipline, but uninterested in the mass of half-believing folk who have valued the Church for generations.

The second concerns *antiquarianism* as a motivating factor in the production of new prayers, together with the thought-patterns of a bygone age, particularly the patristic, which is thought to be far distant from our own. Leslie Houlden, himself a former member of the Church of England Liturgical Commission, is one of the voices of this theme, and with his first-hand knowledge of one branch of the Anglican Communion at work, he speaks with some experience.[10] Why should the Church appear to ignore developments in theology over the past hundred years in favour of anachronistic ways of praying?

The third concerns *ephemerality*, and accuses some of the priorities both in expression of ideas and in ways of selecting scripture passages for lectionaries as being already out of date. The 1960s were a laudable era for student sit-ins, but their theological catchwords are somewhat dated. Tom Baker has given expression to some of these criticisms, overlapping with Houlden from time to time.[11]

The fourth concerns the *methods of prayer-writing*, which have relied too much on the historico-source criticism school of liturgiology, whereby a prayer is made up of different individual units, and analysed as such, whereas it ought also to be seen as a narrative unit in its totality. Stephen Sykes has drawn attention to this,[12] and it clearly links with those who accuse liturgists of being antiquarians in modern dressing.

The fifth concerns the *politics of revision*. No one name stands pre-eminent here, for it has been expressed in many different spheres. The liturgical establishment is in this case seen to be allied with modern synodical bureaucracy. There may even be a touch of academic snobbery to such a view. But it is more about a Church that does not treat liturgy-making with the seriousness that it deserves. These critics, however, question the artistic integrity of prayers that come out of committees, synods, and the like, and suggest that it is not only an unhappy process in itself, but is one in which points of principle may be lost in the horse-trading behind the scenes. The political factor (if one may call it so) can be found in all the major revisions of this century, Roman Catholic included.

In sum, there are, indeed, valid points from each of these five concerns. But it is equally true to say that there are some misconceptions of the nature and process of liturgical development right down through the ages into our own time.

Yes, the quest for 'modern' language in English-speaking Anglicanism is not achieved overnight. Nor is any other language invented as quickly in those (many) parts of the Communion where other tongues are used, perhaps even several at the same celebration. But in reply to these critics, I have to say that Cranmer himself was repeatedly 'edited' over the years, as a perusal of virtually any page of Brightman's *The English Rite* with its parallel columns of the early editions of the Prayer Book and its sources makes clear. In any case, the quest is better endeavoured and persisted in than held back from and shunned. Cranmer, if alive today, might not approve of some of the new service books, but he would be horrified that the Prayer Book had lasted so long.

Yes, it is true that today's knowledge of worship in antiquity is much greater than it was, and it is only inevitable (for example) that if an early version of the Eucharistic Prayer of Basil of Caesarea in an arcane form is rediscovered, and treasured for its ecumenical potential, such a prayer should be used (as it has been in North America) as one that can unite hitherto divided Communions.[13] The key question is that of criteria: Cranmer was not usually dominated by his sources, and it follows that modern Anglican liturgy is only weak where the past is followed for its own sake, rather than because of some particular hermeneutical advantage. The interaction of traditions is a multifaceted business.

Yes, some liturgical texts drafted thirty years ago have a dated ring to them, and some of the 'community'-consciousness of that time sounds a little hollow to worshippers of today. This underlines another issue, namely that the liturgist has to stand, in some sense, for the Church Catholic, and produce in company with the rest of the Church prayers that resound and evoke in a general manner the truths of God as these are identified specifically by different types of worshippers in different contexts. This, it seems to me, is a key truth about the nature of Anglicanism. Ephemerality *has*, it is true, made some of us fall in love with the quickly-disposable text, but the only antidotes to ephemerality are the tests of time, and the collective sanity of the Church at large.

Yes, some drafters of prayers have been over-conscious of sources, and in drafting, for example, a confession, have been too aware of the traditional movements of thought, from address of God, through particular context, to enumeration of sin, and onwards to repentance, and petition for forgiveness and grace to amend. But these are the gridmarks on the map, and there can be few liturgists who are unaware not only of the total character of a prayer, but also of the way in which theological fashions move on, and perspectives shift. To drive a wedge between 'liturgy' and 'prayer' can be dangerously romantic.

Yes, there is an unhealthy taste about some of the political machinations that go on in the formation of committees, and one cannot help noticing that the sheer quality of liturgical work is often in direct disproportion to the time and energy spent to ensure that every single minority group is somehow 'represented', thus producing an even more unnatural milieu for possible creativity than before. But that is the way of the modern Church, and the criticism should be levelled at the structures and the power-sharing in themselves, and not at the liturgies created by them which are but one result. It is reassuring to read, however, of the way in which politics operated in times past, even in that (supposed) haven of liturgical excellence and peace, seventeenth-century England.

The fact is that all liturgies are culture-bound, and one of the beauties about being part of a worldwide and history-deep (and, one hopes, eternally refracted) community is that the worshipper is inherently part of something much bigger, a kind of never-ending swimming-pool in which to swim here and there, rather than in all of it, all the time. There is no such thing as an incomparable liturgy, for a liturgy's best test lies in its use — a process not confined to words. It is a healthy sign of the times that a group of scholars can collaborate in an evaluation of the process of Anglican revision. But because culture is so much part of liturgy, our story would be incomplete without identifying a sixth area of concern about contemporary liturgy that is surfacing in many different places — *context*.

If liturgists can be accused of one fault with considerable justification, it is a preoccupation with the words of the liturgy, almost forgetting that the words have to be 'performed', in some sense, in public. This is a question that is as much to do with the capacity of a liturgical president to adjust well and naturally to many different types of service in an age of pluriformity as it is to do with the current quest for new symbolism. True, symbolism can be applied to words as well as to actions, and many examples can be found of prayers that lack the pictorial and the resonant, through a desire to produce yet another abstract noun.[14] But people are as affected by what they *see* as by what they *say*. There are church buildings in many parts of the Anglican Communion where a good text is wrecked by the context of bad reordering, poor visibility, and a printout of such appalling quality that the worshipper needs a magnifying glass to follow what is going on. Anglicanism has known the poor and the shoddy, but it has a certain reputation for quality of presentation among her sister Churches. As the pastor of a parish in southern England, who has also worked in the rural East Midlands, the urban North-West, and, for a time, the Mid-West of the USA, I have seen both ends of the spectrum, and I cannot put my hand on my heart and say that the way new liturgies are done always reflects the highest of standards and possibilities available. Here is yet one more accident.

The accident of ecclesiology

Commenting on the new American Prayer Book, Aidan Kavanagh, that sagacious observer of things liturgical, has this to say:

> Taking the repertoire of eucharistic prayers together as a whole, one would have to say that it is nothing if not inclusive — moving as it does from Cappadocia and Egypt to Scotland, Rome, and the United States in 1928 and 1976. Because of this one would be hard put to affirm with clarity exactly what a eucharistic theology distinctive of the Episcopal Church really is. The repertoire admits of a variety of formal eucharistic theologies, and this will be regarded by many as its greatest strength. Yet a eucharistic theology inevitably both gives rise to and reenforces a concomitant ecclesiology. I thus foresee a variety of ecclesiologies taking on a new distinctiveness in the Episcopal Church in the

future. The effects of this, both positive and negative, for church order will no doubt receive careful attention from Church agencies in the years to come.[15]

Kavanagh's challenge has to be taken seriously. It can be answered, partially, in a number of ways. Some prayers will drop out of use, or be employed rarely (as has happened with the Roman Catholic Eucharistic Prayer IV). Then, other prayers may well be absorbed into the tradition with greater adaptation (this is already noticeable where different theological emphases are at work, such as eucharistic sacrifice). Finally, pluralism, which is a source of tension in all worldwide Churches today, including over such issues as admission of children to communion, is forcing new kinds of liturgical creativity and distinctiveness in ways that these Churches have not seen before, and must face together. But what, Kavanagh asks, is this variety doing to people? As creatures of the age we live in, there is bound to be for us a degree of consumerism. Prayers are usually written to answer a need, or at any rate a felt need, and they arise out of a particular context, with a series of pressures that may change over the years. One can see this truth in the past as well as the present. Some of Cranmer's best-loved collects that speak of protection from danger have their origin in the Lombard invasions of Italy in the late sixth century at the time of Gregory the Great.[16]

Nonetheless, questions of Anglican identity have to be faced. Three answers to this question have been given, not (it has to be admitted) with regard to liturgy, but to the more general issue of Anglicanism.

One is what might be described as 'the apostolic paradigm',[17] which invests a great deal of value in the notion of the Book of Common Prayer as the expression of what 'the Church' believes and teaches. Such a paradigm always tends to hold before it something of an ideal. It has much to commend it, not least its reliance on the sheer historical fact of Anglicanism as reaching down through the ages and feeding on the fullest traditions. But its fundamental weakness regarding the current liturgical state of play in the Communion is that it just does not engage with what we know in our bones to be reality — namely a Communion that knows considerable doctrinal and liturgical variety, and which at times has grave difficulty in staying together. The accident of Canterbury comes under severe strain. This paradigm, therefore, can be very helpful, but it has its limitations.

Another is what Paul Avis has recently proposed as 'the baptismal paradigm'.[18] Building on the traditional and classical Anglican polity that it all starts at the font, and that Anglicanism began its life in the context of a lay movement against clericalism, this paradigm places its emphasis on the whole community being the Church, sharing in its decisions, and being motivated towards greater service, and deeper spirituality. But its fundamental weakness is similar to the preceding one, namely that it states an ideal, but does not address the actual liturgical problem of variety, much as the new service books place considerable weight on the baptized community as the leaven in the lump of society.

A third paradigm was, paradoxically, worked out earlier this century, and in spite of varying critiques, it has continued to stand the test of time. It is the paradigm of the dying and rising Christ, which finds eloquent expression in Michael Ramsey's *The Gospel and the Catholic Church*.[19] Ramsey recognizes the essential gap between the ideals of the Kingdom of God and the human frailties of a given age. He sees Anglicanism's genius in terms of its incompleteness, which gives the book a strong ecumenical and historical thrust, over against the central authoritarianism of some aspects of the Western Catholic tradition, and the federalism of the Protestant tradition when it tries to embody a worldwide consciousness. Ramsey was, by nature, an optimist about the Church, but he was not blind to its weaknesses, and, indeed, he would have applauded the scholar's rule of thumb from Charles Gore quoted earlier.

Ramsey's paradigm is rooted in a clear authority which is perceived to be passed down in a visible way, but which also addresses itself to specific issues as these occur through history. I want to end by making my own comments, as a way of expressing my conviction that Ramsey was right. Anglicanism needs to address 'substantially' some of these 'accidents'!

First of all, there needs to be a genuine and co-operative *monitoring* of the work of liturgical revision in the Anglican Communion, which means making both the Lambeth Conference and the Anglican Consultative Council the chief forums for airing and reporting on this key area in the Church's life. This is already beginning to happen, and it may be that the second thoughts that are in the air in several of the Provinces will lead to a greater awareness of the need to keep in touch with each other. The appearance of feminist language texts in the USA and the new (very African-looking) Kenyan rite makes this imperative.

Secondly, there needs to be greater *sharing of resources and investment* in liturgical work. For far too long, teachers of liturgy have not been taken seriously and have even been patronized by the older, more established disciplines. Many of the problems we face now over liturgy could have been met earlier had the Communion enough vision. There is already an informal liturgical network. But there has also to be a recognition, especially by the more affluent Provinces, of the need to invest time and money in funding both teachers and researchers with pastoral awareness who will help the Communion forward in its thinking and strategy about the future of the liturgy. The fact that there is no single full-time lecturer in liturgy at an English University is, to some extent, a barometer of the problem on our hands in promoting the viability of our trade. We look with envy at other countries and other churches.

Thirdly, there needs to be a more focused and prayerful awareness of those issues that are *theologically sensitive*.[20] The patristic era wrestled with Christology and the Trinity. The Reformation wrestled with atonement and eucharistic theology. Of this century's many theological advances may be numbered eschatology, ecumenism, and the Eucharist. All have liturgical consequences. They are often skirted round in modern service books. They all appear from time to time in various prayers. But this is where Anglicanism has, potentially, its most crucial role, as a truly ecumenical tradition, which looks critically at the past, and is prepared to learn from other Churches.

Finally, a chief problem-area in ecclesiology today relates to the growing tension over the *rôle of bishop and synod*. It has been a source of tension both in our own Church and in others. It is very much a factor in our own century's nervous compromise over shared leadership. It relates to how power is handled. Perhaps, in the end, a better understanding of the office of bishop in today's Church[21] will emerge, which will limit, in some degree, the more extravagant scope of some of our debating chambers, or at least come to some agreement about precisely what they are supposed to be and do. Synods and Conventions simply do not write good liturgies perforce, and they have a regrettable tendency to flatten language and stifle the prophetic spirit. Good liturgies can only grow organically, as the past tells us again and again. They grow within a living tradition that is conscious of the need to worship as that need is cajoled and checked along its journey through history. One of the roles of the bishop as a teacher of the Church is to foster this process. In a pluralist Communion, this will not be easy, and it may well involve championing the voiceless — those parts of the wider community whose cultural pattern goes against prevailing currents. The history of liturgical development, moreover, teaches us that while, on the one hand, time and sanity get rid of liturgical refuse from the actual diet of the Church, what *does* survive tends to result from a special evolution, the survival of the fittest, but not necessarily the best.[22] Henry Chadwick warns that 'Anglicanism is periodically threatened by a Do-it-yourself spirit of consumerism'.[23] There are, indeed, duties as well as advantages in being a comprehensive Church. One of those is, arguably, the challenge of not just playing to the gallery, but giving it liturgical prose that is both dignified and natural. It is *this* quest that lies behind every worthy step to push the liturgy forward.

'Worship is not so self-contained that it can guarantee its own truth',[24] writes David Power, in an ecumenical volume to commemorate the centenary of the publication of *Lux Mundi*, that landmark of Anglican liberal orthodoxy. No, worship is far from being self-contained.[25] But it is Spirit-filled, and therefore will always emerge where two or three are gathered together. It is offered by human beings, and therefore will always have to exist in particular cultural forms.[26] Its ultimate aim is to praise and serve the Father, through the Son, in the Spirit, as the glorious freedom of the community of the redeemed is celebrated now and for ever. It is the most divine accident of all time.[27]

Notes

1 See Nicholas Brooks, *The Early History of the Church of Canterbury* (Studies in the Early History of Britain; Leicester: Leicester University Press, 1984), pp. 3ff.

2 See Richard F. Buxton, *Eucharist and Institution Narrative* (Alcuin Club Collections 58; Great Wakering: Mayhew-McCrimmon, 1976), pp. 145ff.

3 See Timothy J. Fawcett, *The Liturgy of Comprehension 1689* (Alcuin Club Collections 54; Southend-on-Sea: Mayhew-McCrimmon, 1973), p. 141. On the Simon Patrick collects, see pp. 206ff.

4 Simon Patrick, *Mensa Mystica or a Discourse Concerning the Sacrament of the Lord's Supper . . . The Fifth Edition, In which several Prayers and Thanksgivings, not extant before in any of the former Editions, are now added, to make it of more general use* (London: Tyton, 1684).

5 Charles Gore, *The Body of Christ: An Enquiry into the Institution and Doctrine of Holy Communion* (London: Murray, 1901), p. 239.

6 James Wedderburn, Bishop of Dunblane, and an author of the 1637 Prayer Book, drew attention to Zwinglianism in the 1552 words of administration at communion: see Gordon Donaldson, *The Making of the Scottish Prayer Book of 1637* (Edinburgh: Edinburgh University Press, 1954), p. 52. But the chief exponent of Cranmer as Zwinglian was Gregory Dix: see *The Shape of the Liturgy* (London: Dacre, 1945), pp. 656ff.; see also Kenneth Stevenson, *Gregory Dix — 25 Years On* (Grove Liturgical Study 10; Bramcote: Grove, 1977), pp. 3ff.

7 See, in an otherwise useful essay, Peter Forster, 'Some reflections on the theology of Thomas Cranmer' in Margot Johnson (ed.), *Thomas Cranmer: Essays in Commemoration of the 500th Anniversary of his Birth* (Durham: Turnstone Ventures, 1990), pp. 253–72.

8 See Colin Buchanan, 'Liturgical revision in the Church of England in retrospect' in Kenneth Stevenson (ed.), *Liturgy Reshaped* (London: SPCK, 1982), pp. 146–6.

9 See, for example, the essays in David Martin and Peter Mullen (eds.), *No Alternative: The Prayer Book Controversy* (Oxford: Blackwell, 1981).

10 See J. L. Houlden, 'Liturgy and her companions: a theological appraisal' in R. C. D. Jasper (ed.), *The Eucharist Today: Studies in Series 3* (London: SPCK, 1974), pp. 168–76.

11 T. G. A. Baker, *Questioning Worship* (London: SCM, 1977).

12 See Stephen Sykes, '"Baptisme doth represente unto us oure profession"' in Johnson (ed.), *Thomas Cranmer*, pp. 122–43. The comparison he makes between pages of Brightman's *English Rite* (shown on pp. 124f.) and Abbott and Rushbrooke's *The Common Tradition of the Synoptic Gospels* (shown on pp. 126f.) implies that liturgists today are

firmly in the mindset of Brightman in their work of drafting prayers. Brightman was no keen liturgiographer, and modern prayer-writers have wider perspectives than they are often given credit for. But Sykes makes some valid points about the Prayer Book baptismal rite.

13 See L. L. Mitchell, 'The Alexandrian anaphora of St Basil of Caesarea: ancient source of "A Common Eucharistic Prayer"', *Anglican Theological Review* 58 (1976), pp. 194–206.

14 See, for example, some of the pictorial language in the Eucharistic Prayers contained in *Patterns for Worship: A Report by the Liturgical Commission of the General Synod of the Church of England* (London: Church House Publishing, 1989), pp. 239ff., especially Prayer 'B', pp. 243ff. On the implications of narrative and spirituality, see Frances Young, *The Art of Performance: Towards a Theology of Holy Scripture* (London: Darton, Longman and Todd, 1990).

15 Aidan Kavanagh, '"The draft proposed Book of Common Prayer": A Roman Catholic's appreciation', *Anglican Theological Review* 58 (1976), p. 367.

16 See Henry Ashworth, 'The influence of the Lombard invasions on the Gregorian Sacramentary', *Bulletin of the John Rylands Library* 36 (1954), pp. 305–27. Some of these collects survive into the Sarum Missal, from which Cranmer took them, e.g. Sexagesima, see art. cit., p. 318.

17 See Paul Avis, *Anglicanism and the Christian Church* (Edinburgh: T. & T. Clark, 1989), pp. 79ff., 157ff.

18 Ibid., pp. 300ff.

19 A. M. Ramsey, *The Gospel and the Catholic Church* (London: Longmans, 1936) (reprinted, SPCK, 1990, with foreword by Geoffrey Rowell).

20 See, for example, Kenneth Stevenson, *Eucharist and Offering* (with foreword by Mark Santer) (New York: Pueblo, 1986).

21 See the perceptive analysis of this issue by G. R. Evans, *Authority in the Church* (foreword by Henry McAdoo) (Norwich: Canterbury Press, 1990).

22 See Robert F. Taft, 'The structural analysis of liturgical units: an essay in methodology' and 'How liturgies grow: the evolution of the Byzantine Divine Liturgy' in Robert F. Taft, *Beyond East and West: Problems in Liturgical Understanding* (Washington: Pastoral Press, 1984), pp. 151ff. and 167ff.

23 See Henry Chadwick, 'Newman's significance for the Anglican Church' in David Brown (ed.), *Newman — A Man for Our Time* (London: SPCK, 1990), p. 67.

24 David N. Power, 'The Holy Spirit: scripture, tradition, and interpretation' in Geoffrey Wainwright (ed.), *Keeping the Faith: Essays to Mark the Centenary of Lux Mundi* (London: SPCK, 1989), p. 164.

25 See Kenneth Stevenson, 'Lex orandi and lex credendi — strange bed-fellows?: some reflections on worship and doctrine', *Scottish Journal of Theology* 39 (1986), pp. 225–41.

26 See, for example, David R. Holeton (ed.), *Liturgical Inculturation in the Anglican Communion* (Alcuin/GROW Liturgical Study 15; (Bramcote: Grove, 1990).

27 Some of the points made in Dale Coleman (ed.), Michael Ramsey, *The Anglican Spirit* (London: SPCK, 1991).